The Social Nature of Mental Illness

D0140952

Debate over the true nature of mental illness is polarised between those arguing for a social and those arguing for a physiological aetiology. Psychiatry finds itself at the centre of this debate, its status called into question by those who claim that to treat mental disorder as a physiological ailment is to mask the social origin of the illness.

In *The Social Nature of Mental Illness*, Len Bowers offers an objective and philosophical critique of the theories of mental illness as a social construct. His purpose is to examine the rationality of these theories, what they might mean, and in which cases they are to be accepted or rejected. Previous work on this issue has concentrated upon empirical evidence. All that has been generated from this are opposing interpretations of the data, rather than solutions. This book examines the common ground between the apologists for and critics of psychiatry, and discusses how debate on this issue affects research into and treatment of mental illness. Len Bowers argues that many of the assertions made about the social nature of mental illness are misguided or wrong, but he concludes that they cannot be wholly rejected.

Essential reading for psychiatrists, psychologists, sociologists, psychiatric nurses and social workers, *The Social Nature of Mental Illness* offers new perspectives on the contentious debate around the true nature of mental illness.

Len Bowers is Professor of Psychiatric Nursing at St Bartholomew School of Nursing and Midwifery, City University, London.

MCP HAHNEMANN UNIVERSITY
MOORE LIBRARY

The Social Nature of Mental Illness

Len Bowers

WM
31
B786s
1998

First published 1998
by Routledge
11 New Fetter Lane, London EC4P 4EE

Simultaneously published in the USA and Canada
by Routledge
29 West 35th Street, New York, NY 10001

First published in paperback in 2000

Routledge is an imprint of the Taylor & Francis Group

©1998 Len Bowers

Typeset in Times by Routledge
Printed and bound in Great Britain by
TJ International, Padstow, Cornwall

All rights reserved. No part of this book may be reprinted
or reproduced or utilised in any form or by any electronic,
mechanical, or other means, now known or hereafter
invented, including photocopying and recording, or in any
information storage or retrieval system, without permission in
writing from the publishers.

British Library Cataloguing in Publication Data
A catalogue record for this book is available from the British Library

Library of Congress Cataloguing in Publication Data
Bowers, Len, 1955–
  The social nature of mental illness / Len Bowers.
  p. cm.
  Includes bibliographical references and index.
  1. Mental illness–Etiology–Social aspects.
  [DNLM: 1. Mental Disorders. 2. Social Perception. 3. Psychology,
  Social. WM 31 B7865 1998]
  RC455.B68 1988
  616.89–dc   97–42740
                                               CIP

ISBN 0–415–22777–1

B10870854

$-3.00 Gift

To Eleanor

Contents

Chapter 1

Introduction

Psychiatry is a controversial institution. There may be many reasons for this, from regular scandals about its practice to its interlinking with the law. The reason that concerns us here is the nature of mental illness as a social phenomenon. Debate and criticism on this issue are to be found largely among academics from professional psychiatric backgrounds, and the academic disciplines of history, anthropology, sociology and philosophy. Controversy arises from a number of sources: from the polarisation between those arguing for a social or for a physiological aetiology; from efforts to define the essential nature of mental illness; from historical and anthropological data that appear to show variance in the nature of mental illness; and from arguments about the nature of minds and bodies.

The literature arising from these controversies has a lengthy history. In the 1970s it was characterised as 'anti-psychiatry', but many of the ideas and discussions appearing then had venerable academic histories and continue to be recycled in different forms to the present day. Nowadays these debates surface most frequently in transcultural or historical psychiatric studies and reflections. Some of the most common ideas received their clearest statement in the labelling and deviancy literature of sociology in the 1950s and 1960s, and discussion in this book therefore starts with this topic.

All these arguments circle like moths around one common flame: the nature of mental illness as a social phenomenon. Unlike physical illness, most mental illnesses have no physiological signs or symptoms, and psychiatrists have no recourse to blood tests, cytology or X-rays to determine their presence or severity. Mental illness is determined and defined by the social behaviour of the sufferer. From this deceptively simple beginning, the debate over the status of psychiatry has exploded in every direction. The questions raised continue to rumble and reverberate below the surface, influencing topics and methods of research, interdisciplinary relationships and the treatment offered to the users of psychiatric services.

It has been argued that mental illness is not really an illness at all, and that when we speak in these terms we are, unbeknown to ourselves, talking in metaphors. Thus when mental illness is treated by doctors in hospitals with drugs, the metaphor is being taken literally. Mental illness is really another way of talking about life problems or the effects of social problems. To treat it as a real illness only serves to cover up the true origins of the problems, whether these be in the life choices of the sufferers or in their political predicament. For example, depressed and battered housewives should not be regarded as suffering an illness which needs treating with drugs, but as people in a predicament which requires moral and political solutions. Some would go on to argue on the same grounds that the compulsory detention and treatment of those who are merely socially deviant is immoral and wrong. Such people, instead of being excused from their actions on the basis of some supposed illness, should be held as accountable for their actions as anyone else.

Unsurprisingly, these arguments have been strongly rejected by psychiatric professionals, whose first response has been to point to the very real nature of mental illness and the disastrous effects it has upon people's lives. Two other responses are also to be found in the literature: first, that disordered social behaviour implies disordered brain function, and thus mental illness is really a physiological brain abnormality that merits the title disease; second, that all illness, mental and physical, is determined by social criteria and that mental illness is no less an illness because of this. In support of this argument it is pointed out that most illnesses were identified as such long before any physiological mechanism was known or identified. These defences of psychiatry cannot themselves be easily reconciled with each other, and each solution may be associated with differing ideologies about the purpose, organisation and methods of treatment to be used by psychiatric professionals. On the topic of the social nature of mental illness there is no uniform doctrinaire approach, and ideas elsewhere termed anti-psychiatric sometimes have wide currency within certain sections of the discipline itself.

Some of the more extreme critics of psychiatry from sociological backgrounds have argued that because mental illness is defined by social criteria, it is logically impossible for corresponding physiological entities to be identified. Efforts to do so would be like the attempt to find the specific neurophysiology of lying, burglary, bad manners and other such social phenomena. For the same reasons it is sometimes said that psychiatry will never therefore be a natural science, with the development of causal laws about mental illness. At this point all the arguments against a positivist sociology are brought to bear upon psychiatry on the grounds that it has comparable empirical status to that discipline.

Attempts have been made, largely from within sociology, to analyse and describe the social criteria of mental illness. In order to do this, sociologists have generally considered mental illness to be a smaller subset of what they call, in general terms, 'deviance'. Commonalities between all forms of deviance, or social rule breaking, have then been sought and applied back to mental illness in order to illuminate possible social processes in the identification and treatment of the mentally ill. It is somewhat inevitable that sociologists would seek to understand mental illness in this way, as their major topic of interest is social order. The question that arises is whether mental illness can be analysed in these terms, whether it can be considered as a form of social disorder or social rule violation, in a way that promotes further understanding and does justice to the empirical nature of mental illness as a phenomenon. Furthermore, some sociologists have elevated their consideration of the influence of social processes upon mental illness to the level of a causal explanation. Thus they assert that not only is mental illness determined by social criteria, but that the social behaviour of which it is composed has a wholly social aetiology. If this could be firmly and clearly established, then at least one of the implications would be the discarding of psychiatry as a medical project.

If mental illness is wholly a matter of social processes, what then is its meaning and function? Some have argued that the stigmatisation of the mentally ill is one example of the common human tendency to reject disvalued subgroups and blame them for social troubles. Negative attitudes towards the mentally ill are thus seen as directly parallel to racism and anti-Semitism. For some interpreters these negative social attitudes towards the mentally ill influence the course and outcome of their disorders. Others assert that mental illness has no more reality than the witchcraft of those persecuted under the inquisition – it is socially created in order to provide a group that may act as scapegoat, or an opportunity for ventilation of social frustrations. Thus the argument about the social definition of mental illness ramifies into political interpretations of the institution of psychiatry.

These are not the only deductions which may be drawn from considering mental illness to be a social construction. When imported into social anthropology, it implies that because of social differences mental illness should show extreme variance between different cultures. Whether the variance which is found is to be explained in precisely this way is a matter of dispute. Some scholars take a strong position, asserting that mental illness is completely socially defined, and that its incidence, nature, form, and the efficacy of its treatment vary according to the culture under consideration. One of the implications often drawn from this conclusion is that mental illnesses cannot be properly compared across cultures. For instance, what is considered clinical depression in the West may not be so considered in another culture, may be evidenced in a very different way or may not be present at all. The idea that the aetiological weight of social or cultural factors in a mental illness can be determined by cross-cultural comparison is thus undermined before the attempt is made. Others have, of course, argued completely to the contrary, asserting that mental illness is universal, a position usually coupled with the assertion that mental illness is a physiological brain disorder whose cause has not yet been firmly identified.

Very similar arguments are to be found in the literature on the history of psychiatry. Significant numbers of authorities argue that mental illness is socially defined and has varied significantly from epoch to epoch. Some say, for example, that the huge rises in the numbers of incarcerated insane during the nineteenth century were due to changes in the concept and definition of insanity. If this and other similar arguments were to be accepted, they would imply that the problem of mental illness may be minimised or ameliorated by a change in definitions and their associated social policy.

Upon these common foundations a variety of critiques of psychiatric practice have been constructed. Some have boldly recommended the dismantling of the entire psychiatric enterprise, whereas others have argued for radical reformulations of the nature of mental illness with consequent changes in treatment and research priorities. Yet others have argued for the abandonment of some research methods and strategies in favour of alternative approaches, and some have stipulated limitations upon what can be discovered and known within the realm of psychiatry.

Although these ideas have influenced thinking within psychiatry, they have by and large been rejected by the most influential and powerful professional group in psychiatry: the psychiatrists themselves. Nevertheless, these critiques have influenced the thinking of other psychiatric professionals, and are widely read and absorbed by academic scholars outside the mainstream departments of psychiatry. They thus contribute to internal interprofessional differences and to external appreciations or studies of the institution of psychiatry.

The objective of this book is to uncover and demonstrate the common ground of these interpretations, exposing and tackling their internal logic and consistency, showing much of it to be confused, incoherent or erroneous. All these mainly faulty interpretations circle around the nature of mental illness as a social phenomenon. Some assert a social aetiology for mental illness, some a high degree of influence by social forces and others that mental illness is thoroughly and completely socially constructed. My purpose here is to examine the rationality of these claims, what they might actually mean and in which cases they are to be accepted or rejected. The prime focus will therefore be upon clarification and logical argument. Previous work on this issue has overly concentrated upon arguing from empirical data – all that has been generated from this are opposing interpretations of the data, rather than solutions. These issues cannot be resolved in this way. Clarification can be best achieved by reflection and arranging what we already know. Insofar as this is the case, this book could be characterised as being about the philosophy or theory of psychiatry.

In the course of achieving clarity on these issues, it has been impossible to move without bumping into the cultural furniture of dualism, the nature of evil, life as suffering, the nature of science, etc. The discussion in the following pages is therefore far more wide-ranging than a simple consideration of mental illness alone, and there are implications for a number of areas other than psychiatry. Throughout the following exploration of psychiatric concepts, my guiding light has been the later philosophy of Ludwig Wittgenstein. His technique of dissolving philosophical conundrums through analysis of ordinary language has proved to be of great value in sorting out the conceptual problems of psychiatry. He wrote:

Language is a labyrinth of paths. You approach from one side

and know your way about: you approach the same place from
another side and no longer know your way about.

(Wittgenstein 1958: I, para. 203)

Thus this book returns again and again to a consideration of the
nature of language and of how we use words in order to show the
roots and origins of the confusions that arise when considering
mental illness as a social phenomenon.

Such is the breadth of territory that this book has had to cover
in order to expose the commonality between a variety of traditions
within different disciplines that I am very aware that sometimes
scant attention has been paid to major figures. There is also, I am
sure, much relevant and illustrative material that has been left out.
However, to have concentrated any more on single academic
thinkers or subject areas would have quickly lost the overview which
I have struggled to achieve. One figure that does crop up regularly
in the following pages is that of Thomas Szasz. I make no apology
for repeatedly using him as an exemplar of certain arguments, as he
has more often been rejected than effectively countered.

On the other hand, the work of Laing has not been discussed in
great detail. Although a senior figure of that school of thought
frequently referred to as 'anti-psychiatry', his thinking is of a significantly different nature to that of other scholars considered here.
Laing is largely concerned with presenting an existential, psychological and family systems theory of schizophrenia. His thinking has
more in common with psychotherapeutic theorising, and therefore
his ideas have more overlap with psychotherapy and cognitive
psychology, and less relevance to social constructionism.

Although over the following pages I will be arguing that many of
the assertions made about the social nature of mental illness are
misguided or wrong, this should not be taken to mean that they
should be wholly rejected. Indeed, once clarity has been achieved it
will be seen that in certain senses the claim that mental illness is
socially constructed is eminently correct. This has implications for
psychiatry as an institution which will be detailed in the final
chapter.

Chapter 2

Deviance

Despite its antiquity, the dominant mode of thinking in the sociology of mental illness is still that of the labelling perspective. It continues to be a central plank in the teaching of sociology on nearly all basic courses, and it makes its appearance in the curricula of both social workers and mental health nurses. In the meantime, labelling theory, and the whole heated controversy over it that took place in the 1970s, has been mostly bypassed by psychiatrists and psychiatric researchers. There is a wealth of written material dating mostly from the 1970s, none of which can really be said to have comprehensively settled the question one way or the other. The theoretical and philosophical issues raised by the labelling debate were never resolved, and have therefore been simply left behind, only to re-emerge in different forms and terminologies in the present day.

This approach to mental illness has two major characteristics: first, mental illness is regarded as deviance from social norms and, second, the effect of the reactions of those surrounding the mentally ill person is greatly emphasised.

CLASSIC LABELLING THEORY

Perhaps the clearest statement of 'labelling theory' has been made by Lemert (1951), who made the following tripartite distinction:

1 Primary deviance, the initial deviant act or characteristic.
2 Social reaction, the response of other people to the primary deviance.
3 Secondary deviance, the response of the deviant to the social reaction.

To take then the paradigmal case, the primary deviance of the armed bank robber is the robbing of the bank, the societal reaction is his arrest, conviction and jailing, and his secondary deviance resides in him identifying with other bank robbers and prisoners, committing further crimes and fulfilling the expectations of his custodians and others.

Now the great strength of labelling theory can be seen: the concentration on and description of social process. Labelling theory thus gave birth to a heterogeneous family of sociological studies on marginal and deviant groups and individuals. These studies were able to describe how deviant individuals view themselves, others and their world. Indeed, many of their actions were shown to be guided or constrained by the social reaction to their initial deviance. By carrying out these studies with sympathy, sensitivity and eloquence the sociologists were able to show that sometimes, and in some ways, society's institutions for the management of deviance and deviant individuals had paradoxical effects. Prisons produced criminal recidivists, mental hospitals encouraged crazy behaviour. By a process of selective attention to some aspects of the deviant behaviour combined with exaggeration, descriptions of social process were used to lend support to political cries for reform, revolution or abolition of some of society's institutions. So enamoured with irony did sociologists become that it was made to appear that the criminal justice system produced crime, and that psychiatry produced mental illness. Thus the motivations and intentions of those professional and occupational groups who believed that they had devoted their lives to meaningful and worthwhile work were ignored.

This kind of social critique was afforded further strength by Becker's variation of Lemert's statement of the theory. Becker (1963) made the whole matter of social norms relative by making out a strong case for deviance not being in fact a characteristic of individuals at all. Instead, he argued, it is the making of social rules that creates deviance, and as social rules vary considerably from place to place, culture to culture and epoch to epoch they have no objective, culture-free, ahistorical status. Deviant individuals are, Becker tells us, those who have been labelled as such and treated in accordance with that label. Whether one is to be considered deviant or not therefore becomes a matter of social contingency, rather than a personal characteristic of oneself or one's acts.

APPLICATIONS TO MENTAL ILLNESS: SCHEFF AND GOVE

Scheff (1966) elevated labelling theory into a comprehensive, systematic aetiological theory of mental illness. Mental illness is, to Scheff, publicly labelled residual rule breaking. The picture he has in mind is as follows. Society has a number of residual rules for whose infraction there is no label. These rules are being broken all the time by a variety of people for a number of different reasons and causes. In a small proportion of these cases the residual rule violator is called mentally ill. The psychiatrist is called in, the label confirmed, and under the pressure of the expectations of those around him, the person begins to fulfil the social role of 'being mentally ill'. The publication of Scheff's book, *Being Mentally Ill: A Sociological Theory*, led to a veritable storm of controversy in both psychiatric and sociological circles. Scheff's main critic, Walter Gove, conducted an open battle with him, mainly through papers and letters in the *American Sociological Review* (Scheff 1974, 1975, 1976; Chauncey 1975; Gove 1975, 1976; Imershein and Simons 1976). Gove's main method of argument was to quote empirical studies that countered the tenets of labelling theory. For example, he would describe evidence that there was a tendency for behaviour to be normalised rather than identified as mental illness, that mental illness was partly genetically determined, or that in families with a member suffering from schizophrenia it was that person's actions that determined expectations, rather than vice versa. Unfortunately, the main issue of controversy became the interpretation of various empirical research studies, rather than the coherency of the theory itself. Thus because of the weakness of the empirical evidence the issue was never conclusively resolved, and because the theory was never properly examined for its coherency, its deficits were never exposed.

CURRENT STATUS OF DEVIANCY THEORY

Deviancy and labelling theory remain a potent force in the academic debate over the nature and purpose of psychiatry. Psychiatric professionals, especially social workers and nurses, are taught the theory during their training in a largely uncritical manner. Superficial understanding of the issues at stake has led to confusions, such as the identification of diagnosis with labelling, an issue which has itself become embroiled with interdisciplinary conflicts within the psychiatric establishment. This body of thought converged with and was consolidated by other trends in social psychiatry: for example, the therapeutic communities of Maxwell Jones (see Rapoport 1960), the normalisation methods of Wolfs Wolfensberger (1972), and even the community mental health movement of Gerard Caplan (1964). All these movements emphasised by one means or another the social aetiology of mental illness, or its susceptibility to being influenced by social processes. Insofar as any of these trends were supported and strengthened by deviancy theory, the latter may be said to have had some positive policy outcomes.

Labelling theory continues to play a pivotal role in the sociology of mental illness. Although much attention is now drawn towards the influence of social factors upon the identification and course of mental disorder, the social constructionist viewpoint remains a strong undercurrent, influencing and informing sociological critiques of psychiatry.

Current works on the sociology of mental illness, for example Pilgrim and Rogers (1993), give evidence of the prevailing philosophy of social constructionism, and of labelling theory itself. Although they refer to labelling theory as being 'out of fashion', this contrasts with plentiful coverage elsewhere in their book of its core concepts. In their opening chapter they try to make a distinction between labelling theory on the one hand, and social constructionism on the other. This cannot really be maintained, as social constructionism is labelling theory in another guise. According to Pilgrim and Rogers, a central assumption of social constructionism is that mental illness is a product of human activity, interaction and talk, i.e. a discursive practice in Foucault's terminology. There is no essential difference between this and the more formal tenets of labelling theory which stress how the reality of mental illness is created by the social processes of its identification and treatment. Indeed, when Pilgrim and Rogers go on to refer to the operations of psychiatry as 'moral regulation', it is hard not to hear the echoes of Becker, one of the founding fathers of the sociology of deviance. All these ideas are interrelated, as will be seen. Labelling theory in psychiatry rests upon a conception of mental illness as deviance from the 'moral order' of society, upon the relativity of such social rules, and upon the idea that social reaction creates mental illness. All three of these fundamental concepts

are to be found in what Pilgrim and Rogers call social constructionism. Turner (1992) agrees that contemporary debates about
social constructionism are intimately related to the deviancy theory
of the recent past. So close are these interrelated ideas, and so
pervasive to the analysis of psychiatry in the human sciences, that in
the text that follows I have used the terms 'labelling', 'deviance' and
'social construction' almost interchangeably. As Pilgrim and Rogers
go on to say that social constructionism is revisited in most chapters
of their book, the centrality of labelling theory to current sociological work in the mental health field is clearly evident. If readers still
doubt this, they have only to turn to Samson (1995), where the work
of Lemert, Scheff and others is presented as a matter of current
relevance.

The rest of what now passes for the sociology of mental illness is
a loose bag of many items, including critiques of the legitimacy of
diagnoses, ethical objections to compulsory treatments, poorly
substantiated challenges to the efficacy of physical treatments in
psychiatry, even less well-substantiated arguments for various
psychotherapeutic treatments, arguments purporting to show that
psychiatry is a malign organisation with a negative impact upon
patients, political interpretations of psychiatry representing it as an
instrument of social control – or all the above used to reinterpret
the history of psychiatry. Some of these assertions bear upon social
constructionism, some do not. Those domains of the sociology of
mental illness that relate to the essential nature of mental disorder
are taken up in the chapters that follow.

This chapter will attempt a comprehensive clarification of the
labelling debate. In order to achieve this, the works of each of the
major contributors to the theory are subjected to critical scrutiny.
The origins of the types and ways of thinking used by those
working within the labelling perspective will be shown to originate
in the seminal works of Durkheim, Mead and Blumer. Finally,
some implications and conclusions will be drawn about the nature
of social rules and norms.

DEVIANCE AS DIFFERENCE FROM THE NORM

Lemert (1951) held firmly to a statistical concept of deviance.
Deviance was to be seen as any characteristic or behaviour that was
unusual when compared to the average. This point of view has
many inherent problems. Firstly it leaves deviance imprecisely

defined, for exactly how far does one have to deviate from the norm to be counted as deviant? Any answer to this question has to be pulled out of thin air, as the assumption is that variance occurs on a continuum, rather than there being a categorical difference between deviance and normality. It should be noted at this point that the term 'norm' is, in sociological use, ambiguous. Lemert is very clear that for him it means statistical average, but for others it means the unwritten rules of social conduct. Regardless of this issue, however, Lemert still fails to give us clear criteria for distinguishing deviant individuals from others. This being so, it is impossible for him to build further generalisations about this amorphous group of people.

The second problem with Lemert's statistical conception of deviance brings us to a rather similar terminus. Because he understands deviance to be statistical deviation from the norm, all kinds of things are considered deviant: slang, profanity, obscenity, dialects, argots, ungrammatical expressions, advocacy of unconventional or radical ideas about economic, religious or political institutions or about the whole social structure, genius, artistic creation, religious fanaticism, inventing, blindness, physical handicap, alcoholism, cheque-forging, stuttering and speech defects, prostitution, mental illness, crime, rebellion, addiction, sexual immorality, accidents, sabotage, slow-downs in industry, vandalism. This rapidly leads to the conclusion that, in Lemert's terms, all of us are deviant in one way or another, because we are unique individuals. If all of us are deviant, any descriptive generalisation must apply to us all. It will therefore be so generalised and abstract as to be without content. Lemert might have tightened his theory somewhat by restricting the term deviant to actions and behaviour, excluding physical characteristics. However, this would still not have been enough to define a separate minority population of deviants.

CRIME AS COVERT PARADIGM

Lemert did of course recognise these obvious difficulties with his statistical concept of deviance. He attempted to overcome them by adding that deviance also had the characteristics of being negatively valued and of being sanctioned. This is a considerable advance, made at the cost of the potential threat of relativism. The relativistic implications will be discussed below when Becker's ideas are considered. Ignoring relativism for the present, there are still major difficulties with Lemert's perspective. Nearly all of us still qualify as deviants in one way or another, at one time or another, because we have all broken social rules on occasion. All that Lemert has done, therefore, is to restate the concept of moral behaviour in another terminology. Moreover, he treats morality, moral judgements and negative valuation as a unitary phenomenon. There are in fact many different kinds of rules, moral and otherwise, which are negatively valued and sanctioned. Some of these phenomena are categorically different, in nature, context and consequence. It is possible to differentiate, for example, rules of grammar, of games, of conduct and etiquette, legal rules, rules of mathematics, etc. In each case breaking the rules may have negative consequences, but in very different ways. To treat such circumstances and occurrences all as one generalised phenomenon is to obscure these important differences.

In fact, what Lemert tries to do (as do others of the deviancy/labelling school) is trade off the hidden example of crime. With crime we have a clear moral code translated into laws and put into operation by the criminal justice system. Here we can see very clearly that the moral code has been broken. This is followed by public trial which equates to labelling. And certainly this social reaction has an effect on the subsequent self-definition and behaviour of the criminal. It is when this paradigm is applied to rule breaking in other areas that confusion arises. Can stuttering really precipitate a similar train of events? Can any physical deformity or handicap do so? Where is the public labelling of the mentally ill? The fact that some parallels can be drawn between crime and these other examples does not allow us to say that they are examples of the same thing: deviancy. These are just similarities which are sometimes fresh and illuminating, underscoring important things about the life situations of the mentally ill, for example. However, there are just as many, if not more, very real differences.

APPLICATION OF LEMERT'S THEORY TO MENTAL ILLNESS

Lemert's specific elaborations of his theory in application to mental illness show just how fragile it is. In order to fit with the theory, Lemert can only consider highly socially visible mental illness, therefore having to take psychosis as his exemplar. Thus he never points out that in many mental illnesses, particularly the neuroses, there is little or no social reaction and in fact the sufferer often has to complain quite vociferously to get any help or attention at all. In Lemert's view, the societal reaction is forcible hospitalisation, and he seems to have no appreciation at all of the fact that only a small minority of the mentally ill ever go through this experience. He (Lemert 1967) accompanies his remarks on mental illness with vague and nebulous theorising on the origin of psychosis, mixing psychoanalytic ideas with those of Mead (1936) and Merton (1957) in a largely incomprehensible way. Even his extended discussion 'Paranoia and the dynamics of exclusion' (Lemert 1962) does not really succeed as a good example of his theory – indeed, it only succeeds as a story at all because of his careful choice of example. For this he has chosen to give a generalised description of someone with a paranoid personality, someone who interprets the behaviour of those around him as hostile towards him. This man's interpretation of that behaviour may be unreasonable (he credits them with motivations that people do quite often have, but which they do not on this occasion) but is not totally irrational (he does not believe his workmates are controlling his thoughts with secret X-ray machines, or that they are members of the CIA keeping watch on him). So in this particular context, the reactions of others to his paranoid disposition may appear to confirm his paranoid ideas about them. This far from demonstrates that similar processes take place with other mental illnesses, or even that a similar amplification of paranoid ideas takes place during a severe paranoid psychosis. Certainly, the person with a paranoid psychosis who thinks that the police are following him, that they have agents in the local supermarket and that his telephone is tapped, may find confirmation of his ideas in the actions of his friends and relations to get him help. But even if others do nothing he will find other confirmations and evidence of his delusions in totally innocuous remarks and events. His paranoia is generated from within, and is not dependent upon the reactions of others. Lemert is ambiguous about the inclusion of the psychotically paranoid in his study. He claims to be making generalisations about two cohorts of patients, one group of sixteen compulsorily detained patients, and a later group of eight paranoid patients from which the psychotic were specifically excluded. In any case, his generalisations make no reference to, or interpretation of, psychotic symptomatology.

Coulter (1973) has pointed to two other flaws in Lemert's portrayal of paranoia. First, none of us are totally passive in the face of wrong impressions – we all have a range of techniques for sorting these kinds of misunderstandings out and resolving social difficulties. Second, Lemert gives no explanation of how or why the initial conspiratorial exclusion should lead to 'symbolic fabrication' (i.e. systematic paranoid delusions). It was in this essay on paranoia that Lemert came closest to elaborating his theory of deviancy and social pathology into a comprehensive social–aetiological explanation of mental illness. Despite careful choice of example and language, he signally fails to do just this.

DEVIANCY AND RELATIVITY

Becker (1963) added really only one new thing to the debate over labelling/deviancy theory: the relativisation of deviancy. Such a move was already implicit in Lemert, and was also present in embryonic form in Durkheim's corpus, as we shall see. Nevertheless, Becker stated the position most emphatically and clearly, bequeathing to sociology one of its most oft-quoted statements:

> Social groups create deviance by making rules whose infraction constitutes deviance, and by applying those rules to particular people and labelling them as outsiders. From this point of view, deviance is not a quality of the act the person commits, but rather a consequence of the application by others of rules and sanctions to an offender. The deviant is one to whom that label has been successfully applied; deviant behaviour is behaviour that people so label.
>
> (Becker 1963: 9)

Becker's perspective has been severely criticised for a number of associated reasons. The most common of these is that it rules out the possibility of secret deviance. If the only deviant acts are labelled acts, then those people who have not been labelled because they have kept their deviance secret are not deviants at all, and this position is absurd. Similarly the category of 'falsely accused' is turned into a theoretical *non sequitur*. Critiques along these lines have been mounted with varying success by Pollner (1974), Coulter (1973) and others. Perhaps it is Pollner who couches this argument in the most powerful form when he points out that Becker's position implies that the actor who breaks the rule is in some kind of social vacuum, not knowing or understanding the consequences of his acts, unable even to speak about his rule breaking until he has been labelled. This picture is obviously not true to reality.

IMPACT UPON SOCIOLOGY

This criticism did not stop Becker's work from spawning a multi-tude of curiosity-satisfying ethnographies of groups considered by someone or other to be deviant. Through this literature we can be introduced to the way of life of anyone – from the drug addict to the member of the nudist colony – and be brought to see the world and their life through their own eyes. Consonant with this wealth of material, deviancy/labelling theory was never philosophically well developed. It was, rather, a research programme. Even for Becker himself, only a minor part of his attention was given to theory and its implications, the major part of his work being ethnographic descriptions of minority group life.

Some sociologists viewed this with dismay, arguing that soci-ology was taking the side of deviants as against majority values. This is not necessarily the case, although one can understand why this position might be entertained. To describe the views and life of a deviant subculture with honesty and sensitivity is itself neutral; it is not the same as expressing support for those actions or that way of life. It is in fact Becker's theoretical stance, despite its appearance to the contrary, which is not ethically neutral. By saying that rule-makers create deviance, Becker is trying to undercut our morality. However, all he does is replace it with a moral position that fails to condemn any act at all. Thus he may be criticised for taking up what might be characterised as a completely amoral position. What Becker has failed to understand is that there is no position outside morality, no position of ethical objectivity from which human action can be described.

SCHEFF AND THE CONCEPT OF RESIDUAL RULES

Becker does not directly apply his perspective to the realm of mental illness, his examples of deviant behaviour being homosexu-ality, sadomasochism, drug abuse, juvenile delinquency, criminality and (curiously) being a dance band musician. Contra Becker and Lemert, I am suggesting that mental illness is a specific form of rule breaking, categorically different from crime and other examples. Scheff (1966) can be seen as supporting this assertion with his argu-ment that mental illness is residual rule breaking that is publicly labelled. Unfortunately Scheff is ambiguous about whether there are certain rules which are residual (rules that do not fit within any named category), or certain rule violations which are residual (ways of violating rules which do not fit within any category). If he is asserting that there is a category of rules that are residual, and that the mentally ill person breaks these rules, then he is already off to a false start. The mentally ill person is often bad-mannered, poorly socially skilled, or given to committing minor infractions of the law, but it is the way in which they do so that is irrational and unreasonable. So it is not the rules that are different, but rather the way in which they are broken, the pattern of such violations, the process of rule breaking and its context, social and human.

Coulter (1973) attempts a critique of the alternative interpretation of 'residual rule violation', that which states there is a residue of rule violations for which society has no label. Mental illness is an adequate label, Coulter writes. This was not Scheff's point however. One can describe a system of etiquette and its violations, similarly law and its crimes, but one cannot define the code of normality. It is residual in the sense that when all other explanations have been exhausted and found wanting, then the explanatory category 'mental illness' is used. A better way of tackling Scheff on this issue is to expose the fact that his term 'residual' would be better substituted by 'irrational' or 'inexplicable'. The confusion about whether 'residual' applies to the rule, or to the act of violation, then disappears. Instead 'residual' can be seen as a particular type of 'rule violation'.

Rule violation is a matter of contextual relevance, a point that has been emphasised by Goffman (1972), Blum (1970) and Lemert (1962). Goffman made this point explicitly in his discussion and description of a case of mania, where he gave a rational alternative explanation for the manic person's actions. The force of his argument is that if we knew the entire context of the mentally ill person's actions, we would no longer see them as irrational. Blum makes the same point in another way by demonstrating that, whatever the symptom of mental illness under consideration, a context could always be imagined in which it would be considered both normal and rational. Lemert's essay on paranoia also depends upon the same sort of normalising arguments.

Of course all symptomatic behaviour is normal in some circumstances, because stripping a behaviour of its social context removes much of its meaning and sensibility. Behaviour/action takes place in a social context. It is possible to imagine contexts in which symptomatic behaviour would be normal, but it is also possible to

imagine contexts in which normal behaviour would be very symptomatic. The thing about mental symptoms is that they do not fit,
mesh, or appear properly meaningful in the context in which they
are displayed. And hence they are irrational. They do not become
rational because one can imagine sometime, somewhere, in the most
strange combination of circumstances that one could find the
behaviour reasonable. What is more, coincidence has to be piled on
coincidence to explain chains and combinations of different symptomatic behaviours. Even if one tried, the whole edifice collapses
when you ask the mentally ill to explain and justify their own
behaviour, and they cannot do so in rational terms. Goffman's
particular trick (upon which nearly the whole of his book *Asylums*
rests) of finding reasonable explanations for strange behaviour only
works because he uses isolated individual examples of particular
actions, and fails to check his interpretations by asking the subjects.

Mental illness is no less real because its signs cannot be
subtracted from social context. Goffman and Blum seem to think
that they have pushed the phenomena into some sort of ethereal
realm of 'interaction' or 'sociality', where mental symptoms are
created through talk and action, rather than being natural
phenomena capable of description. There are senses in which
mental illness can be considered to be socially constructed, but this
is not one. Mental illness is not purely a matter of social convention
and hence indeterminate.

SOME MISUNDERSTANDINGS

One of the implications Goffman and Blum are trying to draw is
that mental illness has no underlying reality, no real commonality
between its different instances. So 'it could have been otherwise' –
what we now call mental illness could be considered normal, and if
it could be considered normal it should be, because why should we
compulsorily treat and lock away people whom we could consider
normal? The trouble here is that we can quite easily accept the
premise without accepting any of the following arguments. We
could indeed start to consider deluded and psychotic behaviour
normal, if we so wished. Whether this would be a good, humane
thing to do, whether it would have beneficial consequences for the
deluded/psychotic person and those around him still remains a relevant question. This argument was only perceived to have any weight
in the first place because of a combination of misperceptions of

psychiatry and failings in psychiatric care. The psychiatric care system in the UK has improved considerably since the 1960s, when these critiques had their heyday. Furthermore, it needs to be pointed out that even then, the vast majority of psychiatric patients were treated on a voluntary basis. A good moral case can be made for the operations of psychiatry. The anti-psychiatric sociologists are mistaken in believing that if they show psychiatric symptoms to be socially contexted they may then conclude a politico-moral argument for the abolition of psychiatry. This is not the case. Psychiatry is of course open to political and moral critique at any time, but its operations have not been rationally or logically undercut by the above arguments.

The second implication that has been drawn from this line of argument is that by a matter of logical necessity, mental illness cannot have a genetic/physiological cause. This argument can be found explicitly in Coulter (1975), Blum (1970), Szasz (1987), and in passing in Lemert (1951). The argument is generally applied to schizophrenia as a paradigm case, and it is asserted in two forms:

1   Reliable diagnosis is impossible, because it is a matter of socially contexted judgement. A sample of consistently diagnosed schizophrenia sufferers cannot therefore be generated for research purposes. This being so, research into supposed neuro-chemical causes is impossible.
2   If schizophrenia was a physiologically based disease, its symptoms would be objective and determinate. As they are not, schizophrenia cannot have a physiological basis.

This argument is at fault, and it is easy to show that it must be. However, it is not so easy to say why. It is faulty because diagnoses of toxic confusional state, organic dementias and epilepsy are all made on the basis of socially contexted judgements, yet nobody would dispute that these are physiological disorders. But where is the flaw in the argument? I believe the mistake is to assume that moral/social categories are incommensurable with factual/physical categories. In fact, all our categories are based upon language use. Very few of our words are completely fixed and specific, defined exactly by absolutely determinate objective criteria. Even when they are, such criteria usually have relevance for only a very small area of human actions. Let us take as an example 'ten seconds'. A physicist might for certain purposes use exact criteria for this length of time, based upon rates of atomic decay. However, the fact that I use the same words to say to my wife how long it will be before I vacate the bathroom does not mean (a) that what I have said bears no relation to the real world because it is a socially contexted judgement, or (b) that it bears no relation to the use of the same words by the physicist. In a similar way, showing that psychiatric diagnostic concepts are socially contexted judgements does not rob them of some objective content. How well they relate to the world as conceived in terms of biochemical physiology remains an open question, one that can be empirically investigated. The fact that the initial judgement is social does not rule out the possibility that at a later stage of investigation more precise physiological criteria may be found. If they are, then of course the meaning of the terms in use then begins to change, because they become based upon differing criteria for their application.

SOCIETAL REACTION AS ALL POWERFUL

Lemert portrayed deviance as a tripartite phenomenon: primary deviance, societal reaction and secondary deviance. Scheff (1966) adopted a similar stance, but reduced the importance of the primary deviance and elevated the importance of the societal reaction and secondary deviance. By doing so, his real innovation was to provide a social aetiological theory of mental illness. Primary deviance, he argued, occurs all the time for a diverse number of reasons, and most of the time no great notice is taken of it. However, sometimes (whether this is due to chance or to other reasons) a deviant act is identified as evidence of mental illness and the deviant person receives psychiatric treatment (is labelled mentally ill). Because he is then treated by others around him as mentally ill (the societal reaction) he begins to fulfil their expectations and behaves in a way consonant with the role (secondary deviance). In this way Scheff is able to say that the societal reaction is of significant aetiological importance in mental illness, without denying that other factors may play a role in the production of the primary deviance. He then allows the primary deviance to fall into the background while he describes in detail the nature and effects of the societal reaction.

Before moving on to a critique of Scheff's ideas, it should be noted that his other research into the phenomenon of mental illness is both important and influential. Particularly powerful was his exposure of the superficiality of the compulsory admission proce-

dure in the USA in the late 1950s and early 1960s. His demonstration that people were being compulsorily admitted to psychiatric
hospitals on the basis of five-minute court hearings plus the opinion
of a psychiatrist did much to support mental health legislation
reform in the USA, and perhaps later even the 1983 reform of the
Mental Health Act in the UK.

I have argued earlier that Scheff's idea of 'residual rule breaking'
can retain its sense if it is interpreted as referring to those rule violations or patterns of rule violations for which there is no clear
motivational rationale or explanation. This is still not entirely satisfactory as a description of mental illness as I will show in the next
chapter. However, the main faults of Scheff's theorising lay elsewhere.

The first mistake has to do with the idea of societal reaction, or
what Scheff calls 'labelling'. The problem here is that Scheff offers
us no criteria for the use of his theoretical term 'labelling'. He does
not explain what factors determine whether a person who behaves
oddly is labelled mentally ill or not. Although he asserts that most
odd behaviour remains unlabelled, he does not say why, and under
what circumstances, some is. Others have humorously remarked that
the implication is that the mentally ill suffer from contingencies, not
from mental illness! Scheff also fails to tell us who can label, and
how it takes place. I may well call my boss 'crazy' when he describes
some lunatic scheme for increasing company profits. However, my
attempt to label him mentally ill (if that is what it was) is unlikely to
succeed. Perhaps Scheff intends that labelling should mean being
diagnosed mentally ill by a properly qualified psychiatrist. However,
even to get to the psychiatrist one must be suspected of being
mentally ill, and therefore the labelling process has at least already
started. In any case, if it is necessary to see a psychiatrist to become
labelled 'mad', there cannot by definition be a 'mad' person who
has never seen a psychiatrist. A similar lack of defined criteria
surrounds the use of the term 'label'. True labels belong on parcels,
boxes, bottles and the like. They are visible to everybody, and
indeed determine how we respond to the contents. However, once
'mentally ill' is determined to be a label (in an analogical sense) not
everything remains the same. The most important difference is that
not everybody can see or knows about the label. It is certainly not
stamped on the forehead of the mentally ill person for the public
and everyone he meets to view. Great care is taken in psychiatry via
the professional rules of confidentiality to make sure that as few

people as possible know that an individual is receiving or has received psychiatric treatment. Since not everyone knows about this 'label', the mentally ill are not presented with a unified front of expectations for them to continue behaving abnormally. The question that needs to be asked of Scheff is: how many, and which, people need to know for 'labelling' to have taken place? In fact the absence of criteria for the visibility and application of 'labelling' means that we do not have a theoretically clearly defined subject to analyse.

The second mistake in Scheff's theorising is that it turns the person who is mentally ill into an actor who is fulfilling the expectations of others, rather than somebody who is upset, disturbed, irrational or whatever in their own right. If the mentally ill are responding to societal reaction and fulfilling a well-known social role, their behaviour should match the stereotype and Scheff explicitly states that it does. But in reality it does not, and in fact there is often considerable confusion when someone first becomes psychotic precisely because their behaviour is nothing like the stereotype. The common man's idea of the mad role is very little like the real. If people are fulfilling social roles, why don't they fit the common cultural picture of madness? Instead they do things like invent neologisms, or reckon there are rays controlling them, or that the television is talking about them. The general public is entirely ignorant about these symptoms. If role stereotypes were being fulfilled, then we would have numerous people on our hands pretending to be Napoleon!

This picture of the mentally ill person as fulfilling role expectations is one of the major reasons why those who work in psychiatry find 'labelling' as a theory so unconvincing. Real encounters with psychoticism forcibly show that symptomatic behaviour is unpredictable, not the following of a stereotyped role. The acutely psychotic individual is plainly out of control and in such a state of suffering that it is clear they would not willingly endure it. Moreover, treating the person as sane simply has little or no influence during acute psychosis. All these are reasons why Gove's (1982) most potent answer to Scheff is a chapter giving an account of an episode of mental illness written by the sufferer and her spouse. The implication is that nobody could consider this as in any sense being passive fulfilment of social stereotypes.

OUTCOME OF THE SCHEFF/GOVE DEBATE

The Scheff/Gove debate raged over twelve years. Most of the furious argument was concentrated upon how the empirical evidence was to be interpreted. Little space was given over to assessing the rationality or otherwise of the theory. This whole debate fails to convince either way. It only confirms one's own views. Why is this? First of all, the appeal is to soft and controvertible evidence. There is not enough hard empirical evidence to prove Gove's position, and all Scheff has to show is that Gove's assertion of non-social factors in the genesis of mental illness is not the whole story. Secondly, Gove's real or understated arguments are that anyone with any familiarity with severe mental illness could not possibly mistake it for the phenomenon Scheff is describing. When overtly stated this is the argument that the mentally ill cannot be considered to be passively fulfilling social role expectations, but it is more forceful through the descriptive portrayal of someone who is mentally ill. Hence the paper that provides this harrowing description in Gove's book (Anonymous 1982) is a key one. Both protagonists, in any case, retreat to a position which some have called 'Weak Labelling Theory'. Scheff concedes that the significance of social labelling in aetiology may be only about 10 per cent, but still asserts the importance of societal reaction in determining the conduct of the mentally ill, while Gove concedes that social reaction does influence the course of mental illness.

It must be agreed that all this is not to say that societal reaction has no effect upon the mentally ill person. Of course it does. Because of his medical record held by his family doctor, he may find it more difficult to get a job. In certain circumstances he may be either treated as an invalid by his family or rejected by them. These are not trivial matters, but they are things that everybody knows and has always known. They have not been suddenly uncovered by Scheff much to our surprise. They are consequential, following after the occurrence of mental illness, not aetiological. If they were aetiological, then the manipulation of the societal reaction or removal from it would be curative. Unfortunately this is not so. Normalisation is not a therapy or a treatment and does not claim to be so; it is a rehabilitative strategy and the implementation of a moral perspective.

RECENT EMPIRICAL STUDIES

More recent versions of labelling theory applied to mental illness appear completely to recognise these points. Instead of offering any aetiological role to the societal reaction they investigate and elaborate upon the effects of official labelling (e.g. Mor *et al.* 1984; Link *et al.* 1987, 1991). Put another way, this new labelling literature has stigmatisation and social rejection as its focus, and explores among other things the coping mechanisms used by patients. Evidence is collated showing that sufferers of serious mental illness have more difficulty finding work and getting access to accommodation, and have constricted support networks, not just because of the direct effects of their illness but also because of the responses of others to them. In addition, instead of being portrayed as passive in the face of the labelling process, patients are seen as being able to make efforts to control how others see and respond to them. The new labelling literature has therefore become part of the wider work on stigma initiated by Goffman (1963) and continued now in writings by, for example, Susman (1994). These investigations are not without their theoretical and practical problems, distinguishing, for example, the effects of symptomatic behaviour from that of social stereotyping, as well as failing to define the concept of 'official labelling'. Nevertheless, because they refrain from giving an aetiological role to the societal reaction as Scheff does, they are much more theoretically coherent.

Scheff's entire theory is of course posited upon the exemplary case of schizophrenia. When we come to consider other psychiatric syndromes it can be seen that the theory bears less and less relation to what actually occurs. Let us take depression as an alternative example to schizophrenia. The depressed usually seek out help themselves. Only very rarely do they get compulsorily admitted to hospital. They do not see themselves, and rarely do others see them, as being 'crazy'. Therefore they do not even have the social role of 'madness' to fulfil, and so on. The theory starts to 'fit' actual patterns of conduct and happenings in the real, everyday world less and less well.

ON BEING SANE IN INSANE PLACES

Rosenhan's (1973) famous research study can be interpreted as supportive of Scheff's labelling theory. Rosenhan and his assistants gained admission to psychiatric hospitals in the USA by claiming to hear voices. These 'pseudopatients' then behaved normally and observed the responses of those around them. Most were kept in hospital for some weeks, all were treated with powerful drugs, and all were discharged with a diagnosis of psychosis. This led Rosenhan to assert that psychiatric professionals could not tell the difference between the sane and the insane. 'It is clear that we cannot distinguish the sane from the insane in psychiatric hospitals.' This appeared to support Scheff, implying that societal reaction was the complete explanation for mental illness or, to state the case more clearly, that psychiatric diagnosis really is a matter of contingency: 'psychiatric diagnosis betrays little about the patient, but much about the environment in which an observer finds him'.

The second way in which Rosenhan (this time explicitly) supports labelling theory is when he describes how the normal behaviour of the pseudopatients was accounted symptomatic because they had been diagnosed schizophrenic. However, in this case the term labelling refers to diagnosis and professional expectations, not social labelling as Scheff considered it. Thus what is being described is how psychiatric care shapes the behaviour of the mentally ill, not the aetiology of the mental illness in the first place. It should also be noted that the pseudopatients had given cause for their behaviour to be suspected as symptomatic, because they had laid claim to having some symptoms already. Only two actual examples are given, note-taking and the finding of psychopathological relationships in a pseudopatient's past. On the other hand Rosenhan himself admits that the majority of observations made by staff were not of behaviour seen as symptomatic, but 'these reports [nursing reports on the pseudopatients] uniformly indicate that the patients were "friendly", "cooperative", and "exhibited no abnormal indications"'.

Rosenhan's initial paper was met with a storm of protest, the most potent of which came from Spitzer (1975), who argued that all that had been demonstrated by Rosenhan was that psychiatrists could be fooled by people who pretended to be mentally ill. Following Spitzer's critique, Rosenhan (1975) changed his ground and said that the psychiatrists were right to admit the pseudopatients, but wrong to diagnose them as schizophrenic on so little evidence. This can be readily agreed with, but it is very far from his earlier aggressive claim that psychiatric professionals cannot tell the difference between the sane and insane.

SOME ORIGINS OF DEVIANCY AND LABELLING THEORY

Labelling theory did not appear upon the sociological scene out of a vacuum. Several strands of sociological thought can be identified as leading towards the tenets of labelling theory and the associated sociological criticism of psychiatry. Clarification and elaboration of these demonstrates some of the origins of the above identified errors that can be found in labelling as a theory of mental illness. Description of the theoretical roots of labelling theory illuminates some assumptions frequently made in sociological analyses of different fields. Elucidation of these may have implications for sociological study in areas other than psychiatry.

Durkheim (1938, 1964) was one of the founding thinkers of sociology; his work is of great breadth and complexity. Of necessity, therefore, any discussion of his ideas as they may relate to labelling theory will be incomplete because of its focus and brevity. Nevertheless, there are two elements of Durkheim's thought that appear to provide for labelling theory.

The first is Durkheim's assertion that all social order is a matter of moral facts and regulation. In making this argument Durkheim's concern was to show that social order required a social rather than just a psychological explanation, and to demonstrate that social or moral facts could be objectively defined and scientifically studied. However, in doing this Durkheim made no substantive distinction between law, morals, customs, fashions, standards of taste, articles of faith, religion, etiquette, ceremony and tradition. To Durkheim (1964), 'All moral facts consist in a rule of sanctioned conduct.' As I have argued above, to talk in a broad and generalised fashion like this obscures serious and consequential differences between different categories of rule breaking. Although Durkheim did elsewhere make some rudimentary distinctions between different types of rules, later sociology collapsed all social order into a matter of moral rule-following, under the impression that the underlying structure of the social world had been found and was being described. This subject will be taken up again in the following chapter.

The second element of Durkheim's thought that provides for labelling theory is his moral semi-relativism. There are two conflicting trains of thought in Durkheim's writing about moral order. With one set of arguments he tries to show that all morality has as its object the good of society as a whole. This would imply that morality was fairly uniform and determinate. However, there is also a semi-relativistic strain in Durkheim at several points, particularly when he likens different societies to different species and asserts that different standards of normality will therefore apply. At these points much of Durkheim's reasoning is obscure, and he sometimes appears to be arguing for a sort of proto-functionalist view of society. However, there is clear evidence that he did think in relativistic terms about morality, as he made the following statements, foreshadowing Becker (1963):

> What confers this character upon them is not the intrinsic quality of a given act, but that definition that the collective conscience lends them.
>
> (Durkheim 1938: 70)

> It is not the intrinsic nature of my action that produces the sanction which follows, but the fact that the act violates the rule that forbids it.
>
> (Durkheim 1964: 43)

Thus the labelling theorists were led into the error of making mental illness solely a property of the social process rather than something internal to the rule violator as well.

This same error was further elaborated by G. H. Mead (1936), who struggled to describe how the emergence of 'self' was determined by social process. In doing so he makes statements like the following:

> The individual experiences himself as such, not directly, but only indirectly, from the particular standpoints of other individual members of the same social group.
>
> (Mead 1936: 138)

> The structure of the complete self is a reflection of the complete social process.
>
> (Mead 1936: 144)

Mead therefore saw self and thought as emerging through social interaction. This is entirely correct, but due to Mead's confused elaboration of this idea an error was laid for labelling theory to build upon. A sympathetic reading of Mead shows him to be talking in a more fundamental sense than the labelling theorists. He is explaining the basis of the nature of self and thought – their very existence and essence, as it were. But the labelling theorists take all this framework as given in order to argue that (long after socialisation, long after language acquisition) the way people talk to us or regard us can change our essence (identity, central nature of the self) – we are wholly malleable in the face of the way other people see us, dependent upon them in a fundamental sense for our nature, without defence or self existence, as if we are permeated to our very core by our social interaction with others. Once we are labelled this is what we become. What the labelling theorists are negating here is the reality of our self sufficiency. Although rarely stated by them, these are the kinds of ideas they assume to support their theorising. Taken as a whole, Mead's writings show that he does not mean that the self is continually arising out of the social process, utterly dependent on it for its continued being. What he does mean is that children cannot be people without being brought up in a social community. Labelling theory has not really appreciated this distinction.

The school of sociological work and theorising out of which labelling theory emerged is known as 'symbolic interactionism' and is explicitly indebted to the work of Mead. Blumer (1969) and Hughes (1971) are the two names associated with the development of symbolic interactionism. Neither can be accused of particular errors resulting in labelling theory, but both provided for the development of such a theory in a variety of ways.

Blumer emphasised the importance of the actor's interpretation of his situation and his use of this in his ongoing conduct, in the analysis and description of human conduct. This emphasis upon actors' meaningful behaviour perhaps led to sociologists trying to understand the meaning of insane behaviour, the perspective of the mentally ill person, how they understood the world and constructed their actions in a meaningful sense. To the extent that this was possible, mental illness dropped out of the picture. The phenomenon we call mental illness is to be seen as a reasonable response to extreme social pressure. This method of interpretation supports or underpins the labelling endeavour without specifically providing for it.

Hughes represents a trend in sociology that co-existed with the birth of labelling theory. Hughes' thought arose from the same origins as that of labelling: the increased importance being given to the individual person's point of view, and the falling from favour of functionalism with its emphasis upon formal goals of organisations and institutions. He constructed piercing critiques of professionalisation strategies, occupational cultures and protectionism. By focusing his interest wholly upon the way workers and professionals safeguard their own interests, he was by implication arguing that this was the whole purpose of their organisation. His method is to enter into and understand the personal and social drama of the work situation. The chief topics he describes are the maximisation of status, and the minimisation of effort and difficulties. This is to make the actual overt aims of the occupation play second fiddle to the expressions of personal desires by the workers, thereby ironi-cising the whole venture of work. Although Hughes is not directly quoted by the early labelling theorists, his work had the potential to be linked with labelling theory in such a way as to show that the institution of psychiatry was both self-serving to psychiatric profes-sionals, and damaging to the mentally ill because it was the embodiment of societal reaction. Making this link in a systematic way has been left to Scull (1977, 1979) in his accounts of the devel-opment of psychiatry in the nineteenth century and of community care in the twentieth.

SUMMARY

In this chapter I have described labelling theory as it has been applied to the phenomenon of mental illness. The theory has been shown to be deficient in many respects. In particular, two major areas of defective reasoning have been identified: first, in relation to the concept of rules and social order, and second, in respect of the lack of defined content to the concepts of societal reaction and secondary deviance. The former of these raises important questions about the nature of mental illness and its relation to norms/rules, and this topic will be taken up in the next chapter. To conclude, some of the roots of labelling theory have been identified in the sociological traditions to which it belongs.

Chapter 3

Rules

As I have described in the last chapter, the use made of the concept of social rules or norms is central to the deviancy theory of mental illness. Deviancy theory purports to give (i) an accurate generalised description of the phenomenon of mental illness, and (ii) an explanation of that phenomenon. However, as I will show below, it can in fact do neither of these things, mainly because it works with a confused version of the nature of 'rules'. To see how this is so, we must first examine the sociological conceptions and confusions about rules and rule breaking.

SOCIAL ORDER

The dominant picture in sociology used to be that social order was produced by 'norms' or 'rules'. These two terms are generally used interchangeably within the sociological literature, although 'norm' is in addition occasionally used to refer to statistical averages or modes. Rules or norms have been considered to be mainly unconscious, having been internalised during the process of socialisation. Thus society operated harmoniously and smoothly, all social institutions having a function and all human behaviour gearing together via the shared normative order. This picture is very much associated with the work of Talcott Parsons (1951), although these ideas were widely shared by sociologists and indeed tend to crop up regularly in any discussions of the nature of social order.

Functionalism was toppled from its dominant position by symbolic interactionism and by ethnomethodology. A series of immensely strong arguments have now made it impossible to accept the Parsonian picture in any form. Its most major deficit was that it left no sensible place for the explanations of behaviour given by people themselves. Whatever it was that people thought they were doing and the reasons that they thought they had, they were actually being guided in their conduct by the internalised rules that were producing socially ordered behaviour. The Parsonian picture turned the explanations that people gave for their actions into an epiphenomenon of no importance. It therefore just did not tally with our experience of our lives. We do act upon reasonable considerations, and in doing so we respond to what others give as reasons for their actions. Our actions are not compelled in some mysterious fashion.

The consequence of this more realistic appraisal of what people do and why they do it led to a better appreciation of the nature of rules and norms. Instead of being seen as forcefully compelling regular conduct, it began to be understood that they were used by people in order to act in a meaningful fashion. Garfinkel (1967) expressed this by saying that rules were constitutive of conduct. The main idea here is common to both ethnomethodological and symbolic interactionist writings but is described in slightly differing ways. The former have a clearer perspective because they appreciate that people consciously use and refer to rules in producing meaningful behaviour and understanding the meaningful behaviour of others. An example of this sort of work would be Wieder's (1974) study of how convicted criminals living in a halfway house ordered their activity in conscious relation to the 'convict code' which prohibited informing, confessing guilt, etc. The latter tradition comes closest to an understanding of this in those authors who have used a 'negotiated order' perspective to understand a variety of settings. Strauss *et al.* (1964) do this when they describe the 'continual negotiative activity' between participants within a psychiatric hospital, resulting in 'transitory arrangements' being made to allow the administrative and clinical work to take place.

RULES AS A UNITARY PHENOMENON

The current stress on rule use in socially ordered behaviour has perhaps been given even more impetus by the later philosophy of Wittgenstein. He used the rule use picture to dissolve a number of philosophical problems related to language. However, we are in danger of being totally swept away by the picture of rules. All orderly social behaviour is now understood to be a matter that is constructed using rules. Moreover, a particularly prevalent inaccuracy is to see all order as a moral order, and all rules as moral rules.

Thus if all order is a matter of moral rules, then all deviance (rule breaking) is likewise a unitary phenomenon. Therefore crime, sexual deviance and mental illness and so on are all different exemplars of substantially the same phenomenon, and may be described in the same general terms. This is a pernicious chain of errors that handicaps further sociological thinking and particularly fuels the misunderstandings of mental illness which are made from a labelling perspective.

The first mistake which needs to be swept away is the assumption that all order is a moral order and that all rules are moral rules. Garfinkel (1967) is here particularly at fault for both explicitly endorsing the position that all order is a moral order, and promoting this assumption via his well-known and oft-quoted series of rule breaking experiments. There is a particular game which is played on and off throughout the course of these experiments. It goes like this. Here are some minor and rather trivial rules – let's go out and break them and see what happens. Shock and surprise! Those around us get very upset when we do this. See how we have threatened the moral order of everyday life, because even when we break these trivial rules, our conduct is sanctioned. We are punished for doing wrong.

The deception which is being perpetrated becomes visible when we examine exactly what situations and what rules were being broken. In the experiment where Garfinkel asked his students to behave as boarders in their own homes, the students acted in such a way as to call into question foundational bonds of love, affection and a lifetime of commitment to other people. So of course the scenes exploded. Nothing strange at all here, because these were not some trivial background scheme or irrelevancies, but absolutely fundamental life-and-death issues. A similar ploy operates in the Tic Tac Toe experiment, where the students were instructed to break the rules of the game. It might be thought that these are trivial rules of a trivial, unimportant paper-and-pencil game. However, what the rule breaking was really calling into question was the whole human activity of games, sports and competition. Learning and following the rules of games are a matter of intensive learning during childhood. Likewise in the experiment in which students were instructed to assume hidden motives during a conversation, quite fundamentally damaging attacks were once again made on important personal relationships, so the acute and emotional reactions of the conversational partners are hardly a matter for awed wonder.

Garfinkel's rule breaking experiments are therefore misleading. He appears to want us to believe that what is being contested are the most superficial and frivolous of rules, thus underlining the omnipresence of social order. However, the rules being challenged are in fact highly important ones and it is not surprising that the reactions are severe rather than mild. Superficial rule breaking is ignored, unnoticed or solely a conversation piece. For example, if I tie knots instead of bows in my shoe laces, I am just as much breaking a rule but I do not get sanctioned. In this case my attack upon the 'moral order' of everyday life produces no sanction or breakdown of organised activity.

What this all underlines is that not all order in human activity is a moral order, and not all rules are moral rules. To use the word morality in this way is to stretch its meaning well past breaking point. The word 'moral' belongs with our language games of right and wrong, good and bad, sin, righteousness, guilt, retribution, repentance, confession, forgiveness and the like. To wrench the word morality out of that context and apply it to all regular orderly behaviour from eating breakfast in the morning to going to bed at night, removes much of the meaning from the word. In fact all that is left is the sense that the behaviour under consideration (whatever it might be) is to be considered rule-governed and also that it is therefore possible to break the rule. The word 'moral' is thus redundant in this descriptive scheme, as it adds nothing and carries the potential confusion of invoking its context of origin. Even if the use of the word 'moral' serves to accentuate the fact that these rules are made and imposed by people, rather than imposed from outside as it were, the word is still not required. All that is needed is a correct picture of the nature of 'rule' and 'being in accord with a rule', and this has been provided by Wittgenstein, as we shall see.

As I pointed out in the last chapter, there are actually many different kinds of rules – rules of grammar, rules of games, rules of etiquette, legal rules, rules of mathematics, to name but a few. Likewise there is not one single general response to the breaking of a rule which we can call 'sanction'. There are a whole range of different responses, depending upon what kind of rule has been broken. The appropriate response to someone who adds two and two and gets five is vastly different from the typical response to being punched on the nose. Breaking a rule may result in punishment and sanction, but it may also result in verbal disapproval, negative evaluation, imposing humiliation, retribution, rejection, denunciation, or degradation. There is not enough uniformity here to provide grounds for a generalised description, and this is because there remains some ambiguity about the nature of the concept of 'rule' and how it applies to human conduct.

WITTGENSTEIN ON RULES

In the course of dispelling the philosophical problems related to dualism and cognitivism, Wittgenstein illuminated many aspects of rules which are of great relevance to sociology and to my consideration of the labelling theory of mental illness. Wittgenstein's clarification of the nature of rules and rule following behaviour has implications far beyond this narrowly defined topic, but I will restrict myself to a consideration of those issues which are of direct relevance to the topic in hand.

There is a small but important amount of evidence that Wittgenstein thought of 'rules' as a family resemblance concept (Baker and Hacker 1985). Whether he thought this proposal through or not, this picture certainly helps to illuminate some of the inconsistencies and confusions in the sociological unitary picture of rules and the moral order. Words, Wittgenstein argued, do not directly represent objects. One of the tactics he used to show this was the kind of word he called a 'family resemblance concept', and his favoured example was the word 'game'. There are many different kinds of games, all with different characteristics, but there are no one or two characteristics common to all games. Games resemble each other like the appearance of members of a family where, for example, one set of members has the same hair colour, another and different set has the same body build etc. Thus there are overlapping common characteristics among the things we would call games, but no single item which the word game could be said to represent. Wittgenstein had a range of philosophical points in view to be made out of this argument. For our purposes we may set these to one side, to see how this picture illuminates the diversity of things/practices that we would be willing to call rules.

Rules differ in terms of their appearance, their function, the outcome of following or not following them, degree of schematisation, degree of formality and in the source of their authority. Although criminal law, rules of club membership, and other sorts of rules are written down, it is important to realise that not all rules are verbal. A tape measure is a rule. Casting a fly 'just so' while

trout fishing is a rule. Going to the post office and buying a stamp is
following rules. Conversing with a friend involves rules of taking
turns. Maintaining eye contact during that conversation is a rule of
how to pay attention. Rules are first and foremost regular orderly
human practices. Some are codified and written down, for certain
purposes (usually for agreed commitment of a group or to act as a
source to which one can appeal), but others are not. Wittgenstein
showed that the use of words and the manipulation of language is
itself a matter of rules and their application. To explain the
meaning of a word is to give a rule for its use. Some rules are just
the way things are done. They are traditions or conventions. Others
are highly rigid and formal, carefully defined and given legitimate
authority over the whole community, like the rules and codes of our
legal system.

These rules are not just one method amongst others of
describing human behaviour. The very fact that human behaviour is
orderly means that it cannot only be described but can also be justified and/or explained in relation to some rule or another. A further
consequence is that it can always be shown that human behaviour is
consciously constructed and put together in the light of knowledge
of the relevant rules. When knowledge of the relevant rules is absent
this becomes cause for remark or action by others. This characteristic of rule-guided activity was appreciated by Garfinkel (1967),
who referred to rules as being constitutive of behaviour. Indeed the
very idea of 'human behaviour' or 'human activity' is inseparable
from that of rule following. Disorderly and entirely random actions
by people could hardly be called 'activity' or 'behaviour'.

The consequences of breaking a rule vary enormously, from no
response from others, through verbal correction from friends, to
objections from strangers to the institutionalised punitive responses
of the criminal justice system. On the other hand, breaking rules in
some cases just results in the failure of our endeavours: if we don't
put the baking soda in the cake mix, the cake doesn't rise in the
oven and is inedible; if we fail to follow correctly the instructions
that come with the self-assembly piece of furniture, it doesn't fit
together; if we don't count our money properly, we end up over-
drawn at the bank. Also to be considered is the fact that not all
rules are moral rules, and not all order is a moral order. To assert
that they are is to conflate many different ways of speaking. Bad,
sin, evil, guilt, atonement, revenge and retribution belong to the
language of morality. This is sanctionable disorderliness, although it

merges and overlaps with disorderliness that merits only a correction, like the misuse of a word. There remains all the difference in the world between a slip of the tongue which breaks the rules of grammar, and murder which transgresses our morality and our law.

It is also important to appreciate that human activities can be at one and the same time orderly and in accord with some rules while at the same time breaking others, and that the breaking of rules can itself be orderly, governed by rules and described as such. Let us take the example of the armed robber of the post office. He plans his robbery with great care, endeavouring to ensure that he cannot be filmed and recognised. He threatens the post office clerk in a regular orderly fashion, according to rules so that he and his victim know exactly what he means and intends. For example, he points his sawn-off shotgun at the clerk, not at himself or out of the window. He tells the clerk to 'hand over the money' using the grammatical rules of the language. However, at the same time as carrying out this orderly, rule-governed activity of the hold-up, he is breaking other rules of legality and morality. Another example would be telling a lie. Here the language use is correct and in accord with the rules of grammar. The telling is done correctly, in a perfectly orderly fashion, yet the action transgresses our moral rules. Whether an action is taken to be in accord with rules or not therefore depends upon the purposes of the evaluator and their interests. It is they who determine and select the rules with which to evaluate the conduct in view.

Thus Wittgenstein considered, as I have argued above, that there are many different sorts of rules with many different consequences, and that these types of rules have cross-cutting 'family' resemblances rather than there being some criteria, content or essence which is common to all rules – or to rule breaking, for that matter. This is a valuable corrective to the simplistic view that all orderly human behaviour is produced by the following of a single kind of moral rule or norm. There is not only one sort of rule, the moral norm, and there is not only one sort of rule-breaker, the deviant. It is therefore a mistake to think that speaking in such generalities is informative.

There still remain several other pictures of rules that the work of Wittgenstein warns us to avoid. Rules are not to be seen as causative of behaviour. They are not, as it were, the girders of social structure. To talk about all human action as governed by rules appears to imply that everything is caused by rules, but this is the wrong picture. People use rules to make sense, to make action accountable. They are not driven by rules willy-nilly into certain courses of action. To say this is to raise again the spectre of what Garfinkel (1967) called judgemental dopism, the actor being turned into an unthinking tool of the social rules and norms. People consider quite carefully what they do, and plan their courses of action and the means to their goals in the light of what they know of the enormous variety of rules that relate to their conduct.

A further concern of Wittgenstein was to point out that none of our rules derive directly from the nature of the world in which we live. Our rules are not reflections of the nature of reality. He particularly had in mind here both the rules of logic and of grammar, but the same point applies to all our rules. They are justified or not by their utility. They stand by themselves and are autonomous. In the final analysis, they are the way we do things. As such, they are of course susceptible to change from time to time, and to variation between different social groups and cultures. It is this mundane reality that Becker elevated into the phrase 'rules create deviance'. This phrase is true inasmuch as it underlines that rules are variable and are made by groups of people in concert. However, it is false in the way it is used to imply that sometime, somewhere, there were no rules at all, and the creation of the first rule created the first deviance. Rule following cannot be theoretically extracted from human behaviour in this way. It is and has always been a characteristic of all that we could or would ever call human behaviour and activity.

CONSEQUENCES OF MISTAKEN THINKING ABOUT RULES

We can now be somewhat clearer about the consequences of talking, as do the labelling theorists, about rules in general:

1 The selective attention to certain types of rules neglects many areas of human activity which are rule-governed. Crime in particular is used as the paradigm, instead of careful attention being given to the similarities and differences between different sorts of rules and rule breaking.

2 The term 'deviant' is used to produce a body of people about whom generalisations can be made. But there is no such group,

and there are no generalisations to be made, therefore there is no gain that accrues from this type of theorising.

3 As I shall further show below, the unique character or differences of mental illness are obscured rather than elucidated.

4 Everything is reduced to a matter of morality and moral order, and thus the words 'good' and 'bad', 'right' and 'wrong' are badly used, misapplied and sow confusion into the discussion of human activities. This causes a specific confusion in the case of mental illness where ideas of responsibility for actions are already organised with great complexity.

MENTAL ILLNESS AND RULE BREAKING

I will now attempt to come to a clearer conception of the relationship between mental illness and rule breaking. The connections between the two phenomena are complex and varied, and will involve no small degree of effort in teasing out the different senses of words in common usage. The main points I wish to make are:

1 *Abnormality is not a coterminous concept with rule breaking.* The statistically abnormal is not the same as the breaking of a rule. One might be abnormally tall, have an unusual gait, talk in an unusual tone or volume of voice or have an unusual hobby. None of these things are breaking a rule. Where the confusion arises is that most people for most of the time do follow most of the rules that we have made for ourselves. The person who breaks a rule is therefore unusual, stands out from the crowd, and that rule breaking might then be thought of as unusual. However, it is only abnormal because of its low frequency occurrence, not because of its nature of rule abrogation.

Abnormality is used in another sense to mean not just statistically infrequent or rare, but also to mean warped or unusual in nature and actions. It is applied in the sense of negative valuation when it is not possible to empathise with the person under consideration or with their actions. Either their motives are obscure and opaque, or they are rejected as being insufficient justification for the person's actions. In this fashion the word is often applied to the mentally ill and handicapped. This is related to another usage of the word 'abnormality'. The word is also applied to those with a physical defect or handicap, once again invoking the negative notions of faint nausea, disgust, ugliness or mutation, often coupled with a degree of rejection.

Fabrega (1991) has tried to produce a culture-free definition of mental illness by the use of the term 'human behavioural breakdown'. The root idea here is that of anomalies in human social behaviour. Thus he is like the deviancy theorists, though not entirely so, because his focus is not on rules but 'difference'. To this he adds 'negatively valued', 'not wilful' and 'troublesome to social life'. This all initially seems quite good and fertile ground. Upon further thought, however, the idea of anomaly is exactly the same as that of deviation from the average, except that the latter suggests ever increasing degrees of deviation, whereas anomaly suggests something by itself, an outlier, a categorical difference rather than one of degree. This is a slightly different conception of abnormality, but still not one which is equivalent to rule breaking.

2 *Rule breaking is not the most salient aspect of all that we call mental illness.* It is unfortunate that the labelling theorists concentrated upon only one type of mental illness in their theorising, namely schizophrenia. It is this mental illness that comes closest to fitting the picture of mental illness as rule breaking. Other mental illnesses do not fit the picture nearly so well, if at all. Many do not seem to involve any breaking of rules of any sort. Take anxiety neurosis as an example. We do not have rules that specify given levels of anxiety that the sufferer breaks. Similarly with depression, there are no rules laying down that we should be reasonably happy and content. We could, by stretching our vocabulary and descriptive powers, say that the over-anxious person is acting in ways that are unusual, or we could even say that as a matter of common practice we should not be so anxious. However, no matter how much we twist and turn here, rule breaking does not really capture the essence of anxiety or of depression. We can far more readily see that the most salient aspects of these phenomena are suffering and distress.

3 *When, on occasion, rule breaking is the most salient aspect of a mental illness, it is not the rule breaking itself that is the common denominator, but the lack of reason/explanation for it.* Where mental illness does involve the breaking of rules, as it typically does in schizophrenia, a number of different rules may be broken, for example conversational regularity, language use, criminal or immoral conduct. The sufferers behave in

unpredictable and inexplicable ways. There is no coherent set of 'mental health' or 'normality' rules that they break. They may break any or all of a diverse collection of rules for the orderly conduct of human affairs.

The rule breaking of mental illness differs from other kinds, therefore, in a variety of ways, both in the diversity of rules which are broken, as I have indicated, and in the absence of any reasonable explanation for that rule breaking. In everyday life, people break rules for all kinds of reasons: jokes, experiments, deception, for personal advantage, and so on. What these examples have in common is that there is a reason for the rule breaking, an understandable motivation, and it is precisely this that is absent in the phenomenon of mental illness, causing us to think of categorising a certain rule breaking incident as mental illness.

4 *The rule breaking which is involved in mental illness has specific patterns to it, rather than being random.* That the rule breaking that is part and parcel of some sorts of mental illnesses is without rational explanation does not mean that the rule breaking is random. It does in fact follow certain patterns, and these patterns have been a focus of much study, investigation and analysis by psychiatric professionals. It is these patterns that contribute to the formation of diagnostic categories in psychiatric diagnostic systems. This is not to say that diagnostic symptoms can be mapped onto sets and categories of rules in human conduct, for as has already been argued, there is much about mental illness that does not readily fit a rule breaking paradigm picture. However, there are quite regular ways in which, say, a person suffering from mania will break social rules.

SUMMARY

It must therefore be concluded that rule breaking is not the common denominator, does not capture the essence, does not wholly describe the phenomenon of mental illness. Mentally ill people do indeed break rules, but not always. This is not the essence of mental illness – far, far from it. It is a major error to view the most salient feature of mental illness as rule breaking; this is more correct in analyses of crime. In mental illness the rule breaking is incidental,   unintentional,   sometimes   accidental,   haphazard, unplanned, and largely without sense, not fitting within a socially recognised framework of actions–goals. Certainly it is possible to talk about mental illness in terms of social rules and rule breaking, but this is not tremendously helpful and leads to much confusion. In order to describe some mental illnesses in these terms it is necessary to use linguistic contortions which neglect significant aspects of the phenomena – as when trying to describe anxiety neurosis in this way. Additionally, social rules are diverse in nature, preventing large-scale theorising about mental illness as rule breaking from taking place. Lastly, it is not the rule breaking itself that is characteristic of mental illness, but (among other characteristics to be explored later) the lack of rationale for that rule breaking and its pattern when considered with other actions.

Chapter 4

Culture

The amount of literature on this subject grows almost by the day. It hooks the curiosity of anyone with an interest in psychiatry, because of the range and diversity of human societies and behaviour, and because of the ways in which the phenomenon we call mental illness is located within those settings. In the literature numerous accounts of mental distress in differing cultures jostle for our attention. Descriptions of the structure of Iranian society, the place of women within that structure and their expression of 'heart distress' compete for our attention with case studies of the lives of those traumatised by the cultural revolution in China. At one moment one can be considering the way of life of a small 'primitive' society in New Guinea and how its members meet the painful events in their lives, and the next moment one can be considering similar events and how they affect the lives of Buddhists in Sri Lanka. Such a body of literature cannot fail, at the very least, to engage interest and attention.

With respect to theory, transcultural psychiatry remains rather a battleground upon which basically different paradigms of mental disorder are mauled and fought over. These issues recur in different forms in most disputes about psychiatry. As located in transcultural psychiatry, these disputes are sharpened and slightly more clear cut, thus enabling an attempt at clarification to take place.

IMPORTANCE OF THE PHILOSOPHY OF LANGUAGE

Essential to resolving these disputes is a clear grasp of the nature of language. It is the failure to attain an accurate view of this topic that has bedevilled transcultural psychiatry, and has kept all the arguments floundering in a sea of confusion. Therefore in order to tackle the confusions that have arisen, it is necessary first to consider the philosophy of language. It is probably already clear that I draw much of my philosophical inspiration form the 'ordinary language' school of philosophy and from Wittgenstein's later philosophy. Although I will provide a thumb-nail sketch of that philosophy below, this is not the correct place for a full examination or justification of that position. Further details of the philosophical position I describe can be found in the original works of Wittgenstein (1958), Ryle (1949), Austin (1965), and commentaries upon them by Baker and Hacker (1980) and Hunter (1973). In what follows I provide a preliminary description of this philosophical position, and observe how various complexities and confusions embedded in the literature on transcultural psychiatry all fall away when considered from this point of view.

One of Wittgenstein's key insights was that our vocabulary, rather than being a set of symbols representing objects, actions, relationships and the like, was a tool-box full of verbal resources for accomplishing many varieties of tasks.

> Think of the tools in a tool-box: there is a hammer, pliers, a saw, a screw-driver, a rule, a glue-pot, glue, nails and screws. The functions of words are as diverse as the functions of these objects.
>
> (Wittgenstein 1958: I, para. 11)

For Wittgenstein, language was not just a matter of speaking, but also of how that speaking fitted into regular practices and courses of human activity. It is to this that his famous phrase 'language game' refers: that any one word, term or regular phrase fits within typical contexts of activity within which it makes sense, both word and activity together making a 'language game'. Wittgenstein also used the concept of language games as a heuristic device, creating imaginary languages and contexts of activity in order to illustrate a variety of philosophical points about language use.

Wittgenstein used this picture of language as a set of tools in order to start prising apart our commitment (often unnoticed) to the view of language as some form of symbolic or representational calculus. This had in fact been his own, earlier, philosophical point of view and had been propounded in many complex ways by Frege and Russell. It was from our habitual thinking in this type of way that Wittgenstein attempted to unshackle us. In his later philosophy he saw that many philosophical problems were ultimately derived

from misunderstandings about our own language use. His aim
therefore was, as it were, to 'let the fly out of the bottle', the task of
philosophy being to set us free from our confusions so that we could
carry on with more important tasks.

AN EXAMPLE OF PHILOSOPHICAL CONFUSION

The philosophy of mind is a central area where confusions about
language use generate philosophical perplexity and confusion.
Wittgenstein successfully demonstrated that many words taken to
represent mental states or processes were being consistently misunderstood by philosophical analysts, resulting in the unnecessary
conundrums associated with various 'resolutions' of the mind/body
problem.

> A main source of our failure to understand is that we do not
> command a clear view of the use of our words.
>
> (Wittgenstein 1958: I, para. 122)

As an initial move towards clarification, Wittgenstein first showed
that 'meaning' and 'understanding' were not forms of mysterious
mental phenomena.

It is very natural for us to think of meaning and understanding
as mental processes and phenomena. Words and symbols are after
all quite arbitrary. The vocal noise we make to represent an item
could quite easily have been something other. What gives it meaning
is the mental process of meaning that accompanies its utterance and
the understanding that accompanies its hearing. Additionally, we
have all experienced suddenly understanding something (for
instance, whilst reading a text or listening to a lecture), so it seems
that when we say 'Now I understand' we are reporting an inner
mental phenomenon.

Wittgenstein showed these to be pervasive misconceptions.
Although certain experiences may accompany understanding, they
are not necessary or sufficient for saying understanding has taken
place. No inner experience at all may accompany understanding –
we may just go on to act upon that understanding. Similarly, understanding may be accompanied by thoughts of the logical
connections or reasoning between sets of ideas, but this may occur
even without understanding because it must be applied correctly
before we are willing to grant that understanding has been achieved.
Neither is understanding equivalent to matching up words with

mental images, for this implies not only that there must be an infinite regress of image behind image, but that understanding is like imagining (and do we really have an image of a car in our mind every time we hear and understand the word in the context of a sentence?). Wittgenstein therefore concluded that understanding is an ability. Understanding a mathematical formula is equivalent to having the ability to apply it; understanding a word is to be able to use it correctly. When one says 'I understand', one is not reporting an inner mental process at all, one is avowing an ability to do something. The criterion for saying that someone has understood is that they demonstrate that ability.

Wittgenstein argued that the word 'meaning' was also generally misunderstood to refer to a mental process. The meaning of a word is not its accompaniment by mental images in the mind. Rather the meaning of a word is given by the explanation of its use. Therefore if one wishes to understand what a word means, one must look at the way in which it is actually used.

When this searchlight is turned upon many other words which are generally taken to refer to mental states or processes, it starts to become clear that viewing them as such promotes metaphysical confusion. Take, for example, 'reading'. We sit with a novel, turning the pages in silence and reading it from beginning to end. Reading the book is not looking at its pages alone, or turning them over sequentially. It must therefore be some strange and ethereal mental process, something like a string of images passing through the mind. Very soon this leads us to propound the idea that the mental process of reading is accompanied by all sorts of unconscious information processing, and that if this is not going on then we are not reading. A Wittgenstinian position on reading, as he himself elaborated in the *Philosophical Investigations*, would be very different. Instead of seeking metaphysical criteria for the application of the word reading, we would instead look at the circumstances of the use of the word. In Wittgenstein's terms this would be to describe its logical grammar. How are we able to say that someone has read a book? Well, they will avow that they have done so, but we will not necessarily believe them. We may witness them sitting, concentrating and looking at the pages, but they may just be examining the text and font type. The final criterion for saying someone has read a book is that they are able to talk correctly and coherently about its contents. If they have read *War and Peace* they should be able to talk about the characters that appear in the story and about events in the narrative. This is therefore what 'reading' means. Quite truly, all sorts of inner mental experiences may or may not accompany reading a book, but these are not the criteria we use to apply the word. Similarly, it is quite certain that all kinds of physiological brain processes accompany reading a book, because after all, without a functioning brain one cannot read. But we do not need to look inside somebody's head with a PET scanner to see that they are reading. These are not the criteria for the use of that word, and they are not, therefore, its meaning.

Wittgenstein was very clear that we do not use words to refer to private inner experiences, but that we use them as members of a human community following linguistic rules. He showed quite categorically, with his famous 'Private Language Argument' (1958: I, para. 293), that words could not be used meaningfully if they referred to private inner experience. The argument goes like this. Suppose everybody had a box with something in it, an 'x'. No one can look in anyone else's box, and all say they know what an 'x' is by looking in their own box. This is how we often suppose mental state words are used; for instance, we all know what pain is by looking at our own private inner experience (equals looking at the 'x' in the box). But, as Wittgenstein goes on to point out, everybody might have something completely different in their box, or indeed there might be nothing at all. The word for 'x' cannot therefore have a place in the language of the community. In a similar fashion, words standing for mental states accessible only to those experiencing them can have no place in the language of the community. Therefore these words do not denote private inner experiences, but are used instead according to outward criteria and have their place in human behaviour and practices.

This is not to say that Wittgenstein was a behaviourist. He did not deny the vast range of human experiences and sensations that accompany, for example, thinking, imagining, loving, hating, being in pain, as did Watson and the radical behaviourists who followed him. What he did point out was that our criteria for using those words, or, to put it another way, the meaning of those words, was not a matter of those private inner experiences, whatever they were, but of their observable criteria.

It must be emphasised again that this is a rather crude attempt to represent the ideas of the later Wittgenstein in shortened form. Having done this, we can now pass to examining the application of these ideas to the realm of transcultural psychiatry.

CULTURE AND EXPERIENCE

The most radical argument of transcultural psychiatry, one that recurs again and again in different forms, is that people in some cultures experience themselves and others in a very different way. This is then followed by drawing the conclusion that a mental disorder may be absent or expressed differently. It is also occasionally concluded that mental disorder is an entirely culturally based phenomenon, that certain cultures may protect individuals against some mental disorders, or that there may be culturally specific and effective treatments for certain mental disorders.

These arguments are usually associated with the terms ethnopsychology or ethnopsychiatry. Ethnopsychology refers to the description of psychological beliefs in other cultures, and can include typologies of persons, beliefs about the make-up of persons, typical motivational explanations of behaviour, and so on. It may include both technical/specialist and lay psychologies. If referred back to Western culture, the discipline of academic psychology may be relativised and regarded as a local ethnic cultural product without precedence over any other culture's psychology. Nevertheless, it is interesting to note that what is here called psychology, whatever the culture being described, is that field of interest defined by Western psychology, even if the culture being studied has no comparable category at all. Ethnopsychiatry refers to the description of mental disorders as experienced, treated, and theorised about in different cultures. It draws upon ethnopsychology in order to explain the activities and behaviours with which it is concerned.

THINKING AND FEELING AMONG THE IFALUK

Let us now examine how these ideas find an application in the work and writings which come under the rubric of ethnopsychology or ethnopsychiatry. Lutz (1985) describes the ethnopsychology of the Ifaluk people, a community of approximately four hundred people living upon a Pacific atoll. They share a half-mile-square island and live by fishing and agriculture. According to Lutz, the Ifaluk do not distinguish between thought and emotion. They have one word for both, and are therefore, Lutz argues, internally undivided in a way that Westerners are not. In the West, thoughts are depicted as in battle with unruly emotions. The implication of Lutz's argument is

that the Ifaluk cannot have similar experiences because their particular ethnopsychology fails to draw such a distinction. Thus we are
drawn into the trap of thinking that in some subtle and mysterious
way the Ifaluk experience of themselves, life and the world is
different from our own. How peculiar it must be, we consider, not to
have any difference between thought and emotion! How powerful
cultural shaping must be to produce an experience of self which is
so strangely different! Moreover, given that this is the case, how
different must their experience of depression be. Hardly comparable, therefore, to the phenomenon described by psychiatrists in the
West.

Most of these errors flow naturally from a misunderstanding of
the words 'thought' and 'emotion'. First of all, we must note that
even Westerners do not always make clear distinctions in the use of
these words. A person who has certain feelings is likely to think in
certain ways. The two are not always distinguished by us. To love
someone is to think about them a lot of the time. Only in certain
circumstances do we have any mileage in distinguishing the two.
Thus the two words overlap for Westerners also. In our everyday life
we make these distinctions only when we have a difficult emotion-
laden decision to make, or when we have to justify an impulsive
action or otherwise post-factually account for a now negatively
valued course of action.

Are we really to suppose that the Ifaluk have no equivalent at all
to the following words of advice: look before you leap, use your
head, don't be so impulsive, don't get carried away? All these
appeals to act according to thought instead of feeling must be
absent if the Ifaluk make no distinction. Or to put it in another way,
what would life really be like if the Ifaluk did not distinguish
between thought and emotion? Thinking that two plus two equalled
four would be the same as feeling that two plus two equalled four.
Therefore feelings would be acted on equivalently to thoughts. What
Lutz has done is to strip both our own words 'thought' and
'emotion' from their context, from their location in practices and
typical behaviours of people. The same has been done to the Ifaluk
word for 'thought/emotion'. Then in both cases these words have
been taken to refer to private experiences in the minds of people,
rather than to social actions with outer criteria.

Lutz's depiction of the Ifaluk is not just philosophically and
theoretically faulty, it is also contradicted by her own ethnographic
material. The Ifaluk distinguish thought and emotion too, because

like us, they recommend the grief-stricken to forget their loss and become involved with the living, that is, to control their emotion with thought or rational action (Lutz 1985: 71). In other words they recommend a cognitive strategy! It must be admitted that the description of the Ifaluk people's emotional life by Lutz contains more than these erroneous assertions about thought/feeling distinctions. She does provide a wealth of ethnographic material that allows us to see how the Ifaluk use a range of emotion-descriptive terms that are differently accented from our own and are located in different patterns of action. These are readily understandable when described for us by Lutz. This fact demonstrates the commonality of life and experience between us and the Ifaluk, rather than a gulf of categorical difference.

INDIVIDUALISM VERSUS SOCIOCENTRICITY

Lutz's assertions about thought and emotion among the Ifaluk are well known and widely referred to in the transcultural psychiatric literature. However, a more common argument that appears repeatedly in ethnographic studies of many other cultures revolves around the idea of sociocentricity. Marsella (1982), in his review of the field, drew a clear distinction between the perspectives of Western and Asian/Pacific cultures. In the West, he argues, the self is considered to be distinct, individual, different from others and the source of autonomous actions, whereas in some other cultures the self is not clearly demarcated from others, boundaries are more permeable, and actions are a function of social relationships. One fairly typical example of this is Hardman's (1981) description of the Lohorung Rai of Nepal. The analysis she gives of this Mongoloid hill tribe of some 3,000 rice farmers asserts that they emphasise 'the development of the social, externally controlled person, denying introspection and the significance of an internally derived "self"' (Hardman 1981: 161). This type of argument reaches an extreme form in Lienhardt's (1961) description of the Dinka of southern Sudan, in which it is claimed they do not think of themselves as selves.

All this argument is founded upon a metaphysical reification of the 'self' which is itself the result of a misconception of the nature of language. The word 'self' is not used by us to refer to some essence inside people's heads. It is used instead in complex ways when we wish to distinguish between different people, usually between oneself and others. What would a society be like in which no distinction was made between the self and others? There would be no private property, all marriages would be completely open, people would be as likely to put food in someone else's mouth as their own when they were hungry. They would not have names for each other and would not hold each other responsible for their actions. There would be no private ownership and no preferences, likes or dislikes that were individual and recognised as such by others. Perhaps they might not even realise that they did not all look the same.

Although this is the direct implication of the 'sociocentricity' argument as found in the transcultural psychiatric literature, of course these conclusions are not drawn. The use to which the argument is put is to elicit within the reader a sense of strangeness, and thoughts of how different it must be to live and breathe within such an alien context. Then this sense of strangeness is brought into a consideration of mental disorder and the reader is intended to begin to understand how different the experience of mental disorder must be within cultures like these, or is made ready to accept the assertion that certain mental disorders do not or cannot exist within those cultures. Fabrega (1989) uses exactly this pattern of argument. After quoting many studies on the anthropology of the self, including those referred to above, he concludes that as psychosis involves a destruction of self, its very nature and expression must be culturally influenced.

However, when the ethnographies associated with these arguments are examined in detail, rather than the theoretical analyses of the ethnographic material, a different picture emerges. People do of course distinguish between each other, name each other and so on, whatever the culture, but it would be permissible to say that some societies are more sociocentric than others. This does not mean they have some categorically different 'self' or 'self experience'. What it does mean is that they are more oriented to the group, more often plan courses of action with others in mind and, if asked the reasons for their actions, are more likely to refer to the context of their location within the group. All this we understand, indeed all people do this in all human societies, though some societies may emphasise this more than others.

Some authors in the field of transcultural psychiatry are more realistic in this sense. Schieffelin (1985) describes how among the Kaluli people of New Guinea, men act in an aggressively assertive manner towards one another. He resists the temptation to reify this into a categorical difference in nature, and instead reintroduces (from Bateson 1972) the idea of a dominant cultural ethos. He is therefore able to suggest that there is a different emotional emphasis within Kaluli society, while still maintaining their commonality with us as human beings – although males in our society do not make the dramatic displays of anger that those in Kaluli society do, we still recognise the picture of male assertiveness. What is more, he is then able to describe the ways in which feelings are socially managed among the Kaluli, and to suggest that this management may protect the Kaluli from the experience of depression. He is short of empirical evidence to support this claim, but as culturally specific protective and vulnerability factors have been identified by Brown and Harris (1978) within our own culture, we can readily understand the sense behind this argument.

Still, the kind of misconceived word play described previously is more common, and has the result of unrealistically amplifying cultural differences, or of transforming them from qualitative differences in social action into categorical differences in essential nature. Once this step has been taken, it then follows that because mental states and processes are fundamentally different cross-culturally, so must be mental disorder and its treatment. All this argument is confused, however. Words like 'thought', 'emotion' and 'self' do not stand for things, but have their home as moves in various language games. Their logical grammar is complex, and the words are prone to causing philosophical confusion when removed from their context of use. What differs between cultures is not the nature of some internal essence or experience, but social practices, ways of life and ways of talking to each other that fit within those practices. Mental disorders may still differ, and indeed may differ fundamentally across cultures, but this line of argument has not established that fact.

ESKIMOS AND SNOW

It may now be perceived that the ethnopsychologists above have staked out the same territory previously claimed by Whorf (1964). Although there are many versions of Whorf's arguments, they can all be found in the ethnopsychological literature described above.

An excellent elaboration and analysis of Whorf's teachings has been provided by Cook (1978a, 1978b), who has divided them into three overlapping forms. First, members of other cultures see and experience the world differently because of their different languages and vocabularies. The usual example offered here is that of the Eskimos, who have many different words for different types of snow whereas we have only a few. Therefore they see the world differently from us. Second, as thinking always takes place in a language, the thoughts of those who speak with a different language and grammar are channelled into certain courses by that language, its organisation and vocabulary. Third, different languages and grammars imply different metaphysics and world views. Thus the different verb–tense structures in some American Indian languages are taken to imply a wholly different metaphysical world view of the nature of time and reality.

All three of these propositions are to be rejected on the grounds that they misconceive the nature of language exactly as the ethnopsychologists have been shown to do. Different vocabularies do not mean that the world is seen and experienced differently. Anybody can see different sorts of snow – what is seen and felt is exactly the same. The Eskimos, however, have reasons for making overt distinctions between them, which is why they have and utilise an expanded vocabulary on this topic. What counts as seeing and thinking about the world differently is not some private inner experience, otherwise the Eskimos would not be able to talk about it or act meaningfully with it. Instead they have a different vocabulary which is located within a set of culturally different practices. They make distinctions between different types of snow for a range of entirely practical purposes which we would find thoroughly understandable if they were to be explained to us. This is underlined by the fact that translation can always take place. Whatever the form of words or vocabulary in another language, it is always susceptible to translation, a fact that undermines the assertion that life, thinking and feeling are radically and categorically different among the Eskimos, the Amerindians, or anybody else. At times Whorf implies that language is a kind of cage within which thinking and speaking are imprisoned. This is an incorrect view, for language does not constrain at all; instead it is more like a set of tools out of which we can construct anything we need.

Neither does it make sense, except in certain circumstances, to talk about thinking as being 'in a language'. A full description of the complex logical grammar of 'thinking' would be inappropriate here. It should suffice to point out that if I 'think that Fred is coming to work tomorrow', this might not be associated with any language or mental event. If half an hour later I am asked whether I still think Fred is coming to work tomorrow I would answer 'of course', even though I will not have had the thought continually in mind as some sort of sentence. To take another example, I might be 'thinking of my wife', but such thoughts might take the form of imagining what she looks like in her new dress, and thus be without language. Perhaps one of the only places in which it makes sense to speak of 'thinking in a language' is when we are learning a foreign tongue, but even here all this means is that we have reached a level of facility in the new language so that hesitation is reduced to zero.

So, contrary to the arguments of the ethnopsychologists, different emotional vocabularies do not necessarily indicate different emotional repertoires. Limited vocabularies do not restrict expression. Just because one culture has only two words for negative emotions, 'angry' and 'sad' (Leff 1988) does not mean that this is all they can feel and express. Just because the Ifaluk do not have two separate words for 'thought' and 'emotion' (Lutz 1985) does not mean they cannot distinguish between the two. These and similar assertions misunderstand language and ignore the role of context and non-verbal elements in communication. Moreover, this type of argument even ignores empirical evidence. For instance, people using a language which has four or five colour categories can distinguish colours equally as well as people using an eight or nine colour category language (Conklin 1955, cited in Beeman 1985). People can experience an emotion for which they have no word and also, though a word may be available, the emotion may be only rarely experienced (Levy 1973, cited in Shweder 1985).

CULTURAL TRANSLATION AND CONTEXT STRIPPING

Two misleading types of reasoning are used by the ethnopsychologists and Whorf to support their position on linguistic relativism. First, they use the curious device of cultural or conceptual translation. Instead of giving a direct translation of a word, they provide strange paraphrases in distorted English that are purported to convey the real meaning of the foreign words or sentence. Yet to establish the real meaning of a phrase we must look at the way in which it is used. Moreover, the distorted translations provided by Whorf and the ethnopsychologists are not genuine translations at all; they make only partial sense and have been deliberately constructed in this distorted fashion in order to elicit feelings of strangeness in the reader. A straightforward, practical translation into English instantly dissipates that feeling. Two examples will demonstrate this tactic in Whorf and in Lutz:

1 Whorf translates the Apache words for 'dripping spring' as 'as water, whiteness moves downwards', and concludes that the Apaches think utterly unlike us. However what is 'utterly unlike' is Whorf's peculiar form of translation, not the Apaches' thinking!

2 Lutz's variation on this device is to give a translation, but to slip into the translation the word she is suggesting cannot be expressed correctly in English: e.g. 'Every day I fago my relatives who are away' is offered as a translation of a sentence spoken by a young Ifaluk woman. Alternatively she offers a string of words in translation with the intention that we think that the meaning of the word is some subtle combination of all these: e.g. fago = compassion/love/sadness. Once again these are peculiar forms of translation which import ideas of strangeness.

The second device common to Whorf and the ethnopsychologists is the extraction of words from their spoken context. For example, Whorf claims that because the Hopi language has no singular noun for 'wave' and instead uses a verb form 'waving', it is closer to reality. After all, he argues, we never see one wave, but always a 'surface in ever changing undulating motions'. However, as Cook (1978a, 1978b) points out, Whorf has taken our word 'wave' out of its context of use. When returned to that context it connects quite sufficiently with reality – one can be knocked down by a wave when playing in the water at the seaside, or a freak wave can sink a ship. Whorf has taken both the Hopi and the English expressions out of their context of use, and appropriated them as abstract descriptions of the universe. None of us suspect the Hopi use these everyday words in that strange, philosophically confusing way. In a similar fashion the ethnopsychologists strip ethnic vocabularies of feeling and emotion from their contexts and take them to refer to abstract categories or theories of human nature.

The significance of the above for transcultural psychiatry is that, contrary to the assertions of linguistic and cultural relativists, both symptoms and possibly diagnostic categories can be translated across cultural boundaries. Essentially this is no different from the question whether Frenchmen mean the same thing by the word 'bleu' as we mean by 'blue'. The only way of knowing is by seeing if he uses it in the same way as we do, if he understands what we mean when we make the substitution in translation, if he goes on to act and talk in such a way as shows that comprehension. Exactly the same goes for categorisations of behaviour, for example words like 'jealousy', 'depression' and/or equivalent descriptive phrases.

UNIVERSAL DIAGNOSTIC CATEGORIES

Much of the analytic or theoretical variety of transcultural psychiatric writings is taken up with discussions on the possibility or otherwise of defining and operationalising universal diagnostic categories. Agreement exists that mental illness is a universal phenomenon, but this is perhaps the only statement on which all authorities would agree.

On the one hand we have the anthropological studies of Murphy (1982), plus her review of numerous other anthropological works, that indicate the universal occurrence of psychosis in every society. She also demonstrates that these mental disorders are distinguished from deviance *per se*, and that numerous cross-cultural studies in the field show that far from shamanism being a culturally acceptable role for the psychotic, the two categories are held to be entirely separate. Lastly she shows that sufferers of psychosis are universally put into the hands of healers, whatever the culture, and are therefore identified as being part of the same phenomenon as illness as a whole.

At the other end of the spectrum we have descriptions of what are called 'culture bound syndromes', forms of mental disorder which are said to be culture-specific. Examples of these would be 'koro' (Yap 1965), or 'heart distress' (Good 1977). In addition it is sometimes claimed that what would be accounted as mental disorder in one culture would not be so accounted in another. Kleinman (1988) makes this point about auditory hallucinations – in our culture these are taken to be signs of a psychotic illness, but are for some American Indians a normal part of bereavement. Others point to the evidence that some mental illnesses as categorised in the West fail to occur in certain cultures. The most frequent examples used here are those of anorexia nervosa, agoraphobia and occasionally depression. The conclusion drawn from these arguments is that they undermine the cross-cultural validity of the reliable diagnostic scaling techniques developed in the West from Western culturally-specific notions of mental disorder. It is further argued that these simply do not apply in other cultures, that the rating scales and questions cannot be properly translated into a different cultural setting in any meaningful way, and as a result we do not end up comparing like with like populations.

Despite the conceptual difficulties, transcultural psychiatry continues to fascinate and attract the attention of psychiatric professionals and social anthropologists. It is a very impressionistic and broad generalisation, but it would seem that academic psychiatrists tend to favour universalistic conceptions of mental disorder and support the validity of cross-cultural comparisons, whereas social anthropologists place more weight upon cultural variation and view Western psychiatry as having no special priority amongst all other ethnopsychiatries originating in different cultures. Although these groups may have differing priorities, both understand the potential and importance of cross-cultural psychiatric study. To the degree that mental disorder is culturally produced or influenced, it can feasibly be prevented, treated or cured by psychosocial methods. The degree to which a psychiatric disorder is universal may indicate the relative role of physiological factors in its aetiology and therefore help to guide research into cause and treatment. Detailed description and understanding of ethnopsychiatries is essential in the planning and construction of psychiatric services in developing countries, so that culturally appropriate provision is made. That same information is required in the West to assist in the provision of psychiatric care to immigrant groups. The key question is, can any or all of these very worthy goals be achieved? Whether they can or not depends at least in part upon whether reliable cross-cultural comparisons of mental disorders can be made.

The World Health Organisation (1979) has conducted a renowned international pilot study of schizophrenia (IPSS). This study used standardised methods of diagnosis and analysis of outcome. Nine different centres world-wide were chosen as the focus of the study, and it was discovered that outcome varied widely between the West and the Third World. For example, in the developed nations 15 per cent of all schizophrenic patients studied had a good outcome while 28 per cent fell into the worst outcome group, but in the developing nations 35 per cent of patients had a good outcome, and only 13 per cent fell into the worst outcome group. Such figures are interpreted by some to be strongly suggestive that the cultural environment plays an influential part in determining the prospects for recovery from schizophrenia, but not its overall prevalence.

This study has sometimes been severely criticised as exporting Western notions of schizophrenia and imposing them on other cultures where they might have a lesser or even no validity. Let us examine carefully the process involved in mounting and carrying out the study. First of all, the phenomenon of schizophrenia is described and refined in the West. Clear criteria for that diagnosis are then identified and operationalised. Those scales are checked for their reliability, which is found to be high. Their validity is supported by their ability to predict prognosis and response to treatment, and by showing them to have a high rate of correlation with the diagnosis of schizophrenia made by other (albeit related) methods. These scales were then carefully translated and used in the participating research centres. Again, reliability in diagnoses was demonstrated within and across the centres. Following this, the scales were used to generate samples which could be compared across the differing cultures. All this was undoubtedly one of the most careful, large and rigorous cross-cultural studies of schizophrenia ever undertaken.

The most radical criticism made of the IPSS is that the Western notion of schizophrenia contained in the symptom lists and scales is of validity only in the West. Other cultures may have no comparable conception. This argument is made quite telling by Obeyesekere (1985) with the following example:

> Take the case of a South Asian male . . . who has the following symptoms: drastic weight loss, sexual fantasies, and night emissions and urine discoloration. In South Asia the patient may be diagnosed as suffering from a disease, 'semen loss'. But on the operational level I can find this constellation of symptoms in every society, from China to Peru. If I were to say, however, that I know plenty of Americans suffering from the disease 'semen loss', I would be laughed out of court even though I could 'prove' that this disease is universal. The trouble with my formulation is that while the symptoms exist at random everywhere, they have not been 'fused into a conception' as [semen loss] in American society.

(Obeyesekere 1985: 136)

Obeyesekere offers this as an exact parallel of the methodology of the IPSS and other similar cross-cultural comparative studies. This amusing parallel appears to prove that cross-cultural studies of mental disorder which compare epidemiological data are impossible. It is incorrect for the following reasons:

1   The symptoms of semen loss as described by Obeyesekere do not exist at random, especially not drastic weight loss. When they occur they inevitably have causes and meanings.
2   The syndrome of semen loss is being described at the wrong level of generality. It is as if in the course of the IPSS the researchers had looked for the delusion of 'control by X-rays' across cultures, instead of looking for delusions in general. It might be that if the syndrome of semen loss were described in a more general form, we might see it as having a certain commonality with some forms of illness and suffering in the West.
3   Schizophrenia is colloquially identified universally, as Murphy (1982) has shown; semen loss syndrome is not. There might therefore be different kinds of mental disorders, some of which may be validly cross-culturally compared, and others which may not. One cannot generalise from the example of semen loss alone to all mental illness.
4   The symptoms of semen loss are not universally identified as harmful and worrisome matters requiring medical attention. Persistent delusions, hallucinations and thought disorder accompanied by inability to function socially are so identified.

This is not to say that the IPSS is unproblematic. We need to ask how it can be established that we are talking about the same thing when we speak of schizophrenia in Nigeria, India and Denmark. This is fundamentally the same problem we have of establishing the equivalency of blue and 'bleu' in French. As stated previously, the only way of knowing is by seeing whether the French use it in the same way as we do, whether they understand what we mean when we use the word, whether they go on to act in such a way and to talk in such a way that shows that comprehension. In a similar fashion the success of the translation of a psychiatric diagnostic category like schizophrenia into another language and culture would be judged by the following criteria:

1   Prediction of outcome should be similar in both contexts.
2   Similar treatments should prove to be effective.
3   Similar aetiological factors should be found in the two populations.

4 A similar pattern of prevalence and incidence should be displayed.

5 At a reasonable level of generality the syndrome should be describable in the same way, i.e. similar symptoms.

Any judgement of successful translation would be strongly supported by evidence that the mental disorder in question had a physiological and therefore more culturally-independent basis. The problem with this overall picture is that any differences cross-culturally in items (1)–(5) might either be due to cultural effects overlaying the same basic phenomenon, or constitute evidence that these are categorically different phenomena. The only way to judge, therefore, is to try to assess how the whole picture fits together, whether it makes more sense to see this as one single phenomenon culturally expressed differentially, or whether it makes more sense to see the phenomenon as categorically different in different cultures. My sense of the evidence is that, for schizophrenia at least, given the strength of the similarities in (1)–(5) above, it makes most sense to see it as a culturally universal phenomenon.

Some quantity of cross-cultural uncertainty must, therefore, always be taken into account. Because mental illnesses are defined by social criteria, total assurance that like is being compared with like across cultural boundaries can never be achieved. However, it can legitimately be assumed with a good degree of confidence that if persons identified as suffering from schizophrenia in culture 'A' showed the same symptoms, responded favourably to the same treatment, showed the same pattern of correlating and possibly aeti-ological factors, with similar course and outcome, as in culture 'B', then we are dealing with the same phenomenon. This is, after all, the identical grounds we deploy in order to say that one group of people suffering schizophrenia is the same as another group within the same culture.

Certain types of evidence would call into question the self-sustaining coherent edifice which has been described. If it was proved that schizophrenia did not have a physiological cause or if it was shown, once and for all, that reactive psychosis is a real phenomenon, cultural variation would have to be re-examined in a different light. This would still leave room for arguments for identity of the phenomenon at the level of the forms and structures of human life, although what the relevant issues/structures were would be very much open to question. Unless and until there are physiological criteria, we can never be sure we are talking about exactly the same thing. However, the amount of similarity can be fairly convincing to anyone except those who insist upon final and complete proof.

Some might wish to argue that schizophrenia, as operationalised by studies like the IPSS, has cross-cultural validity because of its specificity and technicality. For example, a precise and technical definition of 'blue' can be given, using wavelengths. However, although the professional psychiatric definition of schizophrenia via the Present State Examination as used in the IPSS may be more technical and precise than everyday conceptions of 'mad' and 'crazy', these definitions are still without a physical reference point. Measures, quantification, qualitative categorical differences in behaviour are all about conduct, not about properties of the physical world. This may appear to leave all social phenomena hanging, as it were, in the air. They can be translated, but cannot be pegged or anchored to any universal physical criteria. The attack on the translatability of diagnostic categories is, in a sense, an attack on the very idea that we can translate from one language to the next. This is patently nonsense, and for the purposes of cross-cultural comparison, this problem does not matter as much as one might think. There are many, many words other than schizophrenia that are in the same position – for example, love, affection, devotion, virtue, work, play – and nothing stops us from translating them with accuracy. Stories, novels, plays and poetry are full to overflowing with this kind of terminology, and yet we see no fundamental problem with translating them. We are able to do this because the ways of life of people in different cultures are so very much the same, full of the same activities, meanings and institutions.

UNIVERSALITY OF DIAGNOSES OTHER THAN SCHIZOPHRENIA

So far only the cross-cultural validity of schizophrenia has been discussed. It has been concluded that the case for this is fairly robust. The situation is very different, though, with respect to other psychiatric diagnostic categories, where in some cases evidence for universal occurrence in any kind of similar form is either sparse or completely lacking. It is tempting to draw immediately the conclusion that in these cases aetiology and identification are psychosocial and culture-specific. Before doing so, however, it needs to be considered whether it is the level of generality at which the phenomenon is being described which is incorrect. Take, for example, the syndrome of 'koro' described by Yap (1965), in which the sufferer believes and fears that his penis is shrinking and that when it is completely gone he will die. It has been found in several ethnic groups in South-East Asia, but is most common among the southern Chinese. Attacks are accompanied by panic, faintness, palpitations, feelings of impending death, breathlessness, tremor, etc. It might be argued that this is a unique and culturally specific psychiatric disorder, but it may equally well be regarded as an anxiety neurosis, the expression of which is via a culturally determined route. Certainly cardiac neurosis in the West and 'koro' in the East could be described as forms of anxiety attack. When the phenomena are described in this way a stronger case can be made for cultural universality and for the potentially useful translation of diagnostic terms.

There is, however, a second question thrown into sharper relief by transcultural psychiatric studies. Depression has been shown to be a vastly different phenomenon in different cultures, not only expressed in different ways but sometimes appearing to be a fundamentally different experience. In some cultures, it is claimed, it either does not occur or is not identified as an illness or any kind of complaint. This has led some to argue that depression is not a psychiatric or mental disorder at all, but a normal part of human life that can sometimes be controlled or not occur at all, depending upon cultural factors. Both these questions, the cultural moulding of mental disorders, and the nature of depression, will be considered in detail further on in this chapter.

OTHER COMPETING PERSPECTIVES

Before turning to these matters, additional complexities of the issue of cross-cultural diagnosis need to be described. Entwined with this discussion is not just the issue of the validity of Western diagnoses in other countries, but also the points that these other countries are (a) imbibing Western culture, capitalism (generally) and scientific technology, and (b) often do not have their own technological vocabulary of psychiatric diagnostic categories. Psychiatric diagnoses are therefore imported as part of the 'modernisation' package. Thus there are undercurrents of politics, as well as claims of cultural colonialism and racism to be considered.

In some Third World or developing countries there are three or more competing systems for categorising and naming mental disorders:

1 Western diagnostic systems as epitomised in DSM IV or ICD 10 (Diagnostic and Statistical Manual/International Classification of Diseases – definitional criteria for psychiatric diagnoses, created with the intention of standardising their meaning and improving communication between psychiatric professionals).
2 Highly systematic but alien categorisation systems like those of traditional Chinese medicine.
3 Rough lay categorisation systems, usually a collection of names with associated vague ideas about aetiology.

The question is, how are these competing viewpoints to be evaluated? There is more than one way in which this question can be asked. First, one can attempt to decide which is more valid. In making this decision one would examine how systematic the categories were, how well differentiated from one another, how specific and predictive of course and outcome they were and how much they were based upon careful observation. Second, one can attempt to evaluate them on the grounds of their utility. Which system provides efficacious treatment within the culture and how acceptable is it to the majority of the population? Third, a consensus between methods could be sought in terms of which suffering individuals are consistently identified by all the categorisation systems. In the final analysis, though, there is no categorical answer, for the same reason that diagnostic categories cannot finally be validated across cultures – there are no physiological markers or discriminators of psychiatric conditions (excluding the organic psychoses).

In this section I have tried to demonstrate that although diagnostic categories cannot be once and for all established to be universally valid or invalid on logical grounds, in specific cases it can be argued that correspondence across cultures is good enough for comparative studies to take place. I have not been trying to chart out some middle path or way between cultural relativism and diagnostic imperialism, as Kleinman (1988) attempts in *Rethinking Psychiatry*. What I believe I have done is to arrange what we already know in such a way as to show how much of the argument is logically sound, how much it is possible to achieve, and the limits of scholarship and empirical study on the matter.

CULTURAL INFLUENCE UPON MENTAL DISORDER

One of the key questions this discussion has been circling is, how does culture affect mental disorder? Most authorities settle for some kind of distinction between those aspects of mental disorder that are influenced by culture, and those that are not. A variety of vocabularies have been used to make this distinction, which is not itself unproblematic:

Culture-free vs. Culture-bound
Form vs. Content
Pathogenic vs. Pathoplastic
Disease vs. Illness
Substrate vs. Shaper/Moulder

Some such parallel distinction is intrinsic to much of the argument above, specifically and overtly in the discussion of 'koro'. On the other hand, Fabrega (1992) has tried to obliterate this distinction, and Kleinman (1980) has brought forward evidence on somaticisation that requires close consideration. Lutz's introduction of the concept of ethnoepistemology has added a further layer of confusion.

Fabrega (1992) wishes us to do without this distinction altogether. He argues that the form/content distinction involves a range of assumptions which cannot be justified. He unpacks the term 'form' and defines it in cognitive and physiological terms. For example, he asserts that 'form' is taken to be constituted by cognitive categories, i.e. beliefs, judgements, perceptions, emotions, etc., and that these are consequently taken to be universal. Then he argues that the 'form' of mental disorder (as opposed to its 'content') consists of physiological disruption of those cognitive categories of behaviour. Fabrega then rejects both these proposals. He opposes the former by recourse to the evidence that what it is to be a person varies by culture, and that the categories of belief, emotion and so on are ethnocentric and belong only within our own culture. It is on these grounds that he argues that mental disorders must be understood using the models and definitions of the culture within which it occurs. His rejection of the latter assertion – that the concept of 'form' implies a universal physiological substrate to mental disorder – is more implicit. The description of how far culture enters into the constitution of mental disorder, and of how culturally variant it is, is intended to demonstrate that there is no universality upon which to base hypothetical culturally-universal physiological disorder.

The fault here is that, as has already been demonstrated, Fabrega is operating using a faulty picture of language. If words such as 'belief' and 'emotion' are taken to stand for cognitive structures (whatever they might be), then use of different or variant vocabularies in different cultures would imply a different cognitive structure. Since it is beliefs and emotions that are disrupted in mental disorder, then mental disorder can be seen as disruption of those cognitive structures. As they vary substantially across cultures, so will mental disorder. Therefore these cognitive structures cannot be the universal 'form' of mental disorder upon which the culturally variant phenomena are overlaid. In fact, though, these words do not stand for some sort of mentalistic cognitive structure, but describe complex, logically organised human behaviour; they are part and parcel of human activities and are therefore eminently translatable. Moreover, it is these human activities which are universal, not some posited cognitive entity. Wherever one goes in this world, human beings believe, think and feel, however different the vocabularies and grammars that form part of those actions.

In a way, Fabrega is quite correct to criticise the identification of 'form' with universal physiological disorder. Just because there is sometimes a universal physiological basis for the shared form of mental disorders whose content varies culturally (e.g. the delusions and hallucinations which occur in delirium tremens or in Alzheimer's disease have a culturally variant content), this does not allow one to argue that every culturally universal form or feature of mental disorder must have a physiological basis. It might, but this remains to be proven or demonstrated. An equally feasible explanation might be the common pattern or forms of human life and existence which lend these phenomena their universality. The use of the terms 'pathogenic' and 'pathoplastic' for the form/content distinction have legitimately been criticised for implying a picture of universal underlying pathophysiology, when in many cases there is little or no evidence for this. In addition it needs to be noted that physiology is not itself necessarily independent of culture. Geographical location, agriculture, diet, hygiene practices, culturally specific forms of medical treatment, marriage practices and consequent gene pools can all have a dramatic influence upon physiology. There are therefore a number of competing explanations for any universal 'form' of mental disorder.

ETHNOEPISTEMOLOGY AND ETHNOTHEORIES

Lutz (1985) made similar mistakes about the use of language in her description of the Ifaluk people. She also makes certain other assertions about the way in which culture shapes mental disorder, or in other words about the nature of the relationship between the form and content of mental disorder. Her argument is that epistemology (beliefs about what can be known and how it can be known) varies across cultures, and that this relates to different pictures of the nature of depression, and indeed is constitutive of the phenomenon.

Although a culture or society may be said to have a dominant belief system, whether this be considered to be religious or otherwise, to elevate this to the level of an epistemology is perhaps going a little too far. It may be questioned whether cultures really have epistemological theories in any kind of congruent philosophical sense. Moreover, the degree of uniformity of beliefs within a culture may vary widely with regard to the phenomenon of mental disorder. There may often be overlapping, sometimes contradictory, sets of theories and explanations of mental disorder. Use of the term ethnoepistemology falsely supports the idea that cultures have a uniform and sophisticated set of philosophical theories. This is not the case, even for our own culture.

Perhaps a better term for Lutz to have used would have been ethnotheories, culturally local explanations of mental disorders. And it has to be agreed, as Kleinman (1980) has comprehensively shown in his studies of the treatment of mental disorder in Taiwan, that these local theories and explanations do influence what sufferers say about their complaint, when and who they go to for help, and therefore the subsequent course of their troubles. The question Lutz is trying to raise is, do such local theories fundamentally alter the nature of the mental disorder? To rephrase this in a way more pertinent to the topic in hand, is there an absence of universal form in the presence of a fully culturally-determined content? As the same question is raised by the work of Kleinman, both will be considered together.

Although Kleinman (1980) comes from a slightly different direction, the question which is posed by his work is exactly the same. He is specifically interested in the phenomenon of depression in Taiwan and the Chinese mainland. In the course of his ethnographic study of Chinese psychiatry, some interesting facts emerge. Where a

Western psychiatrist would diagnose depression, the Chinese use an obsolete Western diagnostic category 'neurasthenia'. More interesting, and perhaps more problematic, is that Chinese patients present with somatic symptoms when they are depressed, rather than complain of dysphoria. This tendency has been widely observed in Asian cultures generally and is known as somaticisation. The question that arises is, does the Chinese person suffering from depression with somatic symptoms have much in common with the depressed Westerner who expresses psychological symptoms? Where is the common 'form' here, as all seems to be 'content'?

Based upon this, a radical argument would be that the experience of Western and Asian patients is fundamentally different, indeed so categorically different as to comprise different phenomena altogether. If this were so, it would be reasonable to assume that the aetiology would be different, that the appropriate treatment would be different and that the phenomena could not be cross-culturally compared.

At first sight, Ordinary Language Philosophy does not appear to help here either. Wittgenstein's Private Language Argument has shown that it makes no sense to talk of private inner experiences. Thus we cannot speak of some ineffable experience of depression common to somaticisers and non-somaticisers alike. All we have to analyse are the psychological or somatic statements of sufferers, which occur within a social context, and within a set of patterned, known-in-common, activities and remedies. And what people say, how they make their complaint and what they do to seek help, all seem to be substantively different between somaticisers and non-somaticisers.

However, treating these as culturally-, historically- and socially-located idioms depends upon some concept of universal underlying distress which is then expressed in different ways. That Kleinman continues to make this form/content distinction is shown by the fact that he calls both the Asian somatic and the Western psychological presentations 'depression'. He is able to do this because of common contexts and situations in which the problem arises, the Chinese patients giving comparable accounts of loss, emotional pain and conflict as do the Western sufferers. His ethnographic accounts show quite clearly that Chinese neurasthenia sufferers make these connections equally as well as Western depression sufferers. It is just that their complaint is somatic, as is the explanatory theory they use to seek a cure and make sense of it. This being established, it makes little sense to go on asking if the inner experience of patients is different, because whatever one could say would make no difference for it would not engage with the world of talk and action or have any possible meaning. The commonalities between depression in the West and neurasthenia in China are in human life and its problems, not in the mystic interior of the human brain or soul.

In this case therefore, form = suffering in the face of the vicissitudes of life, and content = psychological and/or somatic symptoms. It now becomes clear that when we talk about the distinction between form and content in psychiatric disorders we are not always talking in the same way. In the example of depression above, form refers to the context and cause of the disorder, while content refers to the particular kinds of complaints (symptoms) made by the sufferer. However, in the classic presentation of the distinction, form refers to the symptom itself (e.g. delusion) and content refers to the specific culturally-influenced aspect of it (e.g. whether the delusion is about X-rays or about ancestral spirits). We must be clear, therefore, that the form/content distinction refers only to the distinction between what is culturally influenced and what is culturally universal, not specifically at the level of diagnostic entity or of symptom. Moreover, making such a distinction implies no specific explanation as to why phenomena are culturally universal or culturally specific.

One final issue remains to be considered here. If it is being argued that culture influences, shapes or moulds mental disorder, what exactly is being said? Most authors pass quickly over attempts to define culture, in order to be able to get on with cross-cultural comparison. There is a ubiquitous phrase in the transcultural psychiatric literature that goes like this: 'For the purposes of this paper, culture will be taken to be . . . , followed by a one-sentence definition that means little. The reason it is so difficult to define culture is that the term is open-ended. It refers to any difference in psychosocial practices between any cultures. The more differences that are described, the more content the word has. The unfortunate corollary of this is that to say a difference is due to culture is to utter a tautology, for culture is constituted by those differences. Only when one goes on to fill in the detail does it become meaningful. For example, take the difference of presentation of depression in China and Great Britain. To say that this is due to culture is to say, as yet, nothing at all. It is only when one goes on to put this in the context of a coherent and meaningful pattern of differences that a picture begins to emerge. So when Kleinman describes for us the way the Chinese keep their feelings secret and are socially proscribed from expressing them, we can begin to understand how, when they are depressed, they speak in terms of somatic complaints.

SUFFERING AND DEPRESSION AROUND THE WORLD

There is another very important question raised by the cross-cultural studies of depression. In some societies, it is claimed, depression is either not identified, or is not identified as being abnormal or an illness, or runs a relatively harmless course through culturally-provided channels. Schieffelin (1985) describes how depression is rare among the Kaluli of Papua New Guinea because they have plentiful formal opportunities to protest loss and frustration, and says also that suicide is unknown there. Obeyesekere (1985) describes how the Buddhists of Sri Lanka locate depression within the framework of a religion in which all of life is believed to be suffering. Good et al. (1985) describe how in Iran, depression is expressed through the acceptable cultural channels of Shia Islam. If these assertions are accepted, they challenge established beliefs in Western psychiatry, and indicate, first, that viewing depression as an illness is not necessarily the only or best way of dealing with the phenomenon and, second, that the harm caused by depression might be ameliorated by the provision of cultural channels for its expression and ventilation.

Looked at in this way, instead of being seen as a universal physiological disease, depression can be seen more meaningfully as an inextricable part of human life. The nature of human existence, the warp and woof of life itself involves physical pain and suffering, loss of the loved, frustration in achieving one's goals, the stab of conscience and the torture of internal conflict. The opportunities for the experience of these unwelcome feelings are provided differently in different cultures. In different societies different goals are socially approved, different ways of life and commitments provide different opportunities to experience loss and failure. But such opportunities are innate to human society, as there is no human life in which suffering cannot occur. It is the avoidance of despair and unhappiness which is a huge and powerful engine motivating human action. People can find the meaning for their lives in tackling the factors that generate pain and suffering. In a personal sense we all try to arrange our lives to minimise our exposure to such psychological wounds. In a wider sense, many of the caring professions have as their *raison d'être* the reduction or eradication of such consequences. Politics could be interpreted as the attempt to organise humanity's affairs so as to maximise happiness and minimise suffering. Even wars or revolutions may be fought on the grounds that people cannot be happy unless they are free and unoppressed. Depression is therefore inseparable from the human condition.

It is on this basis that we can thoroughly comprehend the predicament of a depressed human being from any culture. Schieffelin's description of the Kaluli woman who is depressed because she has married badly is totally understandable, as are Kleinman's depictions of the experiences of Chinese depressives: frustration of desire, loss of desired object, conflict, anger, humiliation, etc. We all eat, marry, are born, play, work, die, love, hate, envy, desire, become angry, suffer loss, are happy or sad. So much human experience is the same. If not, we could never read, understand or be entertained by novels and stories from other cultures; translation would be impossible because ways of life were so different – instead it is just sometimes difficult. The stuff of human life is universal and accessible to all. The fact that depression is a universal phenomenon does not therefore force us to accept that it must be an illness. There are other forms of universality.

This is, of course, a far from new idea. The eighteenth-century philosopher Giambattista Vico (1725, cited and reviewed by Shotter 1981) argued that cultural universals arise naturally from the properties of human societies and the nature of human activity. He had in mind such natural facts of life as birth, death, sex, the need for food and water, child rearing, care of the old and weak, language and communication. This insight has recently been reintroduced into medical sociology by Turner (1992):

> By virtue of being embodied, human agents are subject to certain common processes which, while having biological, physiological, and generally organic foundations, are necessarily social. These common processes are related to conception, gestation, birth, maturation, death and disintegration. Since so many social practices are based upon such obvious events – marriage, legitimate copulation, socialisation, burial and rituals of grief –

it is strange that sociology has so generally neglected these practices as evidence of our embodiment.

(Turner 1992: 92)

Too often the authors of transcultural psychiatry are tempted to
overstress difference and ignore the commonality of human life.

This picture of depression is not without difficulty. It is not as if
in our own culture we have no difficulty in defining all depression as
illness. In fact psychiatry has grappled, and continues to grapple,
with the attempt to distinguish between depression as illness and
depression as natural response to loss and other calamities. The
struggles to define caseness, cut-off points, the difference between
reactive and psychotic depression, or between mild and serious
depression, all point to the recognition of depression as a natural
response to life events. Most people would probably agree that
serious, psychotic depression, involving delusions, hallucinations
and/or biological symptoms is probably best considered as a
universal illness like schizophrenia, although comparable
supporting evidence for this is not yet available. However, there
seems to be no naturally occurring sign or symptom which would
enable a clear distinction to be made between this and the natural
response to life events. It might be as Beiser (1985) suggests, that
each society creates a threshold for the translation of distress into
illness. This issue will be considered again in a future chapter.

SUMMARY

In this chapter I have shown that the current emphasis in the transcultural psychiatric literature upon different forms of selfhood,
experience, emotion and therefore mental disorder, is misconceived
and rests upon a fundamental misconception of the nature of
language. I have argued that despite the difficulties, it is in some cases
possible to compare psychiatric disorders across cultures. I have
described the circumstances in which this is reasonable and possible,
and the limitations of such study. Clarification of the form/content
distinction has shown it to be valid and possible at the level of individual symptoms and whole syndromes. Where cross-cultural
universality occurs, I have shown that physiological causation does
not necessarily follow. The universality may arise at the level of
common forms of human life. This poses particular challenges to the
way in which we conceive of and respond to depression.

Chapter 5

Diagnosis

Among the writers on transcultural psychiatry, there are many who would wish to place the Western psychiatric diagnostic system at the same level as alternative lay or folk categorisation systems in other cultures. The intention of so doing would be to emphasise that DSM IV or ICD 10 are cultural products in the same way that local indigenous categorisation systems are in other societies. The perceived benefits are that we would become loosened from our commitment to the Western diagnostic system as having any particular priority, that we would be enabled to see psychiatric disorder as profoundly culturally influenced, embedded and sometimes created, and that we would cease from attempts to make quantitative epidemiological cross-cultural studies of mental disorders. Some recent examples of this approach are to be found in Nuckolls (1992) and Gaines (1992). The latter describes the DSMs as cultural constructions derived from Western ethnopsychology, and marshals a range of arguments to show that the concept of self in the DSMs is a Western one which can be clearly distinguished from alternative ethnopsychologies. The arguments used here are exactly the same as those examined in the last chapter.

DIAGNOSTIC SYSTEMS AS CULTURAL PRODUCTS

It has to be admitted that the DSM is a cultural product in that it is derived from Western psychiatric practice and Western ideas and traditions of epistemology and science. However, to admit this is not the same as allowing that the DSM is of the same nature, value or validity as lay categorisation systems elsewhere in the world. Neither is it to admit that there is some peculiarly Western concept of self embedded within that categorisation system. With respect to this latter idea, I would hope that the arguments presented in the last chapter suffice to demonstrate that such a position is philosophically confused about the correct use of the word 'self'. However, the former argument may require more elaboration. Western psychiatric diagnostic classificatory systems are substantively different from all other attempts at classifying psychiatric disorder in any other culture. They are based upon careful, detailed and systematic observation. The products of that observation and analysis of that information have been widely published and submitted to international peer review and critique. Precise criteria for diagnostic categories have been identified and tested for their reliability by different mental health professionals in different countries. The diagnostic categories which have been determined have been shown to be predictive of the course of the disorders and of response to various treatments. No other diagnostic system has been developed and tested in such a rigorous fashion.

In this way the DSM does have embedded Western cultural ideas, but they are not those termed 'ethnopsychology' but are beliefs about the benefits of systematic empirical study. The acquisition of knowledge about a phenomenon usually starts with classification and the creation of a body of technical terms with precise meanings. Linnaeus and the science of biology started here, as did chemistry and many other sciences. Psychiatric diagnosis is therefore an entirely legitimate attempt to increase our knowledge about psychiatric disorder. As Horwitz (1979) has argued, the whole point of psychiatric diagnostic systems is to order the phenomenon, allowing explanation, prediction and control. To the degree that a diagnostic system does this, it is successful, and in these terms Western psychiatric diagnostic systems are the most successful of all.

The DSM is not a lay categorisation system, it is not based upon culturally pervasive ideas about the nature and course of a variety of different psychiatric disorders, and it cannot be compared with loose, lay, traditional systems from other cultures. That is not to say that the DSM is entirely disconnected from lay discourse. The very beginnings of systematic description in psychiatry will have started with lay distinctions, and it is the history of lay definitions of what is to be considered a psychiatric problem that has provided psychiatry with the population which it has subsequently classified. Moreover, the boundaries of psychiatry are permeable, with phenomena moving in and out of the psychiatric domain depending upon political decisions, media presentation and so on. Thus a lay category can become a psychiatric diagnosis and vice versa. Nevertheless, the DSM is based upon a tradition of empirical observation and careful analysis in a way that lay categorisation systems are not, and is therefore very different in stature, authority, reliability and probably validity too.

Consequently, Western diagnostic systems in psychiatry must be accepted both as legitimate exercises and as a significant improvement upon *ad hoc*, lay/folk traditional systems. This does not mean that they are unproblematic, and it is to those problem areas that I now turn.

DOES A DIAGNOSTIC SYSTEM IMPLY AN ILLNESS MODEL?

There are many who reject the idea that psychiatric disorder is an illness like other illnesses, Szasz (1987) being the prime example. This is a highly complex issue which will be the topic of a later chapter. However, many of those who reject the illness picture of mental disorder also reject the diagnostic systems of psychiatry on the grounds that they assume the nature of mental disorder is illness. In answer to this, it must first be pointed out that a classificatory scheme does not by itself imply that it is a classification of illnesses. Classificatory schemes *per se* are therefore legitimate enterprises, whatever mental disorder is or might turn out to be. Secondly, although some categories within diagnostic systems are unequivocal illnesses/diseases, for example the organic dementias, this cannot be taken to mean that all categories in the system are of the same nature. It may be, indeed it seems extremely likely, that psychiatry deals with a very diverse range of phenomena with differing aetiologies, requiring differing treatments.

Nevertheless, Spitzer and Williams' declaration that DSM III 'makes no assumption that a biological abnormality accounts for each of the mental disorders' (1982: 23) rings a little hollow. This is because of the whole vocabulary which is brought into play: 'diagnosis' goes together most readily with ideas of illness, sickness, disease, treatment and prognosis. Moreover, within our society diagnoses are and can only be made by medically trained doctors, so that debate about the nature of mental disorder is prone to become rapidly submerged in issues of professional rivalry. It is therefore no surprise to learn that when DSM III was under discussion and was proposed for incorporation in wider medical diagnostic systems, there were so many objections raised by other mental health professionals that the idea was dropped (Spitzer and Williams 1982). It must therefore be concluded that, despite the legitimacy of classification, there remains a significant objection to the categories being called diagnoses and the system being called diagnostic.

DIAGNOSES, MECHANISMS AND CAUSATION

Diagnosis is frequently understood as being more than a category of disorder. In general medical settings it is also taken to mean getting at the underlying disorder. The patient brings a complaint, and by asking clever questions about the suffering, by looking and performing tests, the doctor finds out the underlying problem. Of course it is only the context which makes this specifically medical. Car mechanics and other occupations whose task is to sort out difficulties all 'diagnose' underlying problems in the same way. The only extra meaning of the word diagnosis in its full sense is that doctors do it, and that the range of problems they do it with are physiological disturbances and disorders. Making a diagnosis thus becomes equivalent to a detective-like function.

All this is very clear in general medicine, but not in psychiatry, for in psychiatry, in most cases, there is no detectable underlying physiological disorder. There are only names of syndromes and statistical prognoses, plus some pragmatic treatments. This has two consequences:

1 *Diagnosis in psychiatry is more akin to naming than to explanation.* Diagnosis in general medicine looks towards the immediate physiological cause of the patient's complaint. For example, the patient is diabetic because she is drowsy, comatose and hyperglycaemic. Why is she drowsy, comatose and hyperglycaemic? Because she has a disorder of the pancreas with insufficient secretion of the hormone insulin . . . . The same thing in psychiatry can be clearly circular. The patient is depressed on the grounds that he is not eating properly or sleeping properly. Why is he not eating or sleeping properly? Because he is depressed. This difference in the meaning of 'to diagnose' between the two domains is purely a function of the fact that the aetiology of many mental disorders remains obscure. Nevertheless, in many cases it is a significant difference because it

means that diagnosis in psychiatry is only the provision of a name, not of a name and an explanation.

2   *Conflation of diagnosis with psychotherapeutic formulations.* As diagnoses are seen as explanatory as well as classificatory, they can be confused with psychological explanations of patient problems and predicaments. Hence there is some ambiguity between making a diagnosis and a formulation in terms of the sufferer's life situation as a whole, with some venerable psychiatric authorities (Menninger 1948, 1963; Meyer 1955) arguing for priority to be given to the latter. The problem here is that although this does often offer an explanation, that explanation rarely has the same reliability and validity as the classification scheme itself. In addition, criticisms of the psychological explanations utilised can then be taken to be criticisms of the diagnostic categorisation system itself, thus bringing the diagnostic system into disrepute.

Mirowsky and Ross (1989) criticised diagnosis in psychiatry for presenting attributes as entities. They meant that psychiatric diagnoses are used and discussed as if they represented something categorical about the subjects, being the name of some underlying mechanism or physiological fault. To the extent that diagnostic terms are used in this way, their criticism is correct, for diagnostic categories in psychiatry are, in the main, descriptive rather than explanatory. Boyle (1990) makes the same point as Mirowsky and Ross, but applies it specifically to schizophrenia. She exposes, at great length and with great vigour, the fact that schizophrenia is a descriptive term without (in her view) any validating physiological criteria.

The provision of speculative mechanisms for psychiatric disorder (e.g. 5HT imbalance in depression) does not make the diagnosis of depression more of an explanation. This is due to the supposed mechanism or underlying disorder being still a matter of guesswork, rather than established fact. However, this does not undermine the utility of diagnosis for other purposes such as research, the prediction of further symptoms/behaviour, the likely course/outcome, and response to treatment. Klerman (1989), in his response to Mirowsky and Ross, is entirely correct to point out that diagnostic systems are not ends in themselves, but are intended to facilitate care, treatment and research.

RIGOUR, UTILITY AND PATTERN

The Mirowsky and Ross critique of diagnosis fails in a number of other respects. They argue, for instance, that the actual clinical features of psychiatric patients do not match diagnostic categories. Using the factor analytic work of Endicott and Spitzer (1972), Spitzer *et al.* (1967, 1970), which show that symptom groupings produced by this method only partially match diagnoses, they argue that psychiatric diagnoses are mythical entities. They then support this argument by drawing a parallel between diagnoses and stellar constellations. They argue that such constellations, of stars or of symptoms, exist only in the mind of the beholder and do not represent real relationships between their elements. There are two mistakes here. The first is that when course and outcome of the disorder are taken into account as well as factor analysis of clinical features, what results is more similar to our current diagnostic system. If the factor analytic groups were that much more predictive and useful in guiding treatment, they would long ago have replaced our traditional diagnoses. In any case, Kendell (1975a) reports that the results of multivariate analyses of this nature are very dependent upon the particular statistical method used. Second, the illustration of stellar constellations sows much confusion, for constellations do not solely exist in the mind of the observer. Stars are not randomly spread across the sky, and identification of groups like the constellations allows us to predict what stars will be near each other at every sunset. It allows us to differentiate the stars, which are virtually unchanging, from the planets, which change location. There is, therefore, a spatial relation between the stars of a constellation which is analogous to the fact that certain psychiatric symptoms typically run together. The force of Mirowsky and Ross' analogy is actually a repetition of their first and correct argument that diagnoses do not necessarily name a hidden causal entity. Just as the interpretation of the patterns of the stars is in the mind of the beholder (the Big Dipper can also be seen as the Plough, or as the Great Bear, or as something else), so are the aetiological theories of most mental disorders (depression might be 5HT depletion, or something else). What still differs between diagnoses and constellations is that we know from empirical scientific study that apart from a spatial relationship, there is no other factor determining patterns in the stars, whereas in psychiatry it seems eminently feasible that in some cases underlying physiological causes for the patterns of symptoms we see may eventually be established.

CONFUSIONS ABOUT DIAGNOSIS AND LABELLING THEORY

Labelling theory has been considered in detail in a previous chapter, and its deficits as an explanation of mental disorder will not be reconsidered here. However, there does exist a certain amount of confusion between the topic of diagnosis and that of labelling, with diagnoses often being referred to as labels, and appeals being made to the labelling theory literature in order to attack the notion of diagnosis. This confusion is ubiquitous, both in everyday psychiatric practice as well as in the literature.

The first point which needs clarification is that the labelling theorists did not have psychiatric diagnoses in view when they spoke about labels. Both Scheff (1966) and Lemert (1951) had in view societal reaction as a whole – social labelling. In other words they were considering the effect upon people of it being widely known that they were psychiatric patients, psychiatric service users, mad, crazy, mentally ill or whatever. These scholars were interested in how that broad societal reaction to the mentally ill constituted or shaped their experience of 'being mentally ill'. As part of that study they were also interested in general lay beliefs and attitudes to mental illness, as these were the factors that determined society's response to the mentally ill person. This is distinct from the issue of diagnosis, although there is a small degree of blurring and overlap. Diagnoses are made after the determination that somebody may have a psychiatric problem or disorder, therefore people may be already considered as socially labelled in deviancy theory terms, before they even receive a diagnosis. Diagnoses are a subset of the category of mental disorder itself, and their currency is mostly restricted to psychiatric professionals rather than to the wider society. To speak of diagnoses as labels is therefore to invoke the debate over social labelling incorrectly.

There is a small degree of overlap between the issue of psychiatric diagnosis and social labelling. Firstly, diagnosis confirms the identity of the person as a legitimate psychiatric patient; the making of a formal diagnosis can therefore be an important marker. It should perhaps be noted that medical diagnosis does not always occur, as many clients are seen by professionals other than psychiatrists. Nevertheless, social labelling always takes place whenever it becomes known that a person is consulting a psychiatric professional. Secondly, there are some rough lay beliefs about diagnoses that are fairly widespread in society, mainly incorrect and mistaken, more general, and largely derived from overall stereotypes of mental illness. Media portrayals of the mentally ill range from distorted pictures of them as narcissistic, parasitic and homicidal, to the more realistic pictures of television documentaries and some fictional works (Hyler *et al.* 1991; Winick 1982; Philo *et al.* 1994; McKeown and Clancy 1995). Surveys like that conducted by Huxley (1993) show that general knowledge about mental illness is rudimentary and patchy, although some respondents were able to use specific diagnostic terms in an accurate way. Thus when diagnoses do leak from the psychiatric system, or are given away by the patient, they may determine some expectations and responses but in a very limited way when compared to the larger effect of such social label as 'mentally ill', 'head-case' and 'nervous breakdown'.

The failure to distinguish social labelling from diagnosis does have consequences for the everyday operations of psychiatry. This misidentification enables a critique of many, if not most, of the actions of psychiatric treatment agencies. Much psychiatric treatment is based upon careful diagnosis as a first step, in order that appropriate and effective treatment can be chosen. If the capacity to diagnose is undermined by the labelling critique, then so is the choice of treatment options based upon it. The abandoning of psychiatric diagnosis on the grounds of labelling can thus lead to irrational, inappropriate interventions which have never been subjected to empirical scrutiny.

It is to be hoped that the above scenario occurs only rarely. Perhaps more often the labelling/diagnosis confusion becomes embroiled in interprofessional rivalries within psychiatry. As the authority and expertise to diagnose is largely vested in medically-trained psychiatrists, the misidentification of diagnoses as labels can be used as a stick with which other professions can beat the medical/psychiatric profession, and as grounds on which to dissent in an unhelpful way from treatment plans for individual clients. Thus what is properly a theoretical or philosophical issue becomes locked into disputes and negotiations about the power to determine what treatment plan is offered to individual clients, and all clarity is lost.

STEREOTYPING WITHIN THE PSYCHIATRIC SYSTEM

There remains a way in which diagnoses can be seen as labels, although this is not the same at all as a deviancy theory version of labelling. Diagnoses can be seen as labels operating within the psychiatric system itself, labels which guide the expectations and reactions of psychiatric staff in relation to the patient. Those reactions and expectations may of course contribute to the shaping of the patient's behaviour. This has both theoretical and practical consequences.

Some diagnostic categories are undoubtedly negative and/or prejudicial within psychiatry. Particularly in the case of psychiatric nurses, the diagnoses of personality disorder, alcoholism and drug addiction produce negative reactions and expectations which may act as self-fulfilling prophecies. There is some evidence for this in the literature about psychiatric nursing (May and Kelly 1982; Kelly and May 1982; Macilwaine 1981), although this area has not been sufficiently investigated by researchers. It should be noted that there are other words, names, stereotypes or labels that operate in this way within psychiatry which are not diagnostic categories at all, for example the term 'problem patient'. However, this is a recognised problem within psychiatric practice. There are readily available practical strategies which are frequently used to prevent the occurrence of negative expectations leading to exacerbation of the problem. For example, sometimes the professional carrying out a psychiatric assessment at a new turning point (e.g. readmission or re-referral) will refuse to look at or consider the existing psychiatric case record, in order to gain a fresh point of view. Alternatively, when workers become bogged down in a particular perspective on a patient's problems, they may seek clinical supervision for new ideas (Hawkins and Shohet 1989), or ask another uninvolved professional to make a fresh assessment of the problem.

The theoretical issue that is highlighted is that the diagnostic system is itself, to a degree, circular. Diagnostic categories are drawn from observations of patient populations. Those categories are then used in the treatment and management of those populations, structuring the expectations of the psychiatric professionals who carry out that care. Those expectations may then shape future patient behaviour, which then in turn shapes refinement of the diagnostic system. Given that this is the case, the key question becomes: to what degree are mental disorders shaped by the social expectations of psychiatric professionals? This question is similar to that considered in the previous chapters about how much social or cultural processes influence mental disorder.

Several considerations would lead one to the conclusion that the

relative weight of influence to be attributed to the psychiatric diagnostic system, as wielded by psychiatric professionals, is not great.
First, it must be pointed out that mental disorder starts, and already
has a form with marked criteria and symptoms, prior to there being
any contact with psychiatry. Thus, these cannot be the effects of
expectations on the part of the professionals. Second, if expectations profoundly affected patients' symptomatic behaviour, then a
closed system should have developed over time, with diagnostic
categories and presentations growing more and more similar. In
fact, this is not the case – diagnosis remains confusing and difficult,
with a substantial number of ambiguous cases. Third, case presentation varies over time in ways which are not predicted by
psychiatric teachings. If expectations guided patient behaviour, then
they should lead any changes in patient presentation, whereas the
opposite is the case. The decrease in catatonic forms of
schizophrenia over the last hundred years (Mahendra 1981;
Johnson 1993) is an example of this process.

Psychiatric categorisation systems are just one example, albeit a
technical one, of the way in which human beings make sense of
their world. Garfinkel (1967) (drawing upon the philosophy of
Mannheim) refers to this sense-making activity as the documentary
method, whereby individual instances are seen as instances or docu-
ments of the underlying pattern, and the idea of the underlying
pattern is used to provide instances exemplifying it. Thus pattern
and instance mutually support and elaborate each other during the
activity of making sense of the world. This is a fundamental part of
human activity: without ordering, typification, categorisation, etc.,
there would be no meaningful activity at all. The following example
shows that this intrinsic feature of human activity cannot be
removed in order to see what the world would be like without it.
Perhaps it would be possible to produce a diagnostically naive
community within which psychiatric patients could be cared for,
and then observe for any difference from patients in standard
psychiatric settings so that the effects of professionals' expectations
could be assessed. An experiment like this would be expensive, ethically dubious, and still unlikely to provide a final answer, for the
members of the community would themselves develop their own
categories for the clients for whom they cared, by drawing similarities between the behaviour of each and by naming those similarities
and elevating them into categories. These would then become expectations of those styles and types of behaviour. Sense-making and

ordering cannot be subtracted; they are natural and fundamental parts of human action. One implication of this is that diagnostic systems, or some such categorising equivalent, will always be used in one form or another.

SELF IMAGE

A final consequence of viewing psychiatric diagnoses as labels in this restrictive sense relates to the patients themselves and their point of view, for they may accept and welcome the diagnosis as a label, and apply it to themselves. Again it must be said that we are not speaking here of labelling theory as described by sociological deviancy theorists. In that particular picture people's acceptance of the label leads to them fulfilling social expectations about mental disorder and accepting a low-status position *vis a vis* others. However, looking at diagnosis as a label within the domain of psychiatry alone, it may be viewed in a different fashion. It may be that this self-labelling is helpful, giving clients access to appropriate treatments and help. Current approaches to psychosocial interventions in schizophrenia are premised upon acceptance of the diagnosis (Falloon and McGill 1984). It could also be argued that acceptance of a diagnostic label may hinder treatment in some cases because patients can blame the label for their behaviour, rather than accepting responsibility for their predicament. This is part of what Baruch and Treacher (1978) have called the 'treatment barrier'. Debate rages in the field of substance misuse as to whether it is necessary for patients to accept the label 'alcoholic' before they can engage in worthwhile treatment, with proponents of motivational interviewing (e.g. Miller and Rollnick 1991) arguing that this is irrelevant. Zubin (1985) and Strauss *et al.* (1989) have argued strongly that negative symptoms in schizophrenia are a consequence of acceptance of the status of mentally ill. Warner *et al.* (1989) and Goldberg (1992) have made some preliminary empirical investigations on self-labelling by patients, with the former finding that rejection of the status 'mentally ill' predicts good self esteem but not improved functioning. How these processes relate to course and outcome of mental disorder therefore remains an interesting field for study.

DIAGNOSTIC TERMINOLOGY AS DEHUMANISING

Before the labelling and diagnosis issue can be left behind, one final argument requires consideration. On some occasions when diagnoses are being criticised as labels, it is not labelling theory which is being invoked at all, but the process of depersonalisation through diagnosis. It is not easy to describe this because it is seldom formalised and rarely overt. Take as an example the diagnosis 'schizophrenia'. Used solely as a category to predict course, outcome and response to treatment, this is unexceptionable. However, when the patient is referred to as a 'schizophrenic', many would object that this was diagnostic labelling. This is objectionable because it can be used derogatorily, in order to group people together as if they were all the same, depersonalising them. This depersonalisation resides in the fact that to call a person 'schizophrenic' can be to regard that as a master category, the most important thing about them, ignoring their status as a person. To think in that way is but one small step from treating the sufferers of schizophrenia in an inhumane fashion. Regarded thus, patients are warehoused in big faceless institutions, herded impersonally from one daily activity to the next (Goffman 1961; Brown 1973). The vocabulary of which 'schizophrenic' is one example fits within a care context of blunt custodialism, offered without warmth or personal regard. The terminology also serves to erect a barrier between us and them, to emphasise our difference. Further reasons for the rejection of this kind of terminology are lay misconceptions, exaggerations and false beliefs which the words sometimes evoke. Thus use of the term 'schizophrenic' might call to mind a range of jokes related to split personality which bears no relationship to the tragedy of the real thing.

Neither of these arguments is an objection to diagnosis *per se*. The latter is an argument for the further general education of the population about the form and nature of psychiatric disorder. The former objection, that the terminology depersonalises, is about the use to which diagnostic language is put, rather than an argument for the abandonment of diagnostic categories. It is doubtful whether simply campaigning to change some of the depersonalising ways in which professionals sometimes speak will make any fundamental difference. For this is a mere branch of the phenomenon of poor treatment of the mentally ill, not the trunk or the roots. The roots are to be found in natural human reactions to illness, deformity and mental illness. But that does not mean that all have to engage in such depersonalisation, particularly psychiatric professionals who should be more aware of themselves and the attitudes to which their vocabulary is giving voice. Perhaps we need to become more sensitive to this. One step along that path would be to disconnect this particular objection from its entanglement with the controversies over the application of social labelling theory to mental illness, so that the issue at stake would be more clearly visible.

PSYCHIATRIC BOUNDARIES

'Who is a psychiatric case?' and 'What sorts of cases are there?', are two questions which are central to any form of categorisation in psychiatry. That these are complex and controversial questions has always been recognised and a substantial quantity of scholarly writing and empirical research has been devoted to producing answers. The theoretical dilemmas involved in these questions are presently most often raised by challenges from transcultural psychiatry and the history of psychiatry. Scholars from both disciplines have at times tried to undercut the diagnostic categorisation enterprise by showing that the answers to these two questions are different at different times and in different places. The phenomenon of the culture-bound syndromes may be taken as an example here. Culture-bound syndromes, as described by transcultural psychiatric studies, are psychiatric disorders which are specific to one culture only, not occurring in others. From showing that the boundary between psychiatric case and normality is substantively different in different cultures, the deduction is made that psychiatric disorder and its identification are culturally constructed rather than universal natural phenomena. Any diagnostic system with its inbuilt definitions of boundaries must therefore be culturally relative. Similar arguments can be made from historical variations in case definition and diagnostic symptoms. The universal validity of any diagnostic system is therefore challenged, and the mistaken conclusion drawn that diagnostic systems are both unscientific and of dubious utility. Even if we agree, however, that there are significant variations in diagnostic systems and psychiatric disorder historically and cross-culturally, the categorisation enterprise can still be rigorously empirically pursued for its utilitarian benefit of giving guidelines for effective treatment.

Before opening up the arguments on boundaries any further, it is also necessary to understand that theoretical description of boundaries in psychiatry is, in part, distinguishable from the practical operations of the psychiatric organisation. Actual referral for psychiatric care often depends upon a range of factors in addition to theoretically defined diagnostic criteria. These factors include the skills of the general practitioner at case recognition, knowledge of psychiatry by the patient, stigma of psychiatry, availability of services, promptness of response by psychiatric services locally, perceived suicide risk, degree of distress expressed, existence of multiple problems (social or physical), especially if they are complicated by psychiatric disorder. Therefore psychiatric caseness as pragmatically defined by who gets psychiatric treatment is very much more loosely defined then any theoretical or research exercise. This fact is well recognised by researchers, who have understood the necessity to conduct community surveys to discover the 'true' prevalence of psychiatric disorder in the population, rather than simply count the number of cases in psychiatric treatment.

In the following discussion about boundaries, the terminology of 'case', 'not a case' and 'caseness criteria' will be used. Terminology is important here as it can invoke differing arguments. The advantage of talking in terms of 'cases' is that this side-steps any of the issues raised by the use of the words 'mentally ill' or 'not mentally ill'. I wish to discuss the idea of illness in psychiatry in a subsequent chapter, and the use of the word 'case' enables me to restrict that debate to that chapter.

The subject of boundaries in psychiatric diagnostic systems can be separated into three different questions:

1 *Boundaries and overlap between the different diagnostic categories.* To establish boundaries between different diagnostic categories has been the main task of diagnostic systems. One of the reasons why mental disorder remains somewhat of an enigma is that no diagnostic system has yet been devised that provides clear and distinct differences accompanied by specific criteria for different categories. Distinctions can be drawn. There are syndromal patterns. But there is significant ambiguity which requires explanation, for there are many patients who show signs of several different categories of disorder. There are five main ways to handle this ambiguity theoretically.

First, it can be claimed that all mental disorder is the same phenomenon expressed in different ways, that there is at root only one mental disorder. This successfully explains the overlapping nature of psychiatric diagnostic categories, and may produce useful hypotheses for a wide variety of research. However, as a practical tool for mental health professionals it is useless, because it provides no guidelines for treatment or prognosis. In order to become useful it needs to be overlaid with a set of categories of different manifestations of that singular root psychiatric disorder. To the extent that this is done the system will resemble current diagnostic schedules.

Second, the search for the ideal classificatory system can continue. This would require further careful description/analysis of mental disorder, followed by testing of the discriminatory power of any new system of categories devised. Whether the difficulty can really be answered in this way remains an open question. Current diagnostic schedules have not changed in any major way for the past hundred years, although it always remains possible that some new and creative analysis and categorisation of mental disorder will resolve the issue.

Third, it is possible to tinker with the current diagnostic system by multiplying the categories available, using finer distinctions and definitions. However, this works only at the cost of a decreased ability to make generalisations and predictions. Again, it does not appear that this enterprise can remove all ambiguity between categories until the level of the individual patient is reached and the system becomes practically worthless.

Fourth, we can wait in the hope that biochemical and genetic research will eventually provide us with objective physiological criteria for distinguishing between disorders. Thus it may be foreseen that in the future a new diagnostic system will emerge, based less on observation of the behaviour of, and self-reports by, patients, and more on physical tests. However, there is currently no guarantee that such tests will ever be found or, if they are, that they will be found for all the phenomena called mental disorder.

Fifth, we can adopt a dimensional model of psychiatric diagnosis. Diagnostic categories could be viewed as poles with continua in between. Individual patients could then be located on those continua. This is not to be confused with a dimensional picture of each category of mental disorder with a continuum between normal and abnormal, slight and severe. That idea is explored below. The dimensions under consideration here are those between different mental disorders. For example, it might be proposed that there is a dimension between schizophrenia and depression, or between manic depressive psychosis and personality disorder.

We are not forced into a dimensional model simply by the fact that some patients show symptoms from two categories. It is quite possible to have two unconnected disorders, for instance, multiple sclerosis (MS) and influenza. But the distribution of flu among MS sufferers must be the same as that in the general population for this to be a realistic explanation. This does not appear to be the case among mental disorders where most patients show some signs of more than one diagnostic category.

It is possible that some mental disorders might run together due to indirect factors – MS weakens the immune system, or the paralysis of MS leads to more respiratory infections, or conversely the fact that MS sufferers do not go out may lead to less flu. This does not weaken the case for regarding flu and MS as separate disorders. Of course, if we knew little or nothing about their cause, origin or underlying mechanisms, we might find that distinction harder to make, and might question the nature of the connection. This would appear to be the case with schizophrenia and depression, where Birchwood *et al.* (1993) have shown that the depression experienced by some schizophrenia sufferers is a result of their own dismay and distress about their psychotic symptoms and their predicament. At the moment it is not possible to tell how much interlinking factors like these explain overlaps in diagnostic categories.

The validity of a dimensional diagnostic system is more seriously questioned by pursuing its implications. If there are presumed to be dimensions between different diagnostic categories, are these supposed to exist between all diagnostic categories? If this is not limited to a restricted number then the pragmatic value of diagnosis in terms of prediction and treatment guide is lost in a wealth of dimensional scales. Moreover, if every diagnostic category represents a pole on dimensions to all other categories, then this implies that really there are no discrete mental disorders at all and we are returned to the first resolution above, that of viewing mental disorder as a unitary phenomenon.

A mix of all five of these tactics is used both by psychiatric researchers and by practising mental health professionals in order to accomplish their work. In the research field, the differing answers given to the points above handicap comparisons between research studies. The continual development of diagnostic systems like the DSM and ICD, plus associated research diagnostic tools, bring more comparability to research. However, these presume that final answers have been discovered to the problems raised by diagnostic ambiguity, when in fact only temporary answers have been given in order to get on with the work in hand.

2 *Boundary between what is or is not a psychiatric case (inclusion or exclusion of the category itself)*. Arguments can be made for inclusions or exclusions from the psychiatric domain. This boundary is indeed permeable – even in the recent past it can be observed how homosexuality has passed from being an identified psychiatric diagnosis to being part of the accepted range of normal human behaviour. Other borderline candidates for inclusion in or exclusion from the psychiatric diagnostic lexicon are shoplifting, grief, jet lag, morbid jealousy and addiction.

There is a range of characteristics that determines which human feelings, experiences and activities may be considered as suitable cases for psychiatric treatment. These characteristics include actions without understandable motives, feelings out of proportion to their stimuli, distress, disability and the apparent presence of diminished responsibility for actions with harmful consequences to self or others. These common denominators of mental disorder will be further explored in Chapter 8, where it will be argued that the presence of some of these characteristics is a necessary but not sufficient reason for a pattern of human activity to be accounted a psychiatric disorder. In a real sense that answer to the question of what is or is not a psychiatric disorder is the topic of this book as a whole, and I shall therefore pass on at this point to the third and final boundary issue in psychiatric diagnosis.

3 *Boundary between what is or is not a psychiatric case (where to draw the line on a dimension/continuum)*. Some mental disorders blend imperceptibly into normal everyday human experience and action. In the absence of any natural discontinuity to serve as a fault-line upon which to divide the psychiatric case from the non-case, arbitrary cut-off decisions have to be made to distinguish who is and who is not a suitable case for psychiatric treatment. There is a dimension or continuum between normality and

mental disorder. This continuum is most clearly visible in anxiety/depression, or perhaps in Alzheimer's disease. Many if not most people experience some mild symptoms of anxiety/depression in the course of their daily life. If a large enough sample of people is drawn and their symptoms assessed, it is found they can be placed on a continuum with the least affected at one end and the severely affected and clearly suffering a mental disorder at the other. The problem emerges in the middle, and there is no natural boundary to separate mental disorder from ordinary everyday experience.

In the absence of a boundary marker, cut-off decisions can be made on several different bases, for example: number of symptoms, severity of symptoms/complaints, presence of indicator complaints/symptoms, duration of complaint, beneficial response to treatment, normative decisions about natural responses to life events/perceived explanatoriness, perceived degree of responsibility for action/predicament, evidence for physiological causation, degree of social disability caused, and help-seeking behaviour. However, given that these decisions are essentially arbitrary, it is not surprising that cut-off points are determined differently by different researchers. Once again this leads to difficulty in comparing research results, although the present situation is much improved because of the widely publicised, used and available symptom scaling instruments. Arguments do still continue over exactly where to draw the line between case and non-case, as this is defined differently by different instruments. Indeed, Dean et al. (1983) applied four different research diagnostic schemes to the same population and generated four selectively different groups of patients. Given that there is no outside, external or objective standard to which to refer, these arguments are unlikely ever to be finally resolved. However, they can be pragmatically resolved, or, should it be said, resolved for practical purposes. There are two ways in which this can take place. First, the cut-off distinction can be made at the point that shows best the causes of the condition. Brown (1981), for example, argues for a particular set of criteria because when applied to groups of cases they show a relationship between depression and social class. Second, the distinction can be made at the point at which patients can be shown to benefit from psychiatric treatment. Substantial ambiguity still remains, however, as the distinction between case and non-case becomes purely a function of the purpose of whoever makes that distinction.

VALUE OF DIAGNOSTIC SYSTEMS

By now the imperfections of the diagnostic system are all too apparent. There is wide disagreement about the numbers, types and criteria for the different diagnostic categories. Many categories overlap, suggesting the possibility of dimensional versus categorical systems of classification. For some disorders there are no objective criteria between the normal and the symptomatic. Moreover, what is considered to be a psychiatric case changes over time and between cultures.

Nevertheless, diagnostic systems remain essential. There is sufficient agreement for research to take place, and that research has provided evidence for a variety of differing aetiologies in differing conditions, and has allowed systematic testing of treatment methods which has improved the efficacy of psychiatric care. To reject the idea of classification or diagnosis in psychiatry means to reject all this. Using a brief descriptive terminology does not represent a real alternative – saying 'suffering delusions and hallucinations' is equivalent to making a diagnosis, but without rigour. It could mean a dementia, a toxic confusional state, schizophrenia or depression, all of which have been shown to require different treatment.

The ambiguities inherent in psychiatric diagnosis should not lead us to rule out a physiological causation for mental disorders. The idea that if mental disorders were physiologically based they should line up in clear and discrete categories, looks appealing but is incorrect. Only those unfamiliar with the ambiguities of diagnosis in general medicine would make such a claim. For example, the distinctions between hypertension and normality, or between diabetes and normality are also arbitrary in the same way as the distinction between depression and normality. Similarly, research sometimes demonstrates that what was thought to be one physiological illness turns out to be two quite different syndromes, or two different illnesses turn out to be different manifestations of the same physiological disorder. The crude uncertainty of practical psychiatric diagnoses, or of their associated prognoses, cannot therefore be used as evidence that mental disorders are not physiologically caused, for exactly the same is true of diagnosis in general medicine.

Mirowsky and Ross (1989) suggest we should abandon diagnostic categories entirely. They recommend that we use instead dimensional scales for each and every symptom or complaint. Their argument for doing so is that much less information would be lost than in the process of categorisation, and that discernment of correlations and cut-off points is statistically stronger with such ordinal rather than nominal data. They also show that relationships between different symptoms would become visible and researchable, their example being perception, mood and arousal in which a diagnosis of depression collapses possible causal relationships, i.e. instead of all three being credited to some underlying entity 'depression', there might be causal linkages between the three to be explored. This move towards a totally dimensional picture is fine as a research strategy, but is simply not possible for clinical practice where limited time for assessment of clinical presentation has to be combined with assessing past psychiatric history and past response to treatment in order to provide a relatively reliable predictive guide for treatment and care. Even as a research strategy it would have to prove its predictive and analytic worth before diagnostic categories could be completely abandoned. Kendell (1975a) points out that similar pleas to replace categorical diagnosis with alternative schemes, whether they be dimensional symptom scales or cognitive tests, behavioural analysis or psychodynamic defence mechanism classifications, have never been carried through into practice. Thus we cannot judge their utility or otherwise.

There remains one final way in which diagnostic systems are misunderstood. They are by no means expansionist charters for psychiatric professionals to increase their power and status. As we have seen, they are derived from rigorous analysis of patients presenting for psychiatric help, and from hard-won empirical data. Having developed rigorous scaling and classification techniques, and demonstrated the worth of psychiatric treatment, it is eminently legitimate for psychiatric professionals to ask how many people in the community at large are not receiving psychiatric treatment and could benefit from so doing. This is not some kind of psychiatric evangelism, but is purely an attempt to reduce human suffering, and can only be wrong if psychiatry cannot deliver effective reductions in suffering by treatment. For example, it would seem clear from research that many people at large suffer from anxiety and/or depression, and fail to receive treatment that could lead to them improving more rapidly. Perhaps this criticism of psychiatric evangelism is slightly more valid when it is claimed that larger and larger realms of socially problematic behaviour are being brought under the psychiatric umbrella. Examples of this might be shoplifting or premenstrual tension. I would argue that in these cases there needs to be careful assessment, category by category, of what positive and negative effects might arise from including these things in the psychiatric disorder lexicon. It must be admitted that such careful consideration and debate rarely takes place.

BOYLE AND SCHIZOPHRENIA

Boyle (1990) uses many of the above points and arguments, plus many more, to attack the value and validity of schizophrenia as a diagnosis. She commences with the simple point that there are no usable physiological criteria for the diagnosis, and that in the absence of those criteria schizophrenia is solely a descriptive term for behaviour of particular kinds. Having made this point she goes on to undermine the evidence for genetic factors in the cause of schizophrenia, and attacks the historical continuity of the term, suggesting that the diagnosis was used for a different population of patients in the past than it is today. Boyle points to a high degree of variability rather than of consistency between those to whom the term is now applied. She concludes that schizophrenia is an illusory pattern of symptoms, the definition of which has been arrived at on a non-scientific and non-rigorous basis.

The upshot of her main arguments is not entirely clear. At first it would appear that she is recommending that we go back to the drawing board with those whom we now consider to be suffering from schizophrenia, and draw up a better system of classification more closely tied to validating criteria such as outcome, treatment response, etc. However, she fails to suggest any alternative classification, and instead suggests that for research purposes we break schizophrenia down into its individual symptoms and study them in isolation. Meanwhile, she recommends that the co-occurrence of these symptoms should be put down to chance. In other words, she is suggesting that the symptoms of what we now call schizophrenia are widely distributed across the population, that the same symptom may arise from very diverse causes (as do many symptoms of physical disease like raised body temperature), and that when they occur together this is by chance. She goes on to suggest that it is not the possession of these symptoms alone that brings people into psychiatric care, but only the possession of symptoms when combined with a collapse in social efficacy or when problems are posed for the daily lives of others. The topic of why failure in social efficacy occurs with some people but not others is, she argues, a priority for research.

The assertion that people who are now being treated for schizophrenia suffer from the chance co-occurrence of symptoms, and that their condition may therefore be overdetermined, having multiple causes, really requires much more evidence than Boyle can currently present. As a research strategy, exploring the nature and treatment of individual symptoms may provide some of this evidence. However, this does not mean that the concept of schizophrenia can be completely abandoned just yet, as it still has real clinical utility. Much evidence does exist on the response to particular medications of people who fit the diagnosis. Some evidence is also available about onset and eventual outcome which is of real benefit to the practice of psychiatry. We cannot, therefore, abandon such a useful diagnosis until we have something better, in practical terms, to put in its place. Until then, there is nothing to prevent researchers investigating individual symptoms.

Boyle's arguments do not undercut the validity of trying to classify psychiatric disorders. All she has done is to show that such classifications are preliminary and always open to revision until validating criteria are established. Quite rightly, she has argued that professional consensus about the existence of syndromal patterns of symptoms is not, by itself, enough to make a diagnosis fully legitimate. It is only a starting-point for further research, and we should be ready to abandon such patterns when it becomes apparent that they are no longer useful or productive.

SUMMARY

To conclude, despite the problems of boundaries involved in classification of psychiatric disorder, that classification is both legitimate and necessary for the provision and improvement of appropriate psychiatric care to those in distress. Social labelling cannot be equated with the process of diagnosis, and therefore diagnoses cannot be criticised as stereotypical labels in anything other than a very restricted sense. The use of the word 'diagnosis' should not be taken to imply that all psychiatric disorders are illnesses, whether they are to be viewed as physiologically caused or not. Neither should the ambiguities of psychiatric diagnostic symptoms be taken as evidence that psychiatric disorders are not illnesses. There are a number of ways to construct diagnostic systems, using dimensions, categories, cut-off points, or combinations of all three as is found in the Goldberg and Huxley (1992) model. All these attempts have equal logical validity, and are therefore to be evaluated according to what can be achieved with them, for their utilitarian and research benefits.

Chapter 6

History

In recent decades the history of psychiatry has shown every sign of becoming an academic growth area. Early writings on the subject authored by practising psychiatrists like Walk (1954), and Hunter and Macalpine (1963), made enduring contributions to the subject. At the same time Kathleen Jones' work appeared (1955, 1960), charting changes in the law and the process of reform of policy in UK psychiatry. However, it was in the 1970s and 1980s that renewed interest in the field began to be shown in an increasing number of publications. This interest may have been spurred by the unique and original contributions of Foucault (1967) and Castel (1976, published in English translation 1988) in France, and Szasz (1971) in the USA. The main contributor to the trend in the UK has undoubtedly been Andrew Scull (1979, 1989) who has not only made major contributions to the study of the history of psychiatry in the UK, but has also encouraged many other scholars from differing backgrounds both to study and to publish in the field. Important and substantial contributions have also been made in recent years by Bynum (e.g. 1981) and Porter (e.g. 1987).

Much of this latter and now dominant style of historical psychiatry contains assertions that mental illness is a fluid phenomenon which has been differently socially constructed in different epochs. Scull (1979), for example, argues that the construction and opening of the asylums operated to 'induce a wider conception of the nature of insanity'. Even more strongly, Bynum et al. (1985) support the position that 'the recognition and interpretation of mental illness, indeed its whole meaning, are culture-bound, and change profoundly from epoch to epoch'. This picture of mental disorder as a culturally-relative phenomenon with no real historical universality is of course precisely the same picture which is in the frame in transcultural psychiatric studies. The issues and arguments that arise therefore parallel the debates in cross-cultural studies. However, despite their assertions of the historical relativity of mental disorder, few historians have attempted to tackle the topic seriously. Transcultural scholars can, after all, visit different cultures, ask questions and observe their people. Historical scholars have to rely almost solely on written historical sources, as well as their own powers of interpretation and analysis. Direct comparisons of mental disorder now and at some point in the past are therefore fraught with difficulty, although not completely impossible. The early history of psychiatry was mainly preoccupied with formal government policy. In the later period historians have concentrated upon the professional organisation of psychiatry and its development. The nature of mental disorder as a phenomenon has largely been left as a side issue, although not an unimportant one. Some examinations of the topic have been made, and it is to these that we now turn.

TEMPORAL DEVELOPMENT OF PSYCHIATRIC DIAGNOSES

Some authors, mainly academic psychiatrists, have attempted to get to grips with the diagnostic systems of psychiatry from the point of view of their historical development. For example, Pichot (1994) has described the temporal development of psychiatric diagnoses, dating the birth of the modern diagnostic system to one hundred years ago with the work of Kraepelin. It would, however, be fairly accurate to say that Pichot assumes the historical continuity and universality of the phenomenon of mental disorder. For him, the question does not seem to arise as to whether mental disorder has itself changed in form or nature. Instead he is concerned with the changing conceptions, interpretations and classifications of mental disorder. He wishes to illuminate the origins of our current diagnostic systems and persuade us that it may be possible to improve upon current conceptions and classifications. He fears that development of the ICD and DSM could lead to an over-rigidity in our thinking which might blind us to advances in the classification of mental disorders.

Although this argument may be valid, because of Pichot's assumption of historical continuity, his perspective is limited. He does not appreciate the challenge of the new historical psychiatrists who insist that mental disorder is a wholly socially-defined and therefore malleable phenomenon. Pichot proceeds with his descriptions of diagnostic categories in the past as if these are entirely separable from the ways in which people, both lay and professional, reacted and responded to them. He assumes that it is unproblematic for us to identify, for example, melancholia in the past with affective disorder today, or dementia praecox with schizophrenia. Unfortunately, the only grounds available for making such identifications are the descriptive accounts left behind by previous generations. This is an indirect access at best, as we cannot subject the past accounts to cross-examination. In addition, it may well be that psychiatric diagnostic categories/descriptions can remain the same over a long period of time while their meaning changes, or that the terms can stand for a theory or explanation of behaviour rather than the behaviour itself.

These latter two problems are firmly grasped and well described by other writers. Parry-Jones (1972) provides an instance of the former with his almost incidental description of how the term imbecility has changed in meaning. Using original sources relating to early nineteenth-century private madhouses, he shows that imbecility was a term used to describe disturbances of mental state secondary to physical disorder. In comparison, by the end of that same century the word was being used consistently to describe mental handicap of a lesser degree than idiocy.

An example of diagnostic terms referring to theories rather than clinical presentations is Foucault's (1967) historical analysis of the term melancholia, demonstrating that it covered an enormous range of symptoms whose only real unity appears to have been their theoretical explanation, not their syndromal relationship. Foucault provides evidence that melancholia has been considered to be evidenced at one time or another by nihilistic delusions, fear of death, delusions of being an animal, delusions of guilt, long persistent delirium without fever, obsession by only one thought, and sadness. He provides a similar analysis and description of the term mania, conveying clearly how the causes and nature of this disorder have been variously thought of and explained. By describing the pictures and metaphors used in the explanatory theories Foucault is able to link these to the differing observations which were made and the treatments which were applied. Although he does not deny that there is a natural order to the phenomenon of mental illness, his arguments do come close to a perspective similar to that of Kuhn's analysis of scientific advances (1962), where explanatory theory determines what is or is not observed. Kuhn suggests that the dominant paradigm, or explanatory theory, determines what scientists look for and see in their experimental evidence. Foucault is advancing rather similar ideas when he describes how what was seen in the behaviour of the insane was determined to a degree by the explanatory theory in use.

A further illustration of the difficulties involved in determining the nature of psychiatric disorder across historical periods is provided by scholarly attempts at retrospective diagnosis of historical figures. Using historical sources, some have tried to project modern diagnostic categories and sometimes modern psychopathological theorising into the past. Freud's work on Moses (1939) and Leonardo da Vinci (1910) are early examples of this form of scholarship. Macalpine and Hunter's (1969) analysis of the illnesses of George III is another. This particular work is helped by the availability of copious amounts of source material due to the prominence of the subject. Mainly on the grounds of evidence of concurrent physical and mental symptoms in the king, plus some genetic detective work with his surviving descendants, they are able to conclude with a high degree of credibility that he suffered from porphyria. The richness of the historical record for this personage is seldom matched, however. Porter's (1985) examination of the life of Samuel Johnson wisely refrains from 'slapping a retrospective psychiatric diagnosis on the deviant dead', but even he cannot refrain from the overwhelming temptation to explore all the diagnostic and psychopathological possibilities. The problems that arise are of course exactly the same as those encountered in trying to bring into alignment diagnostic terminology of the past with that in present use. Only limited amounts of source material are available for the compilation of a list of signs and symptoms. Questions that arise about the precise nature of some reported symptoms cannot be cross-checked, as the historical sources are all that we have. It is hard to be certain whether descriptive terms used in the historical sources mean the same as they do today, and it is almost impossible to be sure how much of what is described in the sources and appears to be abnormal behaviour or behaviour worthy of remark was actually so in the eyes of contemporaries. Questions of historical retrospective diagnoses can therefore never be finally answered.

RELATIVITY VERSUS CONTINUITY

The problems which surround the debate about historical relativity versus continuity of psychiatric descriptive terms are variously grasped by different authors. In a series of papers Berrios (1984, 1985a, 1985b) displays great scholarship in his depiction of changes in psychiatric diagnoses and their associated psychopathological theorising. His survey of the whole field of change in psychopathological thinking in Europe over the past two centuries is brilliant, as is the scope of his detailed description of changes in the psychopathology of affectivity and his analysis of terminological changes in the description of obsessional disorder. Berrios has tried to make links between these changes and parallel developments in philosophy and psychology. It is hard to see, however, how these links can be any more than speculative as in most cases it cannot be determined in which field of endeavour ideas started to change first, let alone what or who was the primary influence. The links Berrios draws are suggestive and interesting, but never final.

Although Berrios acknowledges that the historical continuity of mental disorder can be questioned, he does not seem to think it a serious challenge to the task he has set himself of 'calibrating' the diagnostic languages of different historical periods. His basis for rejecting the challenge is the constancy and stability of a number of symptoms of mental disorder throughout history. He does not specify these but probably has in mind the common symptoms of the organic and functional psychoses such as hallucinations, delusions, agitation, overactivity, retardation, and furor. Not only do these symptoms remain historically constant, but their content also remains remarkably similar – delusions of grandeur, for instance, as well as persecution, guilt and somatic changes. In his most recent and wide-ranging work, Berrios (1996) confirms this picture of continuity. Although variously construed, since the nineteenth century hallucinations, delusions, obsessional behaviour, depression, mania and many other symptoms have been considered as mental disorder. The argument for the continuity of mental disorder is strengthened when it is considered that at no time in history has there been an era when mental disorder was not recognised and described. This argument for the stability of mental illness is not weakened by evidence, for example, that catatonia has dramatically declined in frequency over the past hundred years. As Mahendra (1981) and Johnson (1993) show, this is most likely to be due to a decease in the infectious and other physiological causes of the condition, rather than psychosocial changes. Berrios is therefore undoubtedly right to argue from the constancy of symptoms to the historical continuity of mental disorder. He even advances a historical parallel to the pathoplastic versus pathogenic distinction of transcultural psychiatry, referring to the pathoplastic elements of mental disorder as 'social noise'. He is wrong, however, to assume that the historical continuity of symptoms constitutes evidence for biological causation when this regularity may well be founded equally in historically-constant forms of human social life.

Historical continuity is not restricted to the psychotic symptoms. Even for those mental disorders which have been considered to be recent social constructions whose aetiology is entirely psychosocial, evidence is now beginning to emerge that they have always been with us. For example, anorexia nervosa is often considered to be a psychiatric disorder of recent origin. However, Banks (1992) shows that a syndrome identifiable as anorexia dates back at least to the middle ages, and possibly before. Likewise Sournia's (1990) description of the history of alcoholism shows that the phenomenon of alcohol dependency has been a constant feature of human societies, although its identification as a psychiatric disorder is relatively recent. Can we therefore say that anorexia nervosa existed prior to its description by Gull in the nineteenth century? This is not the same question as, for example, whether Pluto existed before its description by Percival Lowell and subsequent discovery by Clyde Tombaugh, for what is now called anorexia nervosa is not just self-starvation, it is self-starvation in the context of a particular and historically-local set of meanings around femininity, slimming and psychiatric disorder. Both the sufferer and those around her construct the experience in certain ways because of the beliefs and actions to which they respond. So though in one sense it is quite right to assert that anorexia nervosa did not exist as such prior to its description and identification, this is really only to reassert once again a distinction between the pathogenic and pathoplastic. As is known from Banks (1992), young girls did starve themselves for obscure reasons prior to the description of anorexia nervosa, just as lives were ruined by alcohol dependency before the word 'alcoholism' was coined. These tragedies were not always considered 'madness' or 'insanity', but were nevertheless a consistent and continuous thread in human social experience.

INFLUENCE OF CONCEPTS UPON EXPERIENCE

While this interaction between sociocultural factors and mental disorder is a primary area of focus and interest in transcultural psychiatry, the history of psychiatry has as yet shown only passing interest in the way in which past conceptions of mental disorder may have shaped both the experience of, as well as social responses to it. Perhaps part of the reason for this is the paucity of historical sources on the experience of mental disorder in past ages. Peterson (1982) has collected together and reviewed many historical accounts of psychiatric illness, but remarks that many of the older of these are preoccupied with controversies and scandals surrounding detentions in various institutions and the kind of treatment meted out there. Where those accounts do touch upon the personal experience of psychosis, as in the well-known Perceval's narrative (Bateson 1974), what is described is strikingly similar to the sufferers of today. Most of this material is from the eighteenth and nineteenth centuries, and was part and parcel of the movement humanising the insane, a topic to be discussed in more detail below.

It is interesting to speculate, however, how the explanations of madness and the treatments used in the past actually may have affected the behaviour and understanding of the actual sufferers of mental disorder. A number of competing explanations and theories of madness were in use at different times in the past. It is dangerous to assume simplistic retrospective pictures that suggest one idea as dominant or current at one period. Indeed, the historical record appears to show that the explanation of mental disorder has always been controversial with numerous ideas in circulation at any one time, a situation which continues today. It is hard to find any historical scholarship which takes this as its topic, apart from the work of Berrios which is focused upon professional rather than lay views. There are, however, isolated pieces on particular ideas and explanations.

Porter (1987) gives an overview of some of these interpretations of mental disorder. His evidence shows that madness has been viewed in many different ways, as:

1 A response to trouble and stress.
2 A physical illness (based on humoral theory).
3 Reduction of the human to the level of the animal.
4 A consequence of libertarian individualism.
5 The overthrow of reason's control over the passions.

It is interesting to note the common threads in these pictures of mental disorder. These are ideas of 'loss of control' and of 'diminished responsibility', and they remain central to current conceptions of mental disorder. However, what does not always come through in Porter's and other historians' accounts is that an interpretation of mental disorder has many different ramifications. The most obvious of these is the way the sufferer is treated, and many have linked the perception of the mad as close to beasts to their treatment by whipping and chaining. Less often remarked upon is how the sufferers too might have believed these ideas: they may have entered into their delusions and hallucinations in such a way as to confirm the picture for those who were charged with their care. A third level of import can be found in the way in which these interpretations can be transformed into moral imperatives.

Many examples are available here. The picture of madness as being the overthrow of reason by the passions and impulses was common in the eighteenth century, and Porter (1987) is able to marshal a wide range of evidence from various sources. However, this interpretation of the cause of madness becomes a moral injunction to control the impulses and passions lest they drive one to madness. This is one of the central lessons of Hogarth's *The Rake's Progress*, in which the main character finds himself incarcerated in Bethlem as a final result of a debauched lifestyle. Perhaps a more obvious example of the path from psychiatric theorising to moral recommendations is that displayed in the tale of masturbatory insanity. This popular interpretation in the late nineteenth century of the cause of mental disorder led transparently to a moral campaign for continence. This theory had great utility, as due to the widespread nature of the behaviour it was always available as an explanation, should mental disorder occur. Szasz (1971) describes how this theory led to some terrible treatments, up to and including major surgery.

Another idea current at the same period was that of degeneracy, an explanation particularly associated with the work of Morel (1857), a French psychiatrist. Morel argued that, over the generations, alcohol abuse and poor nutrition led to mental disorder, mental handicap, epilepsy and eventual sterility. Dowbiggin (1985) describes how these ideas were widespread among psychiatrists of the period. The ideas carry clear moral and political implications, although Dowbiggin does not make apparent whether they were treated in this way. Some current commentators upon psychiatry argue that this translation of aetiological theorising into moral imperative is not something that has been restricted to past eras. Rose (1986) argues that the mental hygiene movement of the early twentieth century developed and expanded the concept of mental disorder taking on personal unhappiness and social inefficiency, thus removing them from the domain of moral and consequential behaviour to that of illness and diminished responsibility. Castel *et al.* (1982) develop a very similar critique of the community mental health movement in the USA of the 1960s. These ideas will be taken up in more detail in the following chapter.

FOUCAULT AND CHANGING CONCEPTIONS OF MENTAL ILLNESS

It has already been mentioned that Foucault collates some interesting historical material relating to different conceptions and treatments of particular diagnostic categories over historical periods. This is however a minor theme in his work on psychiatry. His major book is more wide ranging, abstract and difficult to define. It too relates to the nature of mental disorder over time, but as a whole rather than as specific syndromes or diagnostic categories. Foucault makes these arguments in a very forceful and poetic form, tempting Scull to call his prose 'idiosyncratic and self-consciously opaque pyrotechnics'.

Foucault appears to be arguing that there has been a transformation in the way people think and act towards the phenomenon of madness, and that this transformation has been both subtle and fundamental. He suggests that prior to the seventeenth century, madness was viewed as a liberation of the animal within. At that time people perceived themselves as surrounded by unreason or madness, which threatened both to overwhelm and liberate them. Subsequently, madness came to be perceived rather differently as the absence of responsibility or free will, a state in which behaviour was not determined by the person. Harking back to that pre-seventeenth-century picture of madness, Foucault paints a poetic picture of madness as wisdom, non-being, liberation, freedom, communicating what is deepest in man.

There are many problems with the way Foucault portrays the history of madness, not least its overall coherence and intelligibility. His method of argument is not painstakingly to establish a case with historical evidence, but to assert and then illustrate it with various opaque comments on isolated works of literature, drama or art. At first glance it appears that he is drawing from the materials, but in fact he is not. Instead he appears to have no serious interest in his sources. It is in this way that he is able to read back into the past the ideas of existentialist philosophy. Foucault's use of existentialism is very visible in statements like 'madness has become man's possibility of abolishing both man and the world'. His debt to modern French philosophy, Husserl and Nietzsche is acknowledged by all his major commentators and supporters including Sheridan (1980). The identification of madness with unreason and wisdom can be seen as parallel to the rejection by existentialists of abstract Hegelian idealism. Instead of trying to analyse the nature or essence of madness, Foucault regards it as a form of human existence or being. His praise of the state of madness, or folly as he sometimes calls it in order to evoke Erasmus and other earlier writers (e.g. Tertullian) who assert Christian faith as a form of absurdity, suggests that he sees it as a form of existential authenticity. This is false for two weighty reasons. Firstly, it elevates madness into a chosen state rather than the affliction it is. It removes the irrationality from madness, converting it into a meaningful rather than meaningless experience, and describes a state which cannot be matched with the explanations or non-explanations given by the seriously mentally ill about their condition. Only in the case of depression can mental disorder be found to have a coherent existentialist explanation of its experience. Secondly, this portrayal by Foucault of madness as a crisis of authentic choice, as a consciousness of the essentially meaningless irrational nature of human life, corrupts and obscures those concepts which are so central to existentialism. Existentialism is committed to the idea that human beings create value and meaning out of their lives. To equate this with madness is to imply that the path from existential crisis of meaninglessness to authentic, creative and chosen human action is a path that is founded upon irrationality.

Perhaps the best way to show the vacuity of Foucault's interpretation of madness as the wisdom of unreason is to ask exactly how did this show itself in the way the mad were regarded prior to the seventeenth century? Did people take their problems to the insane for solution? Did they consult them on business matters? Or was their advice sought for family problems and arguments? The answers are of course 'No' in each and every case. Additionally, perhaps, we may assume Foucault did not try to tap the wisdom of the insane in the writing of his own works. The truth is more likely that insanity has been a curse in every era and every age.

Foucault's work boils with ideas and interpretations of the history of madness. Though the view of madness as a beneficial existential experience is only one strand in his writing, it is the one that attempts to challenge the historical continuity of madness. Unfortunately, it is hard to identify the real world of mental disorder in Foucault's romantic portrayals of the wisdom of unreason and its closeness to artistic creativity. Foucault has in fact betrayed the mad by failing to accept the reality of their suffering and disability, choosing instead to interpret the nature of mental disorder as something that is a beneficial gift to mankind. He is not the first to do this, and in so doing he shows the kinship of his ideas with those of Laing (1965), whose thinking is also grounded in existentialist philosophy, and who interprets madness as a voyage of self-discovery and personal growth.

PSYCHIATRIC EXPANSIONISM

Scull's (1979, 1989) attack upon the historical continuity of mental disorder takes a significantly different tack. He argues, from the rising numbers of the insane in the nineteenth century, that conceptions of insanity change according to social factors and requirements. More specifically, he suggests that the idea of insanity was broadened by the psychiatric profession in order to accumulate more resources and power. Unlike Foucault, Scull makes excellent use of historical sources, arguing from them that there was an initially low prevalence of mental disorder in the early nineteenth century, and that the gross increase in numbers of incarcerated insane during the period is not accounted for by social discontinuity and change, rising numbers of paupers or the supposedly poor quality of the early statistical data. In the UK, rates of certified cases of mental illness rose from 12.66 per 10,000 (1844) to 29.6 per 10,000 (1890). Having removed what he sees as the alternative explanations of the increase, Scull deduces that it was the concept of insanity itself that changed, rather than any objective rate of mental illness. Scull thus mounts a powerful argument that mental disorder is not a determinate, objective affair, but is dependent upon historically varying definitions and interpretations. The implication is that what is considered to be mental disorder now might be wholly different to what was considered mental disorder in another era, and, moreover, that our current conceptions should therefore be open to challenge and change.

There are, however, two reasons why Scull's account does not necessarily stand up to critical scrutiny. The first is that although he establishes very clearly and with good evidence the real nature of the figures indicating a rise in numbers of the insane, and couples this with the assertion of a broadening of definitions and conceptions, he is unable to say precisely how the concept of insanity broadened. He fails to provide any evidence on what new deviant behaviours were arising and being brought into the psychiatric fold. All he can point to is a vagueness in medical definitions of insanity current at the time, coupled with the argument that the psychiatric profession had a clear motive to increase their power by increasing the number of patients in their control. However, the vagueness in the definition of insanity in the nineteenth century continues to the present day, indeed from one perspective this is the main topic of this book. This does not mean that what is, or is not, mental disorder is arbitrary, as Scull attempts to assert. Clinicians of the nineteenth century could with reasonable ease determine cases of imbecility, dementia praecox, melancholia, mania and the like. As a practical task this was not so problematic. The definition difficulty arises when one tries to say what all these differing human problems have in common, what makes them examples of the concept of insanity. In the context of this argument, what is important here is that differing views, definitions and ambiguities about the general nature of insanity do not necessarily have direct practical implications for the task of defining cases for treatment in the clinical arena. For Scull's argument to succeed, he would have to show in precisely what way the practices of psychiatrists in defining suitable cases for treatment actually changed over the nineteenth century, exactly what new human behaviours were now considered evidence of mental disorder which were not before. This kind of evidence is strikingly absent from Scull's presentation.

Second, although Scull deals with some alternative explanations for the rising numbers, other than changes in definitions, he does not consider them all. He does show that the rise cannot be accounted for by statistical error, rising populations or numbers of paupers. He considers evidence that decreased mortality rates within the asylums, together with an accumulation of chronic cases, partly contributed to the rise in numbers, but argues that these do not fully explain such a large increase. One thing he does not seriously consider is that there may have been a real rise in the numbers of the insane, particularly those suffering from schizophrenia. Of course it would be very difficult to demonstrate this retrospectively, but it remains a potential explanation. Recent preliminary evidence (Der *et al.* 1990; Eagles 1991) that the incidence of schizophrenia may be declining would support this as an explanation. However, perhaps the most likely explanation is that over the course of the nineteenth century the asylums began to take responsibility for the care of widely varying groups of disabled people who were unable to work and required full-time supervision. This would include the senile aged, the mentally handicapped, the epileptic, those suffering brain damage following infection, other physical disorder or injury, the severely physically handicapped, dietary deficiency syndromes and poisoning from industrial work or pollution. Busfield (1986) agrees that the rising numbers of lunatics in the asylums (at least, in the UK) was a process driven by the operation of the Poor Law combined with economic and practical necessities facing families. In fact, when Scull arrives at the close of his argument, we see that he too admits the force of this interpretation of events. In his later reworking of the argument (Scull 1993) this is even more apparent, and he produces plentiful historical evidence that it was not the definition of insanity that changed over this period, but the practical pressures upon poor families and relative economic costs of various welfare options.

Does this mean that the concept of insanity changed, as Scull would have us believe? If insanity is defined by who has had an episode of care in an asylum, then perhaps it has. However, insanity can be defined by the criteria for its diagnosis by psychiatrists. In fact, this is the definition Scull himself is working with, as it is psychiatrists' definitions that Scull argues have changed under the motivation of professional aggrandisement. It is precisely on this point of psychiatrists' definitions of insanity that Scull's argument fails. In order to substantiate it, he must be able to show that in the early nineteenth century epilepsy or mental handicap, for example, were not considered by psychiatrists to be instances of insanity whereas by the close of the century they were. He does not do this. Instead he quotes psychiatrists of the era who were clearly aware that a proportion of asylum residents were not insane as such at all.

In addition the sin of anachronism must be avoided. Perhaps we can say retrospectively that some of the asylum residents, although displaying symptoms of serious mental disorder, were actually suffering a variety of physiological disorders, injuries or poisonings – but this does not mean the psychiatrists of the time were able to make that distinction. Thus although physiological disorders interfering with brain dysfunction may account for some of the nineteenth-century rise in numbers of the insane, it cannot be concluded that the concept of insanity itself changed at all.

It is for these reasons that Scull cannot be said to have established the historical relativity of mental disorder. As he takes his argument into wilder and wilder territory, it becomes more and more tendentious. His assertion that asylum expansion created new demand is simply ludicrous. If this was so asylums should have continuously suffered from overcapacity as their expansion preceded demand, rather than the reverse situation of overcrowding which was actually the case. A last and most interesting point remains to be made. Scull has examined only the rising numbers of insane in the nineteenth century, whereas it is a matter of record that these numbers continued to rise right through into the 1940s, not just in the UK, but throughout Europe and the USA. It is an open question as to why this happened, although it may lend support to the argument that there has been a real increase in the incidence of schizophrenia that continued through the first half of the twentieth century.

LABELLING AND DEVIANCY THEORY IN THE HISTORY OF PSYCHIATRY

Throughout his works on the history of psychiatry, not just in respect of the debate over the nature of insanity, Scull makes a great deal out of the professionalisation of medical psychiatry. In common with many other of the current historians of psychiatry, Scull sees as one of his main tasks the destruction of the 'Whiggish' version of the development of institutional psychiatry. That development, he would argue, has not been one of linear scientific, moral and policy progress towards modern humanitarian psychiatry. Instead he interprets the rise of psychiatry in the light of structural class and interest group conflicts, calling such scholarship the 'Historical Sociology of Psychiatry' (1989).

The roots of Scull's thinking in the sociology of deviance are clearly visible here, his very language and terminology reflecting accurately the work of Becker (1963). This influence can be seen in Scull's consideration of the nature of mental disorder described above. The insane are purely, by the application of rules, made by others, rules which vary from time to time and from place to place, rules which create rather than respond to deviance. However, Scull's dependence upon Becker does not stop there, but continues in his interpretation of medical psychiatrists as moral entrepreneurs. He argues that psychiatrists sought to gain a monopoly control over the care of the insane for personal and professional gain. Acting as a unified interest group, he thinks, they resisted interference in their work, technologised and mystified treatments, asserted the efficacy of treatment without firm evidence, and fought to extend their legal rights in the certification process, all in order to strengthen their dominance in the 'mad trade'. Thus many events and episodes in the history of psychiatry are interpreted by Scull in terms of the self-interest of medical psychiatrists. Nineteenth-century arguments for a somatic basis to mental disorder become in Scull's eyes mere props and rationales for treatment by doctors, rather than attempts to advance knowledge and promote cure. Research by asylum superintendents becomes merely an excuse to get away from real patients. This cynical view of occupational and professional life can be traced back not only to Becker but also to the sociology of Hughes (1971), who ironicised the development of institutions and occupations, recasting them as accounts of how workers sought to maximise their status while minimising effort and difficulties.

The problem with this perspective is not that it is entirely wrong but that it is entirely one-sided. At no point is Scull ready to admit that on occasion psychiatrists and other professionals are motivated by a desire to help and improve the lot of others. He thus loses his grip upon the perspective of the historical persons he is studying, substituting 'sociological man' whose only interests are power, wealth and status. This loss of insight must be considered all the greater because Scull's extensive familiarity with original sources could have produced a much more well-rounded account of the development of psychiatry. This is exemplified by Castel (1988) who admits the possibility of good intentions on the part of psychiatric professionals, coupling this with the insight that those actions may have good or bad outcomes nevertheless, i.e. that policies and arguments can have unintended as well as intended results. This enables Castel to give a far more realistic and complex picture of the evolution of psychiatry in France over the identical historical period as that considered by Scull.

MORAL TREATMENT AND CONCEPTS OF INSANITY

Scull thus explains the development of psychiatry with reference to the self-interested motivation of the medical profession. Foucault maintains that the conception of madness has radically altered, and Porter offers a more diverse and less specific account. Each, in their different ways, is trying to explain or come to terms with that transition in psychiatric development, that movement to humanitarian care known as moral treatment. All without exception identify this as a key event or turning-point.

Moral therapy is usually dated to the foundation of the York Retreat in 1792 by William Tuke as an establishment for the care and treatment of mentally disturbed Quakers. Through the promulgation of the ideas of moral therapy, the York Retreat became internationally famous, influencing the practice of psychiatry all over the Western world. However, it is not easy to say exactly what moral therapy was, as practised by the Retreat, nor easy to say what it became over the course of the nineteenth century as it was applied in different contexts. Moral therapy at the York Retreat appears to have consisted of two central ideas or practices. The first was that the insane should be cared for with a minimum of physical restraint. Before this change, it was a matter of routine for the mad to be chained and manacled. The second was that by use of praise and reward the insane were to be induced and assisted to control their own behaviour. More recent historical scholarship by Parry-Jones (1972) and Scull (1979) has shown that these ideas were not unique to the York Retreat, but were being applied at a number of locations during the eighteenth century. Nevertheless, the beginnings of this reform have long been credited to the York Retreat, which certainly played a key role in its dissemination, receiving many visitors from other parts of England and abroad. This reform was neither instant nor uniform. It is not always appreciated that chains and physical restraint were still used as a last resort at the Retreat and that the move to total non-restraint did not emerge for some time, eliciting considerable resistance from asylum proprietors along the way. By the late nineteenth century the meaning of moral therapy had expanded to include the abolition of restraint, separation of different groups of patients, provision of amusements, facilities for exercise, religious activities and light, well-ventilated surroundings (Parry-Jones 1972). It would appear that just like the term 'case management' today, moral therapy came conceptually to include all improvements in psychiatric care.

The question of whose morality was in view when the term moral therapy was used remains ambiguous. If it was the patient's morality, then the main emphasis seems to be the attempt to persuade patients to internalise moral norms, to want to behave and control their 'morbid propensities'. On the other hand, the emphasis could be on the morality of the keepers of the insane. This would then highlight the way in which care and treatment became a matter of kindness and humanity rather than beatings and cruelty. Accounts of moral therapy show no consciousness of this ambiguity and make reference to both emphases.

Foucault (1967) criticises moral therapy as a subtle fraud. He argues that moral therapy was neither an advance nor a liberation. He suggests that all moral therapy does is to transform overt physical control into a different form, one that is psychological, internal and moral. Indeed it must be agreed that moral therapy was not a change from control of the insane to a full state of freedom. Nevertheless, it is still a liberation, still a massive revolution, to treat the mad with the respect a human being deserves, making him one with the moral community of men, no longer like an animal to be tied up, fed, watered and beaten. It is Foucault's desire to eulogise the state of madness (as was discussed above) that leads him to express a preference for free madness rather than responsible behaviour. However, this is almost like saying black is white. The sufferers of mental disorder rarely seek by preference to stay in that state, neither do those who love them seek it for them. Psychiatric institutions and wards are not overwhelmed with requests from patients to be physically restrained rather than be verbally persuaded to conform. Thus Foucault's account of moral therapy, describing it as a manipulative technique, simply does not match the evaluations of that care made by sufferers themselves and their relatives. Furthermore, Foucault's account has been criticised on the grounds that the aims of physical restraint and punishment were no less than the internalisation of norms, and therefore equally as psychologically intrusive and controlling.

Another way this transformation has been described is as a change in the way the insane were conceptualised. Before moral therapy they were seen as having lost their essential humanity, having become insensitive animals or beasts. Hence they were treated in the same way animals were treated in those days – tied up, and whipped when misbehaving. Then, at the dawn of the nine-teenth century the conception changed, with the insane being seen as human beings struggling to regain their reason. Hence moral therapy developed with the absence of restraint and the use of psychological rewards for self-control. The question may still be asked, however, as to why moral therapy sprang up at just that historical period. Scull (1979) suggests that the internalisation of norms required by the then new labour market both led and paral-leled the development of moral therapy. Alternative views are possible. Tuke's organisation of moral therapy at the York Retreat could be seen as a creative act, as one of invention, or as a working out of the peaceful non-violent principles of Quakerism applied to the care of the insane. Tuke then treated the mad as human beings and showed that it could be done. Prior to this demonstration such methods of caring for the insane could always be dismissed as unre-alistic and contrary to the practical necessities of confinement.

RESPONSIBILITY AND MENTAL ILLNESS

What moral therapy illustrates, for the purpose of this book, is how the non-responsibility of the mentally ill is not a monolithic, black-and-white issue such as is suggested by legal judgements of insanity which exonerate the sufferer from any responsibility. Instead there are continua, graduations, grey areas of part-responsibility. The attribution of responsibility for behaviour can be different in different contexts, like for example the community versus the inside of the psychiatric hospital. And that attribution is motivated; it is not a judgement based solely on evidence, or belief about the nature of mental disorder. It can be utilitarian, to produce a strategy by which the difficult behaviour of patients can be managed without resort to physical pain or restraint to accomplish that management.

There is something paradoxical here. It is behaviour, that because of context, circumstances and absence of reason, suggests that the actor is not responsible, that provides candidates for consideration as being possibly mentally ill. Then individuals are admitted to hospital, and one of the main strategies of care is to start treating them as responsible in order to manipulate their behaviour. This shows the complexity of negotiating responsibility, not just on the basis of individual instances or people, but also in terms of the social policy of psychiatry. The inception of moral therapy is just one historical example showing how the complex agreement between society, psychiatry and the mentally ill about who is to be held responsible for their actions and under what circumstances and with what consequences, can undergo significant changes. Despite this room for negotiation, the boundaries of change remain the same. They are that irresponsible actions may indicate the presence of mental disorder, which absolves, at least in part, responsibility for actions. By moral therapy, psychiatry created a space within those boundaries that allowed the humane and kind treatment of the mentally disturbed.

Such changes and transformations may have an immense impact upon the practice of psychiatry and upon the behaviours and actions of the mentally ill. Moral therapy demonstrated that kindness worked better than cruelty, that the chains and beatings had themselves to a large degree created aggressive and violent responses from the mentally ill. But this is not to say that mental disorder itself changed in nature. The afflicted continued to be deluded, hallucinated, agitated, stuporous and the like. Only their response to themselves and to their keepers changed. Certainly, this is no small thing, but neither is it a substantive change in the nature of mental disorder.

TURNING-POINTS AND HISTORICAL CHANGE

The intense focus on the analysis of the meaning of the change to moral therapy illustrates the preoccupation with turning-points which recurs regularly in the literature on the history of psychiatry. Two well-known examples of this preoccupation are Foucault's (1967) assertion that lunacy took over where leprosy left off, and Szasz's (1971, 1972) assertion that society's preoccupation with witchcraft became a preoccupation with madness.

Both imply a deviancy version of madness, but this is most explicit in Szasz, and only implicit in Foucault. In fact in Foucault this supposed transformation from leprosaria to lunatic asylums forms only a small part of his book. It has nevertheless been seized upon by others because it is so easy, using historical sources, to prove untrue. In fact there was a gap of several hundred years between the decline in leprosy and leprosaria in Europe, and the inception of lunatic asylums (Scull 1989). Foucault's misuse of history is similarly exposed in his romantic account of the 'narrenschiff' or ship of fools, which he suggests was used to export lunatics from one town to another in medieval Europe. This detail, too, has no basis in historical evidence (Jones and Fowles 1984). Nevertheless, these arguments of Foucault's critics miss the target, partly because such matters of historical fact are peripheral to his main arguments about the changing conception of madness, and perhaps because he is suggesting that lunacy took over the social function of leprosy. Szasz certainly says this explicitly in his argument about witchcraft and lunacy.

What kind of evidence could be found to support assertions of such social transformations? There are in fact two ways in which such arguments can be taken. Either they assert that witchcraft trials specifically gave way to institutional psychiatry, or that both are examples of practices which fulfil a social function which have been popular in different eras. Let us take the former argument first. For it to succeed it must be shown that the witchcraft trials of the middle ages have more points of similarity with the institutions of psychiatry now, than either phenomenon has with anything else. The way in which Szasz tries to support his assertion that 'Institutional Psychiatry is a continuation of the Inquisition' is by making the following connections:

1   *Both serve the interests of a specific professional group.* This is both a non-specific and ironical comparison. Professions and occupations all exist to carry out delimited tasks, therefore every task can be said to serve their interests. This cannot mean, however, that the occupational group got together first and then found a task in order to provide themselves with a *raison d'être.* For the same reason it is incorrect morally to condemn an occupation by this reversal of logic. Mental illness no more serves the interests of mental health professionals than does mass starvation the interests of Oxfam, or child abuse the interests of social workers, or cancer the interests of oncologists.

2   *Both witches and the mentally ill are defined as such by others.* This is again a non-specific and incorrect argument. Generally speaking all criminals are defined as such by others, as are geniuses, Nobel prize-winners, war heroes and a multitude of others; therefore the criterion does not apply specifically to witchcraft and mental illness. Second, the vast majority of the mentally ill are defined as such by themselves, by the help they seek from their family doctors. Only a minute fraction reject the category and are compulsorily treated. In any case this issue is far more complex than Szasz is willing to entertain, as many will

seek and receive psychiatric help without ever calling themselves, or being called, mentally ill. Others will use the lay terminology of 'nervous breakdown' rather than the stigmatising words 'mentally ill'. All are still psychiatric patients, defined as such by themselves.

3 *Most people accused of witchcraft then, or hysteria now, are women.* It will be immediately noticed that in order to draw this parallel, Szasz has had to ignore mental disorder as a whole, instead restricting himself to the rather uncommon syndrome of hysteria. The same does not hold for other psychiatric disorders like schizophrenia, manic depressive psychosis, Alzheimer's disease, etc. Although overall psychiatry treats roughly twice as many women as men, and may be open to the charge of gender bias, this is not a specific similarity to the Inquisition. As popular and academic feminism has shown, bias and discrimination against women exists in nearly every social domain.

4 *Most persons accused are of the lower classes and powerless.* Again, simple similarity because of social class distribution is not a specific resemblance between the Inquisition and psychiatry. Most crime, mental handicap, physical illness, physical handicap, disability and neonatal death are class-distributed in the same way. Moreover, Szasz is implying that more mental illness is identified among the lower classes because they lack the power and resources to reject the identification. This is interesting but lacks supporting evidence showing that the rich and powerful behave oddly but do not get psychiatrically diagnosed.

5 *Both psychiatry and witchcraft trials claim to benefit the people with whom they deal, but in reality do not.* Szasz erects a complex web of arguments here. At the most simple level it can be pointed out that there is a significant difference between temporary involuntary detention in a psychiatric hospital and burning at the stake. Even then, as has already been pointed out, only a small minority of patients are involuntarily treated. Szasz, however, wishes to counter that justification of psychiatry based upon the assertion that it benefits the patient. Witchfinders too, he shows, claimed the same motivation, arguing that they were saving the eternal souls of witches. Other than a rejection of Szasz's anachronism of reading his current moral values back into the past, this supposed similarity between the Inquisition and psychiatry can be dissolved in two ways. First, there is no empirical evidence of the pervasive practice of witchcraft or of its

being harmful to other people. The historical record shows that some people were aware of this at the time of the witchcraft trials and their arguments eventually held sway, as shown by the dying out of the Inquisition. On the other hand, mental illness, whatever its nature really is, definitely both exists and has profound negative consequences for the sufferer and those around him. Thus claims to benefit the identified person in the former case must be vacuous, but in the latter case may have a real basis. Second, the scale of values by which the Inquisition and psychiatry are to be judged is not made explicit. On a secular and materialist scale of values (e.g. longevity, health, comfort and freedom) the Inquisition did not benefit witches. On that same set of values, though, psychiatry does benefit its subjects. One may choose to criticise both on the basis of some alternate set of values, but these must be made explicit for the argument to be evaluated. Part of that calculation would be what would happen to the mentally disordered if the practice of psychiatry was abandoned.

6 *Both witchcraft and mental illness provide a rationale for events.* Witchcraft was certainly invoked as an explanation. It provided a cause or rationale for, typically, diseases of men or animals, accidents or personal misfortunes, and provided a theory about how that worked. Evans-Pritchard's (1976) description of witchcraft and magic among the Azande of Sudan gives many examples of the types of events ascribed to witchcraft: blight of crops, collapse of buildings, wasting diseases, death and failure to find game when hunting. These are very similar to events ascribed to witchcraft in the middle ages. Mental illness, however, is significantly different. It is not an explanation of events but an explanation only of behaviours. It is a partial and tentative explanation, or it can be seen as a set of competing theories. Mainly it is a class of human activities with certain characteristics, a name or category more than an explanation.

7 *The Inquisition created witchcraft, as psychiatry has created mental illness.* As evidence of this Szasz quotes the rise in number of witches following the Inquisition, and the rise in the numbers of mentally ill in the nineteenth century. This argument is simply specious. The invention of new techniques of deep sea fishing increases catches, but does not create increasing numbers of fish in the sea. Szasz has not appreciated that there may be differences between real and identified rates of mental illness. As

for witchcraft, the relevant question is whether there was there a real rate at all – empirical evidence suggests there was not.

Szasz makes a number of other parallels between the Inquisition and psychiatry, but these are even weaker than those dealt with above. In doing so he has to obscure very real distinctions between mental state examinations and confession of witchcraft under torture, illness and witchcraft, projective psychometric testing and the finding of witch's marks, and others. It becomes clear that Szasz has to put psychiatry and the Inquisition on parallel procrustean beds in order to make identifications between them. The first version of his argument therefore fails.

This still leaves the second, wider, version intact. Witchcraft and mental illness may serve similar social functions, as may leprosy if we are to follow Foucault. Chief in view here is the idea that human societies have the trans-historical property of rejecting, excluding and segregating disvalued subgroups. The issue of whether witchcraft specifically is one example of this phenomenon thus becomes less weighty. Far more important for the sake of this book is whether mental illness has, as this would assume, a political explanation or basis for it. This argument will therefore be taken up in the following chapter.

SUMMARY

This chapter has selected for discussion those facets of writings on the history of psychiatry which carry implications about the nature of mental disorder. This is a small and rather obscure proportion of the literature as a whole. Recent years have seen an explosion of historical scholarship in the field, much of which has consisted of careful descriptive work based on original sources. This work is of high quality and illuminates current psychiatric practice and the recurrence, at regular intervals, of many common ideas. A realistic rather than hagiographical account of the contributions of key figures has been provided, reconnecting psychiatry with its past. The value of this flurry of work should not be underestimated.

The more radical historians have, however, failed to substantiate their arguments that mental disorder is a historically-relative, socially constructed phenomenon. To succeed in this they would need to establish the limitation of a major psychiatric disorder to one historical period. Instead they can only point to dubious, ambiguous, peripheral and rare syndromes that do not require large-scale social responses. As Berrios (1984) asserts and most historians of psychiatry admit, the actual phenomenon of mental disorder has remained stubbornly the same across the centuries of human existence. History does show that social factors influence the presentation, conception and treatment of mental disorder, just as transcultural comparisons do, and as do the deviancy scholars in their work on social reaction to mental disorder. However, none of this work delivers coherent evidence that mental illness is entirely and comprehensively socially constructed.

The history of psychiatry has reflected ongoing debates on the nature of mental disorder in the human sciences, just as transcultural psychiatry and sociology have. In all three can be found traces of deviancy theory and existential approaches, the former being the most popular. The evidence indicates, nevertheless, that there is a serious core of mental disorder, historically and cross-culturally universal. There may be boundary disputes about what should and should not be accounted a psychiatric case. In addition, mental disorders may include a number of phenomena very different in cause and nature. Still, the historical evidence indicates significant continuity rather than gross fracture and change.

Chapter 7

Politics

Political interpretations of mental disorder have followed two broad but strikingly different highways. Straightforward social and political theorising has been found generally inadequate for the task, resulting in strange alliances between political domains. The first of these to be examined is the melding of deviancy sociology with a functionalist perspective of social institutions. These are two particularly unusual bedfellows, given that deviancy theory sprang out of the symbolic interactionism of Blumer which was itself a reaction against the functionalism of Talcott Parsons. It is, however, hard to shed completely functionalist modes of interpretation, for reasons which will be explored below. The second applicable theory combination is that of Freudian psychoanalysis and Marxist theorising. This has a more venerable history, such attempts at resolving the two bodies of theoretical knowledge being as old as psychoanalysis. These efforts have unfortunately seldom concentrated upon interpretations of mental disorder. What thinking on this matter does exist will be examined in this chapter.

I use the word 'politics' in this chapter in its broadest possible sense. Both functionalism and Marxism can be regarded as sociological theories, in that they try to explain how and why human societies organise themselves in the ways that they do. However, both are also replete with political implications. This is most obvious with Marxism, which has been widely politically applied in the twentieth century, but functionalism too can be, and occasionally has been, interpreted as a political theory. As such, its view of the social system as a finely balanced and tuned machine based upon a social value consensus can be perceived in conservative or right-wing political ideologies. Examples would be repeated calls for the return to or upholding of traditional values, or the concern with maintaining the stability of society and resisting change. Gouldner (1970) has argued that functionalism's assertion that the operation of society is based upon a consensus of values between its members serves only to legitimate the position of the dominant group. Functionalism also explicitly justifies the system of social stratification on the grounds that it organises the allocation of appropriately skilled people to different positions and occupations, and functionalism's arguments and theories are drawn upon by the right to justify social inequalities.

There are further dimensions to the relationship between politics and mental health issues, some of which have been raised in a preliminary form in the preceding chapter. Aetiological theorising can, when acted upon, translate into political regulation and action. Similarly, political action influences the practice of psychiatry in a variety of ways. These ideas too will receive critical elaboration here.

THE FUNCTION OF PSYCHIATRY

One cannot deny that social institutions have functions. There are overt reasons for their existence: the Post Office and delivery of mail, for example, or power companies and the provision of electricity, the police and apprehension of criminals, the fire brigade and the putting out of fires. This does not hold just for work organisations but also for the institution of wage labour itself, the family, education, the health service, etc. All this is another way of saying that these activities are purposeful, that people engage in them for good reasons and with a range of expected outcomes. These ideas are elaborations on the nature of orderly human activity, and are therefore innate to that orderly activity. This is perhaps why sociologists, although able to perceive the deficits of functionalist sociology, are unable to unshackle themselves from its fundamental basis.

The general rejection of functionalism by sociology does, however, have very good grounds. The functionalist sociology of the 1950s, epitomised by the theoretical works of Talcott Parsons (1951), asserted that social institutions have functions of which individual members of society are unaware, functions grasped only by the sociological observer. For example, the function of the family was to socialise children into the norms of that society, and social stratification has the function of upholding a society's value consensus. These and many other functionalist ideas have been subjected to much criticism within sociology itself. The most important and final criticism from the point of view of mental illness is that functionalism in this form denies the implacable reality of human agency. To uphold a functionalist interpretation of an institution it is necessary to assert that the people carrying out the activities of that institution are unaware of its purposes, or in other words are acting unconsciously. This is not only untrue to our lived experience (we do know rather well what we do and why, generally having good conscious reasons for our actions), but also fundamentally undermines the notion of function – when applied to the activities of people, speaking of function is only another way of talking about the purposes of people who carry out those activities. As I have argued above, institutions or organised activities only have functions in relation to the purposes of people. So either functionalism must uphold the *non sequitur* that we can be unaware of our purposes, or the whole idea of sociological function must disappear. The problem is that once we remove ourselves from talking about the purposes of actual people and suggest that society has purposes that give functions to institutions, then the false move has been made and, as it were, our argumentative feet have completely left the ground. Society can have no purposes separate from those of the individual people of which it is comprised.

Admittedly there are a still a variety of other ways in which institutions can have functions of which some people who contribute to their activities may be unaware. For example, there may be secondary gains for a group of the participants like employment, security or financial reward. Other participants may be only partly aware or even unaware of this. Nevertheless, these subsidiary functions are just that, subsidiary; the institution has that function only for that particular group, not for people at large. The purpose or function is not granted to an institution by such a subgroup (nor by an observing sociologist), but by what people do and say in relation to the organisation. The fact that people write letters and put them in post boxes indicates, and indeed makes, the Post Office the institution for the delivery of letters. Additionally the organisation itself, by what it does, says what it is. The Post Office and postmen do not call to mend the leak in my roof, for instance.

One further point remains to be made before passing on to the application of these ideas to psychiatry and mental disorder. Social institutions and formal organisations have not been distinguished from each other in the above discussion because both are examples of orderly human social activity which may justifiably be said to have common sense functions. We also speak of natural objects as having functions, though again this is only in relation to the purposes of human beings. Thus the function of an object depends upon how it is integrated with or used in human activities. For example, a mountain has no natural function for people as such, but it can become an object to climb, or a place to pasture sheep or mine minerals. It can therefore have a multitude of different functions depending on how it is utilised in the activities of human beings. This, though – being functional – is only one way in which objects enter into human activities. There are other relationships of natural objects to people. To take the example of the mountain again, it might be an obstacle to the person who wishes to get to the other side. The importance of this distinction is that mental disorder may be variously accounted for, as a social institution or as a natural object. Various interpretations of its 'function' hang upon this distinction.

It remains to try to explain why deviancy sociologists and those influenced by such thinking have found it necessary to reincorporate functionalist ideas in order to round off their accounts of psychiatry and mental disorder. One reason might be that despite the rejection of the functionalism of the 1950s, with its hidden metaphor of society as a body comprised of organs having both structure and function, the simple logic of orderly activity makes it plain that organisations and institutions can be readily spoken of as having functions – albeit not in the sense of functionalist sociology. Another reason might be that deviancy theory by itself does not appear to offer a comprehensive explanation of mental illness. Perhaps the most weighty reason is that similarities have been drawn between the rejection of many different subgroups by different societies in different eras, just as Szasz has drawn parallels between the persecution of witches and the treatment of the mentally ill. The apparent universality of the phenomenon without evident explanation or cause, often morally reprehensible to the liberal scholar, seems to beg for some kind of functionalist explanation. In making his case about mental disorder, Szasz covers the three main variants of the functionalist explanations of psychiatry and mental illness. In the review that follows we shall therefore use his arguments as a framework for discussion.

EXPLAINING AWAY MORAL PROBLEMS

Szasz (1972) argues that psychiatry uses the term 'mental illness' as a false explanation in order to conceal difficult moral and social problems. By doing so, psychiatry acts as a social tranquilliser, removing sources of strain, tension and conflict within society. An example of this process might be the psychiatric treatment of a woman following a pregnancy termination. The woman might be depressed, anxious about having made the right decision, and guilty. Psychiatry diagnoses her as suffering from a depressive illness for which she has no responsibility, and treats her with antidepressant medication. Thus any moral conflict is short-circuited and the difficulty is explained away as being one of illness rather than of right and wrong. Ingleby (1980) supports this argument, suggesting that psychiatry has the political function of converting the suffering produced by work, family, education and politics into an individual problem. This argument is persistent and crops up again in Lyon (1996) linked to the debate over the use of Prozac. Lyon writes that the prescribing of this new antidepressant is leading to the medicalisation of social–structural problems.

It is important to realise that psychiatry might have this effect and outcome without it being its function. As argued previously, functions are determined by human purposes. Neither the psychiatric patient nor the psychiatric professional acts with the intention of explaining away moral problems, but with the intention of seeking and offering relief from distress, pain and discomfort. Nevertheless, even though relief from moral dilemmas is not the function of psychiatry, it may well still be one of its effects. Scheper-Hughes (1988) gives an example of this process in Brazil which is painful to contemplate. She describes the plight of a community of plantation workers in north-east Brazil who live in abject poverty. These sugar cane workers exist in a state of chronic and continuous malnutrition. That malnutrition causes nervousness, anxiety, weakness and fatigue. However, instead of protesting about their life conditions and their exploitation by the plantation owners (which would in any case result in severe reprisals and even death), these unfortunate people are diagnosed by themselves and by their pharmacists as suffering from a psychiatric condition locally called 'nervios', for which they are treated with tranquillisers. Scheper-Hughes' paper breathes her anger and outrage at this situation, and the tale she has to relate is truly terrible. Nevertheless, however reprehensible this situation it does not demonstrate that the function of psychiatry is to divert political protest into medical pathways. In fact Scheper-Hughes' own evidence shows that the sufferers are unaware of the connection between their suffering and their hunger, as are their landlords and exploiters. Even if we accept the innocence of psychiatry in this case, it is still open to condemnation on these grounds as, regardless of the intent and purposes of the people involved, this is the effect it is having.

Similar arguments can be mounted about psychiatry in the UK, although the situation is less outrageous. Psychiatry can be seen as converting distress from poverty, poor housing, unemployment, wife battering and child abuse into a medical, rather than a social and political issue. This needs rather careful disentangling before it can be concluded to what degree psychiatry actually does this, for many of the activities of psychiatry quite clearly have nothing to do with the conversion of social, political and moral dilemmas into matters of physiological brain disease. The care of many thousands of people suffering from Alzheimer's disease or other organic dementias, for example, can hardly be seen as this kind of process. Scheper-Hughes' depiction of 'nervios' in north-east Brazil succeeds so well because she describes a specific political dilemma, its effects, and how those effects are treated as a psychiatric neurophysiological disease instead of the political dilemma they are. To establish the same about psychiatry in the UK or the Western world generally, it is necessary to consider specific moral or political issues and how they relate to the treatment of specific syndromes by psychiatry. The construction of sweeping generalisations about the operations of psychiatry simply will not do to establish a charge of such gravity.

There are two interlinked arguments which are drawn upon to support this kind of superficial generalisation. It is argued first of all that as psychiatry calls its subject matter 'mental illness', it therefore considers all the matters with which it deals to be pathological abnormalities of brain function or diseases. As some mental illnesses are clearly linked to social stress, particularly neurotic depression and anxiety, the case that psychiatry turns political problems into matters of physiology appears proven. Second, it is assumed that as a matter of empirical practice, psychiatry has no interest in, or ignores, social, moral and political factors in the generation of mental illness.

Both of these assertions are false. The use of the word 'illness' does not necessarily imply notions of physiological abnormality or malfunction, as will be comprehensively demonstrated in the next chapter. As for the second assertion, even brief acquaintance with the practice of psychiatry in the UK and its published writings indicates that the role of social and psychological factors in the genesis of depression is very well appreciated. There are of course other psychiatric disorders for which this is not so, but psychiatry cannot properly be charged with ignoring the social distress and moral dilemmas which can precipitate some mental disorders. Just because something is accounted an illness does not mean its social roots are ignored. Even in the realms of physiological disorders like tuberculosis the role of poverty and diet is well acknowledged and understood, and has led to social and political change.

Nevertheless, although the position just described of the role of social factors being appreciated by psychiatry does seem to be true as a generalisation, based upon an appreciation of the content of the psychiatric literature, there does remain a significant faction of psychiatric practitioners who emphasise physiological cause and treatment. To the extent, for example, that these practitioners and others are treating with antidepressants those who are depressed due to the poor condition of their housing, and promulgating overtly or covertly the view that their patients are suffering a brain disorder, then psychiatry is short-circuiting or medicalising what is really a sociopolitical problem. In the UK, perhaps most prescribing of antidepressants in these circumstances is carried out by general practitioners, who treat the majority (approximately 80 per cent) of cases of anxiety/depression that they identify without referring on to formal psychiatric services (Goldberg and Huxley 1980). Still, the practice of prescribing in these circumstances is recommended to general practitioners by the psychiatric establishment, via training courses, publications and systematic campaigns. It may, therefore, properly be seen as the responsibility of psychiatry.

The extent to which this scenario occurs is also strongly influenced by where the boundary is placed between what is or is not a psychiatric case. As described in a previous chapter, these judgements are ultimately arbitrary, and boundaries cannot be determined from the nature of the phenomena. Distress due to life problems merges imperceptibly into distress considered to be excessive, out of proportion, irrational or overtly psychotic. The more inclusive the criteria for 'psychiatric' status, the more likely it would be that for some people in some cases psychiatry would have the unintended effect of medicalising their social problems. Therefore a major factor that needs to be taken into account when drawing such boundaries would be the maximal exclusion from psychiatric care of those whose distress was clearly a sensible, rational and human response to their life situation.

The position of Szasz (1972) must then be acknowledged to be potentially partially correct. Although it is not the function of psychiatry, at some times and on some occasions psychiatry may be having the effect of transforming social and moral problems into matters of disease and medical treatment. Whether it actually does so to a significant degree would require careful empirical study of particular social problems, their manifestation and treatment as specific psychiatric disorders.

VENTILATION OF EMOTION

Szasz argues that psychiatry allows the public ventilation of two main sorts of emotions – hypocritical righteous indignation and displaced anger. Both arguments appear to fit witchcraft and the Inquisition better than they do the operations of modern psychiatry. For example, by punishing witches Szasz suggests that the public were able to demonstrate an adherence to a moral sexual code which was largely disregarded in private. He uses the ceremonial decanting of alcoholic drinks during the Prohibition era as a further example. When he moves on to suggesting that public executions of witches gave vent to feelings of anger, he proposes that the true target of this anger were women and the lower classes.

Notwithstanding the fact that these theses would be very hard to prove empirically in the face of statements from the people involved that they were acting according to quite different purposes, there is still the problem of drawing a parallel with psychiatry and mental illness. It should be noted that there is no real equivalent of the public trial in psychiatry, save in rarely occurring criminal trials. In all other domains of psychiatry great value is placed on secrecy and confidentiality. Therefore most of the operations of psychiatry cannot have the function of public ventilation of any emotion. Furthermore, when it comes to the expression of righteous indignation it is not the mentally ill that tend to be the target, but rather those professionals who care for them. Hence, as Martin (1984) has described, the great public scandals which have always attached to the care of the mentally ill have not been about the mentally ill themselves, but about the failures of the professions.

MENTALLY ILL TAKE THE BLAME FOR SOCIAL PROBLEMS

In his final and most forceful argument for a social function of psychiatry, Szasz suggests that it is but one example of a much wider human phenomenon, that of the rejection of disvalued subgroups. Subgroups can be blamed for social problems, which are then seen as solved by the elimination, domination or subjugation of the subgroup. This theory suggests that the mentally ill are merely scapegoats for problems for which they have no responsibility, a role which Szasz and many others would argue has been held by a variety of groups throughout human history. Under this type of explanation he includes anti-Semitism and all deviancy or difference. Szasz strives to make into a unity witches, Jews and insanity, all of whom fulfil the same social function by being blamed in the same kind of way for the same social evils.

This argument has a strong and a weak version. The strong version, argued by Szasz, is that mental illness has no more reality than witchcraft had in the middle ages, and that the whole practice of psychiatry creates the roles of the mentally ill and finds ways to fill them, just as the Inquisition 'discovered' witches. The weaker version of this argument admits the existence of mental illness but still maintains that the mentally ill are persecuted and blamed for social problems. These arguments are precise equivalents of strong and weak deviancy theory, as discussed in a previous chapter. Strong deviancy theory, as promoted by Scheff (1966), came close to asserting that mental illness was created by the responses and expectations of others following an incident of rule breaking. In a similar fashion Szasz is here arguing that mental illness has no more reality than witchcraft, both being created and produced by the social process of their identification and treatment. Weak deviancy theory acknowledges the stubborn reality of mental illness but emphasises its malleability in the face of social responses. Although the chapter on deviancy described why strong deviancy theory was to be rejected, it did not proceed to examine why the negative evaluation of the mentally ill was as widespread and universal as mental disorder itself. One possible explanation is the political displacement of blame described by Szasz.

To talk in terms of blame suggests that the mentally ill are either punished or persecuted. This is not in fact the case at all in Western societies. Considerable resources are devoted to the humane care and support of those suffering mental disorder. They are specifically excluded from punishment for criminal acts, receiving care and treatment instead of retribution. Neither are the mentally ill blamed for social problems. Bubonic plague and the poisoning of wells were blamed upon witches. Recession, inflation and unemployment were blamed upon the Jews in Nazi Germany. But it is impossible to find any equivalent for the mentally ill today.

Nevertheless, the reality of the stigmatisation and rejection of the mentally ill must also be acknowledged. Although they are neither punished nor persecuted, they are still feared and excluded from normal social life. If the reason for this is not to be found in their receiving the blame for social problems, what is its source?

Deviancy theory generally would imply that the sanctioning of contra-normative behaviour was a product of the maintenance of social order. The fact that human beings build a social order means that disorder exists to some degree. To make a social order, disorder must be repressed, controlled and managed. There are many ways of doing this: the family, education and socialisation are positive, proactive methods, whereas deterrent and sanction are reactive methods. Sanctions vary, from moderate to extreme, and extreme sanctions include exclusion. All this follows from the fact of orderly human life together. However, deviancy theory lumps together under its heading all forms of difference and norm breaking. In fact, as I have argued in a previous chapter, there are significantly different kinds of disorder – different in cause, different in nature, and therefore with very different social response. For some forms sanctions barely exist, while for others sanctions merge imperceptibly into strategies for the management of behaviour that causes trouble for orderly life. Mental illness and psychiatry make up one of these bodies of social practices. Although related to other social ways of dealing with disorder, its subject matter is significantly different and thus may be discussed and considered separately from other forms of deviance/disorder. Interestingly, this perspective implies that social order itself is not unitary, that in fact we have many different kinds of social orders, rather than just one, and that these are built up out of orderly or regular human practices. It may also be concluded that there are no such general phenomena as the rejection of deviant subgroups, but this conclusion is not without difficulties. Regardless of the fact that it cannot be theoretically provided for or justified on the grounds of the maintenance of social order, the rejection and indeed persecution of subgroups has been universally present in human behaviour.

In order to understand this a little more fully, the concept of group membership needs to be used. At all levels and in all contexts human social behaviour is characterised by the formation of groups, as well as by order. There cannot be a group without a boundary, without some people being left out. There cannot be an 'us' without a 'them'. Remove this universal out-group rejection and you remove the possibility of any groups whatsoever. This is the logic of groups that overlaps the logic of order. Disorder, deviance and difference do not necessarily cause the rejection of the Other, but they do provide candidates for such a rejection. Which group gets picked out is contingent upon popular belief and ideas in circulation, events, rumour, news and gossip. The rejection, exclusion and casting out of the outsider is a pattern of behaviour endlessly played out at multiple levels in all human affairs. The degree and consequences of the rejection vary depending upon the nature, extent and power of the dominating groups. It takes place on a small scale in school playgrounds, and on larger scales within organisational hierarchies, and sometimes throughout nations as a whole or even between nations and races. Sometimes the conflict reflects the general values of a society or group, at other times things become values through the conflict, or almost seem to be created for it. It thus remains a matter for moral argument as to what should be the boundary markers for various groups and on what basis. This has been part of mankind's struggle with itself for the duration of its existence. In fact these very arguments about boundaries, who is to set them, how, and where, become in- and out-group markers themselves and are subsumed in the conflicts which they try to shift.

A full account of the rejection and stigmatisation of the mentally ill has still not been provided. In order to complete the picture the justifications offered and used for that rejection must be examined. These are many and various, being an intricate web of belief, reasoning and natural human reaction. There are several senses in which the phenomenon of mental illness gives rise to fear and anxiety. Despite the fact that the mentally ill commit relatively few crimes of violence (Steering Committee of the Confidential Inquiry into Homicides and Suicides by Mentally Ill People 1994) they are generally feared for their unpredictability in this respect. The inexplicability of mental illness also arouses fear, as it is not susceptible

to rational explanation – and our lives are completely based upon patterned networks of logical, reasonable behaviour. The mad threaten us with a breakdown of this commitment, demonstrating how fragile our human society is and showing us a potentiality for madness within ourselves that we generally deny, impulses that we hold in check, odd thoughts that we thrust out of mind, transient moods and feelings which we endeavour to overcome. Again, the mentally ill may arouse the fear of contamination, that to be with them is to become like them, like getting dirty from working with cars and engines. In addition to these fears, mental disorder lessens the essential humanity of the sufferer: competence and resilience in the face of stress is lost, weaknesses of character displayed and the full range of human social ability diminished. Finally, mental illness arouses natural feelings of revulsion, just as do deformity, disfigurement and ugliness. It turns the human being into a phenomenon which is both alien and inexplicable, eliciting responses of distaste and disgust.

These beliefs and feelings can be overcome, may be appealed against and countered with argument and evidence. Yet they are both widespread and natural responses. Together with the disorder to everyday life posed by the mentally ill, and humanity's tendency to form groups and reject others as outsiders, this provides a convincing account of the stigmatisation of the mentally ill. Barham (1992) describes this process as one of dehumanisation, and argues that the mentally ill are seen as less than full persons because of their attributes and disabilities. He suggests that it is therefore but a small step from here to the view of the mentally ill as a burden on society, and hence moves towards their eradication.

This scenario is potentially susceptible to political exploitation. These feelings can be politically whipped up, made larger and taken advantage of in order to accrue power. This might be accompanied by public humiliations, eugenic control, persecution, mandatory sterilisation, murders and death camps. At present other targets find more ready exploitation, particularly racial ones. However, even in the case of anti-Semitism in Nazi Germany, which constitutes the paradigm case for both Szasz (1972) and Wolfensberger (1987), such political exploitation is by no means a simple matter. If the work of Hannah Arendt (1966) does nothing else, it underscores once and for all the uniqueness of totalitarianism in the history of the world. Arendt's depiction of totalitarianism and the death camps stresses how different this phenomenon was from anything

occurring before or since. She describes it as a mass movement in which individuals surrendered and sacrificed their autonomy to an ideology that permeated and then controlled their lives, judgements and consciousness. She does not see Nazi anti-Semitism as driven by class interests – for her the motivator of persecution was not the blame for social ills that was laid at the door of the Jews. Instead she sees the Holocaust as part and parcel of a mass movement of people who felt cut off, superfluous, unimportant and who were therefore ready to devote themselves to the ideology of Nazism because of the purpose it gave to their lives. To portray the Jews as scapegoats is therefore far too simplistic a theory to explain comprehensively the rise to power of National Socialism in Germany, or the consequent Holocaust.

We cannot therefore say that the function of psychiatry is to produce some form of sociopsychic equilibrium by picking on a weak subgroup and rejecting them. This interpretation not only tramples over the accounts of very nearly all the people involved, but also oversimplifies a complex pattern of human activities. Human societies do reject subgroups in a variety of different ways, with a variety of different reasons and a variety of different outcomes. This behaviour is implicit in orderly activity and the human capacity to form groups. Coupled with beliefs about mental illness and various natural reactions and fears, this accounts for the stigmatisation of the mentally ill. Nevertheless, to argue or imply that the function of mental illness is to provide for that rejection is to place the cart before the horse. Instead we should see that the rejection or stigmatisation of the mentally ill follow from beliefs, fears and reactions about it; they are not driven by social forces which command rejection of some group in order to maintain equilibrium. The rejection of a subgroup based on some difference can be both politically created and exploited, but there is not a shred of evidence that this is the case, here and now, with mental illness. That is not, therefore, its function for anybody.

OTHER POSSIBLE FUNCTIONS OF PSYCHIATRY

Nor can it properly be argued that the function of psychiatry is purely the maintenance of social order through social control plus the upholding of value consensus. This can be said about the criminal justice system, but not so easily about psychiatry. Sometimes psychiatry can be said to maintain social order, when it deals with

those persons who are disturbed, irrational, making difficulties for the everyday lives of others, and in extreme circumstances threatening violence. However, most psychiatric activity has no such specific aim, and only by the most tortured use of language can it be said to do so. The same goes for the upholding of a value consensus. Certainly the police can be said to do this when they apprehend the burglar, but surely not the psychiatrist who treats the depressed. Talk of some consensual value of average human happiness which is being upheld by the psychiatrist is plainly to do an injustice to the accounts which would be given by him or his patient about what was happening.

It could be argued that although the function of psychiatry is not to uphold a value consensus, it might actually be having this effect. For example, a psychiatrist as part of treatment may insist that the depressed woman should be content in her social role of housewife. If this was the case generally, then perhaps psychiatry could be considered to be upholding some form of value consensus. However, it would have to be shown that psychiatrists and other psychiatric professionals regularly and repeatedly made these demands of women who were actually depressed because of their social role. Personally, I suspect that these and similar events only happen on an occasional basis and are evidence of bad practice, for nowhere in the psychiatric literature is the giving of such advice laid down as a principle of appropriate or good treatment. The majority of the psychiatric literature prescribes precisely the opposite – that the patient should be helped to clarify the issues in their own mind and make their own decisions.

Lastly, the contention that the function of mental disorder and psychiatry is to provide roles, occupation and status for the psychiatric professions, must also be rejected. This explanation most cynically disregards the temporal development of psychiatry as well as the reasons and justifications of those who participate in it.

To be able to say properly what is the function of psychiatry we must engage with the stated purposes of the participants themselves, patients, relatives and professionals. At a very general level this purpose or function might be stated as the relief of suffering and distress, although obviously the picture is far more varied and complicated than such a simple statement would cover.

If we try to speak about the function of mental illness itself it becomes very easy to get confused. As with much else, a great deal hinges upon the nature of mental illness itself. If it is considered to

be a physiological disease or malfunction, then it is a natural object. As a natural object it can only have a function in relation to the purposes of people. Generally speaking, mental illness is not used by people in purposive action, and the mentally ill are not used to accomplish any kind of goal-directed activity. Instead it is seen more as an affliction, burden, obstacle and tragedy. The complications in a functional view of mental illness arise when we leave this organic model and consider other explanations. Immediately one is immersed in the maelstrom of psychological and sociopsychological theories about the genesis and aetiology of mental disorder, for if mental disorder is this kind of phenomenon, then to describe its aetiology is to define its function. Thus each psychotherapeutic or theoretical model will confer a different function upon mental disorder, whether it be the maintenance of inner psychological equilibrium (psychodynamic psychotherapy) or the maintenance of social homeostasis in the family (family therapy), to mention but two out of numerous theories. Some of these theories can potentially be linked to or translated into political strategies and ideologies, although generally speaking they are not. In the previous chapter it was described how the theory of masturbatory insanity led to widespread moral injunctions. Similarly Morel's theory of degeneracy influenced political policy in the management of the poor and deprived. Modern parallels are, however, hard to find.

MARX, FREUD AND PSYCHIATRY

The second major highway of political interpretation of psychiatry has been via the combination of Marxist and Freudian theorising. Marxism by itself has been unable to provide a thoroughgoing political explanation of mental disorder. It is perhaps Basaglia who has made the bravest attempt in this direction. Franco Basaglia was the leader of the revolution in mental health care that took place in Italy during the 1960s and 1970s. His ideas, derived from Marxism and other sources, drove the transformation from asylum to community care in that country. It is only relatively recently that his writings have been translated into English, and are now available in a collection of his works edited by Lovell and Scheper-Hughes (1986). Unfortunately his writings present an unsystematic and poorly integrated collection of arguments about the nature of mental illness and psychiatry, and these are explored only in a limited fashion. Basaglia uses deviancy and functional explanations,

too, although such ideas are criticised by him for not prescribing political action. Indeed, it would appear that political action rather more than theoretical coherence was Basaglia's forte. Nevertheless, there are a number of ideas within Basaglia's writings, loosely derived from Marxism, that while not fitting together neatly do recur from time to time in the debate about mental disorder as a political phenomenon.

First and foremost is the idea that asylum-based psychiatry is a form of violent oppression of the lower class poor. The conclusion drawn is that the asylum needs to be 'negated' – demolished or undone – rather than reformed. This perspective is at its most forceful when considering the poorly run, understaffed, abuse-ridden asylums of the era which gave birth to it. Within the context of the isolated asylum where abuse of patients by staff is embedded within the culture, this idea seems startlingly true. It seems less forceful in the context of a well-run, well-staffed district psychiatric unit backed up by community services. In fact, the reforms initiated by Basaglia gave birth to exactly this pattern of psychiatric services (Ramon 1983; White 1989).

The class analysis of psychiatry that Basaglia provides is basic and superficial. Even in its most complex presentation, mental illness is interpreted as simply the misery of the working class poor. This begs many questions like 'Why aren't all the working class poor thus considered mad?', or 'Why do the wealthy rich suffer from madness?'. Perhaps the kernel of truth in this assertion is that working class life may well provide more toxic stress and life events, thus causing more mental illness. It is certainly true that serious mental illness has a much higher frequency among the working class, but the reasons for this are disputed.

Basaglia's writings borrow and incorporate many different ideas from different origins. Strong traces of deviancy theory are to be found (although this is at one point rejected because it does not mandate political action), as well as the scapegoat theories of Szasz and the therapeutic community ideals of Maxwell Jones. Basaglia deliberately refused to ally himself to a unitary ideological and theoretical perspective, fearing that if he did it would be absorbed into the system and become fossilised. Perhaps he should be remembered less as a theoretician and more as a political activist seeking to establish everybody's right to humane, non-punitive psychiatric treatment. One thing his writings do make clear at the theoretical level is that Marxism by itself cannot produce a comprehensive account of mental disorder. It has been this difficulty that has driven Marxist psychiatric thinkers towards the incorporation of Freudian psychoanalysis.

Reich's (1949) harmonisation of Marxism and psychoanalysis is not really an attempt to explain mental illness using Marxism, nor, vice versa, an attempt to support Marxism by invoking arguments and rationales from psychoanalysis. He argued instead that both mental illness and the oppression of one class by another had their explanation in the same source: the authoritarian, patriarchal family. The root cause of both is the submissive character structures produced through the repressive wielding of power by fathers. In the case of mental illness, such character structures are argued to inhibit orgastic capacity and thus produce mental ill health. In the case of Marxism, the production of such submissive character structures by institutional means provides a populace ready to be ruled. Reich went even further by arguing that all these forms of oppression are functionally identical, i.e. neurosis = character structure = patriarchal oppression = class oppression.

Reich's ideas have been widely rejected by psychiatry and by Marxism. As an explanation of mental illness these theories have been seriously criticised. There is no empirical evidence for a link, or even a correlation, between orgastic capacity and any mental illness. Even if there was such a link, there would be a great deal of difficulty determining the direction of causality between the two. Similarly, no empirical evidence has been advanced for the concept of character armour, or for its generation by authoritarian families.

Indeed, Reich's explanatory theory of mental illness is not so much a political explanation as one rooted in the institution of the family and its dynamics. This idea is a common one, popular in a different form with the family therapists of today. Although Reich argued that psychological disorder and political oppression were functionally identical, this does not mean he saw the latter as causing the former. Rather his argument was that they were parallel, similar, and originating in the same source. It would be all too easy to claim that these were actually different forms of the same phenomenon, that interpersonal oppression equalled intrapersonal repression. This is overly simplistic, and was not Reich's thesis, but it does facilitate political sloganising in the psychiatric sphere and the use of mental disorder as a stick to beat capitalist social structures. This argument maintains its currency despite the fact that for many mental disorders there is no evidence of any link between oppression and the genesis of the disorder, or if there is a link it is far more complex than simple causality.

Freud (1985) himself equated civilisation with repression. Repression had to take place for civilisation to occur. In the absence of repression, society would fall back into barbarism and chaos. Hence the political interpretations of psychoanalysis, apart from those of Reich and Marcuse, had a tendency to be inherently conservative in outlook. The conditions for the formation of neurosis are inherent in all civilised society by this view. No political preventative strategy is therefore possible without relinquishing orderly social existence.

Marcuse (1966) can best be seen as attempting to rescue Freud from the arms of the reactionaries. Contrary to traditional interpretations of his ideas, Marcuse saw them as being truly revolutionary in their implications. He draws largely upon Freud's body of metahistorical writings and in so doing creates a synthesis between the ideas of Freud and those of Marx. By combining Freud's hydraulic concept of the mind with that of repression, Marcuse was able to argue that there was a surplus of repression from which society could be relieved without disintegration into chaos. In addition, by using the Freudian concept of the reality principle of mental functioning, Marcuse was able to produce a psychoanalytic description or version of the Marxist concept of alienation. The precise details of these ideas cannot be fully explored here, save to illustrate the method by which Marcuse married up psychoanalysis and Marxism. Marcuse uses the synthesis of ideas that he produces in order to define the goals of human fulfilment and to argue that these are likely to be attained only through revolutionary change.

Unlike Reich, Marcuse does not express any direct concern with mental illness or its treatment. Mental illness is perhaps perceived as a side effect of the repressive nature of political structures, rather than being the central issue. However, by linking Freudian and Marxist ideas in the way that he does, Marcuse does imply that mental disorder is produced at least in part by the repressive operations of the State. Having taken this step, and found a way out of the Freudian view that this is inevitable for the production of civilisation, it is impossible not to conclude that mental disorder can be ameliorated or prevented by political change. The political change Marcuse had in mind was of course a Marxist revolution, albeit reinterpreted as the formation of a non-repressive state coupled with the decline in need for labour due to automation.

In more recent years Banton *et al*. (1985) have been among the few who have continued to try to provide Marxist interpretations of mental illness, and to define a new radical agenda for psychiatric practice. Like those before them, they endeavour to link Marxist class analysis to an aetiological theory of mental illness. In order to avoid a simple stress-diathesis model (i.e. that exploitation causes increased stress which causes increased rates of mental illness), they too invoke psychoanalysis and argue that early infant socialisation builds societal contradictions, particularly class conflict, into the psyche. Unfortunately they do not seem to perceive that, were this so and were this the cause of mental illness, then most of us would be mentally ill. Neither do they draw the corollary that any associated psychotherapy should therefore be more akin to political-consciousness raising. Instead their concept of therapy seems to consist of analysis of leadership dynamics within groups.

Theories like those of Reich and Marcuse stand or fall with the basic tenets of Freudian theory itself, in particular Freud's theories on sexuality and the development and structure of the personality. These have been heavily criticised from empirical evidence (Eysenck 1985) and on a philosophical basis (Popper 1963). Debate on the validity or otherwise of Freudian ideas has become much less prominent over the past decade, as has serious Marxist theorising. Thus interest in political Freudianism appears to have declined from both sides.

MENTAL HEALTH SERVICE USERS' MOVEMENT

The user movement in psychiatry has drawn upon (and probably contributed to) many of the ideas explored in this book. The development of organised groups of mental health service users is described in Chamberlin (1977), Haafkens *et al*. (1986) and Rogers and Pilgrim (1991). The influence of user groups has become pervasive. It is *de rigeur* at the moment to believe that the user viewpoint is sacrosanct and of prime importance to those involved in the delivery of psychiatric services. In my own profession of psychiatric nursing, a recent government review asserted that the profession's foundation was working in partnership with service users (Department of Health 1994). These days, everything that psychiatric professionals do pays homage to the idea of user involvement. If a conference is held, then users must give a presentation, or must at the very least be invited to attend. If new service developments are planned, then a user must be on the committee. It is said that users should help devise the curricula for the education of psychiatric professionals, and should be providing some of their training (English National Board for Nursing Midwifery and Health Visiting 1996). Even when research is conducted, it is recommended by some that users should contribute to prioritising topics, and the management and operation of projects. Everywhere you go, the refrain of 'user involvement' is heard.

User groups represent a highly diverse range of views about the true nature of mental disorder, and how it should be dealt with by society. Some take a fairly conservative stance, and are supportive of traditional psychiatric services and the psychiatric professions. At the other end of the scale, some user groups call for the abolition of compulsory treatment and accuse psychiatry of being a form of political oppression. Chamberlin (1977) represents the more radical end of the spectrum, and takes on board the ideas of Scheff, Szasz and the Marxist psychotherapists in a largely uncritical way. She couples these critiques with individual stories of cruel and brutal treatment of patients within the psychiatric system, plus tales of the compulsory detention of obviously sane persons. These pleas to the authority of writers such as Szasz, combined with individual accounts of bad psychiatric practice which are generalised to the whole psychiatric system, are used as a base to argue that service users should construct for themselves alternative forms of help and mutual support.

Although Chamberlin's work may be quite radical, it contains three strands which are ubiquitous in the user literature. First, more primacy is given to the role of the individual's social and psychological situation in the production of the distress which is considered by the psychiatric system to be mental illness. Rogers *et al.* (1993) have shown in their interview study of 516 service users that few were willing to accept that their problems were due to an 'illness', instead seeing their problems as arising out of their social situation combined with their individual predisposition. In addition, psychiatric symptoms tend to be normalised by some user groups, as auditory hallucinations are by the 'Hearing Voices' movement (Romme and Escher 1993). These ideas fit neatly with those of Szasz as explored in this chapter and elsewhere in this book. However, unlike Szasz, the writings of the user movement spell out in some detail the kind of alternative service they wish to see. This constitutes the second strand to the user literature as a whole – its emphasis upon the provision of alternative, user-controlled services. These range from self-help groups to crisis services (Wallcraft 1996) and residential houses providing alternatives to hospitalisation (Chamberlin 1977). These are not widespread, and the current state of play in this area is well described and catalogued by Lindow (1994). The third strand which is present in all the user literature is the emphasis upon the right of the service users to be heard, their right to self-determination, and their right to influence the pattern and content of psychiatric services as a whole.

Part of the problem with attempting a critique of the user movement is that it does not have one single, solid and coherent set of arguments to be examined. Insofar as they follow Szasz, the arguments about mental illness stand and fall with his. However, the user literature is superior to that of Szasz, for unlike his writings it does describe an alternative to current psychiatric practice. Not all user groups or literature go as far as Szasz in denying that mental illness is an illness, and thus they converge with a large and dominant body of psychiatric literature that accepts the role of social and psychological factors in the generation of mental disorder. The assertion that alternative, user-controlled services are required is more of a practical issue. What matters here is that such services can show that they can provide safe and effective care to a high standard. The fact that all such services so far have had to institute rules that enable difficult people to be excluded indicates that such services are developing in a way that is supplementary rather than alternative to psychiatry. As to user power and influence, this is a complex organisational issue. The right of users to make a contribution is now widely accepted, but user groups and the psychiatric services need to grapple with the issues of the degree of representativeness of user groups, and the extent to which they can claim expertise that is of equal value to that of service managers and the professionals' knowledge base.

POLITICAL REPRESSION

Psychiatry, or mental illness, as the form or result of oppression has been highlighted by the Marxists. Indeed, the political abuse of psychiatry is always a possibility. One way this might occur has been described above, that politicians might attempt to exploit the stigmatisation of the mentally ill in order to scapegoat them for problems originating elsewhere. There is another potential political abuse of psychiatry, in that powers of compulsory detention and treatment may be utilised as a means of suppressing political dissent. Wing (1978) and many others have described how psychiatry was abused in this way in the former USSR in the 1960s and 1970s, with political dissidents being locked away in mental hospitals and treated with neuroleptic drugs on the grounds that they were deluded and psychotic.

This is not to say, as some do, that all mental illness is in reality political protest. Sedgwick (1972) points out that mental illness does not constitute much of a political threat in any sense whatsoever, and that dissent can take far more powerful forms. In other words, he suggests that no political structure has any need to fear and control the mentally ill as if they constituted some sort of protest and threat. Reznek (1991) elaborates the same point when he argues that the sufferer of schizophrenia is hardly likely to rock the foundations of society, and that mental health is probably a requirement for constituting a threat to the political system. Ingleby's (1980) defence that all mental illness is ineffective political protest does not hold water. Effective or ineffective, if some behaviour is a political protest then the protesters should be able to explain their behaviour with reference to the protest they are making. This the mentally ill cannot and do not do. A more reasonable interpretation of Ingleby is to see him as arguing that we should understand the discomfort of the mentally ill as a consequence of political factors, and which therefore should be interpreted as protest. His argument can then simply be seen as an assertion that mental illness is caused by certain unspecified political factors – an assertion that can be subjected to empirical test. It can readily be seen that this argument converges with the argument of Szasz that psychiatry explains away social problems.

It might still be argued that there is no essential difference between the political protester who is psychiatrically treated for his deviant political beliefs, and the schizophrenia sufferer who is treated for his delusions. Indeed, the obscurity and ambiguity that exists allowed psychiatrists in the former USSR seriously to believe they were treating psychotic illness when dealing with political dissidents. Nevertheless, clear thinking shows that there are definite, universal differences between the delusions of psychosis, and political dissent. The most obvious is that the political dissenters' beliefs are political, whereas most psychotic delusions are not. In addition, the political dissenter can engage in reasoned argument about his beliefs, justifying them with evidence and logic, and is often willing to take the opponents' point of view seriously in order to undermine it. The deluded, however, do not do this. Often they cannot provide any kind of reasoned grounds for their beliefs, or the kind of reasoning they operate with makes no sense to others. In addition to these qualities, the psychotic may suffer other symptoms such as hallucinations, agitation, insomnia and perplexity; the political dissenter does not. Most of us could therefore discriminate readily between an opponent of the political system and a sufferer of mental illness. The justifications offered by USSR psychiatrists were therefore most likely due to the political constraints within which they themselves operated.

PSYCHIATRY AS A POLITICAL MOVEMENT OR PRODUCT

It is possible to view psychiatry itself as a political movement. Something like this view is propounded from a critical perspective by Rose (1986), Castel *et al.* (1982) and Prior (1993). All these authorities would suggest that in the twentieth century psychiatry has expanded its domain, broadening the concept of insanity or mental illness to incorporate the minor mental illnesses or neuroses. This expansion, out of the restricted practice of the asylum and into the community, is linked by them to the development of community care as a policy, and the inception of a range of out-patient services. However, none of these authorities are able to support a claim that the concept of mental illness has undergone significant change, although this does not undermine the assertion that psychiatric services have expanded. Minor mental illness or neurosis has been recognised and treated for many hundreds of years, and was not a creation of twentieth-century psychiatry. Porter (1987) describes its prevalence in the eighteenth century and Bynum (1985) its prevalence in the nineteenth. During those periods few were able to afford professional treatment of any sort, and indeed these disorders were not always recognised as matters for psychiatry. The expansion of psychiatry that took place in the twentieth century can be better understood, not as a change in the concept of insanity, but as the growth of wealth, education and welfare services providing the opportunity for more people to obtain treatment for their suffering.

This critique of psychiatry as an expansionist political movement is frequently coupled with the argument that these minor disorders are not illnesses at all, but responses to distressing psychological or social circumstances. By incorporating these as illnesses, psychiatry is said to be defusing political action and protest. This is the same argument as the first version of Szasz above, and hinges upon whether, when and how it is justifiable to call these sufferings illnesses. Further discussion on this issue is deferred to the next chapter.

Psychiatric practice, and mental illness itself, can be viewed as a political product. Psychiatric services operate within a legal context and in the UK – as part of the National Health Service – they follow policy set by central government. The psychiatric professions themselves are, to a degree, politically regulated. Thus politics shapes psychiatry at every level. Mental illness itself may be viewed as politically defined – within certain limitations. Governments can, but seldom do, promulgate specific definitions as to what should and should not be considered mental disorder. One such definition is incorporated in the Mental Health Act (1983). Sentencing policies of the courts with respect to offenders considered mentally ill also contribute to the definition of mental disorder. It must be accepted, however, that these are relatively small influences compared to professional definitions adhered to by well-organised and powerful professional groups. Public demand for services and assistance also contributes to the final definition of mental illness, as does the content of the media. In combination these determine, within limits, what mental illness turns out to be. The limitations on such public, professional and political definitions of mental illness are that the major mental illnesses brook no real alternative definition. If they are not illnesses, or matters for psychiatry, they still need to be dealt with compassionately and they still obviously excuse from responsibility for actions. Thus debate, movement of definitions and the like occur mainly at the boundaries of psychiatric practice rather than in its mainstream. So the definition of mental disorder is a political process in many different ways, and it is hard to see how it could be otherwise. Only if mental illnesses were once and for all established as physiological diseases defined by clear-cut physiological criteria would they be removed from the professional–political domain into the professional–scientific arena. As we shall see from the following chapters, such a transition is by no means assured.

SUMMARY

It has been established that it is reasonable and justifiable, within certain restrictions, to speak of social institutions having functions. Szasz has combined the description of psychiatry in these function- alist terms with deviancy theory to produce three possible political functions. The first is that psychiatry has the function of explaining away unpalatable moral or social problems. Careful analysis revealed that although this could not be said to be the function of psychiatry as a whole, it may have this effect and impact in certain areas, which would thus require further empirical study. Second, psychiatry has the function of allowing ventilation of displaced indignation and anger. This interpretation simply did not fit the facts about psychiatry. Third, the mentally ill take the blame for social problems. Again this was seen not as a function of psychiatry, but a result of the nature of social order, group formation and natural responses to the phenomenon of mental illness. Other authorities have sought to combine Marxist and Freudian theory in ways that imply political interpretations of mental illness. These interpretations do not offer useful or coherent guidance to psychi- atric practice in most cases. Evidence and argument that undermines either foundation (Marxist or Freudian) brings the whole edifice down. Sundry other ways in which psychiatry can be said to have an impact upon politics, or vice versa, have been explored. Most relevant to the topic of this book are the ways in which political processes influence the definition and boundaries of appropriate tasks for the institution of psychiatry, thereby contributing to the definition of mental illness itself.

Chapter 8

Illness

Few topics in the philosophy of psychiatry, or perhaps of medicine generally, have generated so many words, essays, papers and even books. Yet it is fair to say that the product has been more heat than light, more confusion than clarity. On the one hand Szasz claims that 'mental illness' is a metaphorical phrase and that all illnesses are physiological malfunctions or not illnesses at all (Szasz 1987: ch. 5). On the other side of the divide Sedgwick claims all illnesses are socially defined, suggesting that 'there are no illnesses or diseases in nature' (Sedgwick 1982: 30). Others have looked to definitions based upon psychological or cognitive malfunctions as the key criteria of 'mental illness'. Some have fought a reductionist battle making cognitive malfunctions equivalent to physiological brain malfunctions, based upon a materialist monist philosophy of mind. Yet others have sought to draw up lists of criteria or defining qualities of illness. No work or body of ideas has been definitive or set any form of intellectual benchmark within this debate, save perhaps for Szasz, who has provided less of a solution and more of a target to criticise.

Nevertheless, and somewhat mysteriously given the above confusion, the institution of psychiatry continues to function seemingly quite happily without a definition of its subject matter. Millions of people receive psychiatric help every year, varying from out-patient care to lengthy in-patient hospital stays. Thousands of professionals are trained and employed to provide that care. Millions of pounds are spent by governments or insurance companies to underwrite the operations of psychiatry. How can this be? If the nature of mental illness is such a mystery, why do sensible people fund, vote for, use and provide a service the content of which appears to be fundamentally unknown?

A PHILOSOPHICAL PROBLEM

This has the typical form of a philosophical rather than of a practical problem. It is akin to those famous philosophical problems like the nature of mind, understanding and meaning, and its source is in the same location: misconceptions about the nature of language. Just as we manage quite contentedly in our day-to-day lives with references to minds and bodies, understanding, thinking, feeling and the like, so psychiatry manages satisfactorily with multiplex activities referring to 'mental illness', disease, disorder and so on. In both cases, however, theoretical and philosophical reflection produces a wealth of ambiguity and confusion to the point of the cognitive equivalent of gridlock. Wittgenstein and the other ordinary language philosophers dissolved the former confusions through elaborating on the use, meaning and nature of language. I believe, and will attempt to show below, that those same lessons properly applied to psychiatry result in a similar evaporation of perplexity. Therefore instead of diving directly into the deep end of debate on the nature of 'mental illness', whatever that may turn out to be, it is perhaps more important to consider first the various ways in which language may be used.

LANGUAGE AND REPRESENTATION

In trying to decide what any word or phrase means, 'mental illness' included, a whole host of problems are caused by the assumption that words represent or are signs for objects, qualities or actions. Yet this is the picture of language we so often have in mind and which tends to mislead our thinking. We consider that our early learning of language is all about attaching word labels to things, thus by pointing and saying 'table', the young child is taught and learns to associate the word 'table' with flat objects having generally four static legs, off which one eats one's dinner or on which one plays games. This picture of language seduces us into thinking that the essence of a statement or sentence is description, portraying in symbolic form the way something is, or could be, in the world. Wittgenstein regarded this way of thinking about language as a pernicious philosophical weed, liable to crop up anywhere, and certainly present in the linguistic philosophies of Frege, Russell and his earlier self, as well as in everyday consideration and reflection.

Wittgenstein conducted a detailed destruction of this picture of language. But what is precisely wrong with the picture? It is relatively easy to view the results in endless philosophical discussion about mind, or the nature of cognitive processes, or indeed in the confusion surrounding the term 'mental illness'. Specifying the exact route by which we end up in such thinking culs-de-sac is rather more difficult.

When a definition of 'mental illness' is requested, this is not a pragmatic question on all occasions. A pragmatic question would be: 'How severely must one be depressed and what symptoms must one have to be considered mentally ill and referred to psychiatric services by one's GP?'. More often what is being sought is a definition, something that all cases of 'mental illness' must have in common, some list of necessary and sufficient criteria that will distinguish 'mental illness' from similar things for theoretical discussion. In other words, what is sought is some 'thing', of which 'mental illness' is the label. However, in everyday psychiatry, professionals use and explain the term 'mental illness' without a problem. Statements like 'He is mentally ill' can be made, and if it is asked what that means, say, in the context of a ward round, we are able to respond quite readily that it means that the person concerned should continue to receive psychiatric treatment and is in need of care and attention to prevent harm coming to him. Yet when we ask the abstract question 'What is mental illness?', we immediately become confused. This demonstrates that what is really needed here is a good grasp of what constitutes an explanation. Once this is understood, it will be seen that we do not need some super improved form of explanation that competes with our everyday ones.

Wittgenstein taught that meaning is given by explanation of meaning. The meaning of 'mental illness' is not something hidden or esoteric which is to be found by theoretic reflection. Instead, all we have to consider is how 'mental illness' is explained in concrete circumstances. And there are many kinds of explanations, from pointing to someone and saying 'Well, he is mentally ill', to offering a paraphrase or a contrast. Lists of necessary and sufficient criteria are only one restricted form of explanation which is not privileged over any other. Explanations may be given by providing examples, giving instructions for locating, producing or manufacturing examples, or by describing 'ideal types', providing restrictions, describing special cases and many other practices.

Meaning is what is given in the explanation of a word, rather than a strange mental act that accompanies its utterance. 'Mental illness' is not an essence held in mind by the speaker when he utters the words. There is no cognitive correlate that shadows in our minds the speaking of the words. The idea that the true nature of 'mental illness' can be discovered there, like a pot of gold at the end of a rainbow, must be abandoned. Instead, meaning is its use. Its meaning is displayed by the context of its deployment, verbally and socially.

What the explanation provides is a rule or rules for the use of the words. It is those rules held in common by the whole language-speaking community that support the meaningful use of words. The meaning of words is founded in the public practice of applying them in accord with their explanations. Indeed, for language to exist and function, there must be this agreement in definitions, otherwise no communication would be possible. The standard of a satisfactory explanation is that the person to whom it is given goes on to use the words concerned appropriately, accurately and without error. If they do, then we are justified in saying they have understood our explanation, and in saying that our explanation was correct. Whether a definition by lists of necessary and sufficient criteria is any more complete can only be judged within specific contexts, as it is relative to circumstances. In most everyday situations this is not required. If this is the only standard of explanation to be accepted, then most of us must be judged to be generally incapable of giving explanations of words at all. For it requires only simple reflection for us to realise that we cannot provide on demand definitions for most of our vocabulary by lists of necessary and sufficient criteria. This can lead to puzzlement about how we manage to use these words properly when we do not seem able to explain them. Very soon we can be on the road to philosophical hell by making bizarre deductions like supposing that our use of words is governed by rules of which we are ignorant, or unconscious, or that we know them but cannot speak of them.

SYSTEMATIC AMBIGUITY

No. There are some words and phrases, and I believe 'mental illness' is among them, which cannot be explained solely by the provision of lists of necessary and sufficient criteria. Two types of examples suffice to show that words are not labels attached to things by such lists, known or unknown, conscious or unconscious.

The first example is provided by Baker and Hacker (1980), the preposition 'on':

> 'on the table', 'on the agenda', 'on the air', 'on call', 'on further reflection', 'on Monday'.
>
> (Baker and Hacker 1980: 41)

There is no way to provide a complete explanation of these usages, if by complete we mean a list of necessary and sufficient criteria. If we are to provide an explanation of 'on', we need further information about the context of its use; then we are able to explain its meaning. Yet we use this word and others like it, to good effect, with the understanding of others around us, all the time. The second example is Wittgenstein's own elaboration of the concept of family resemblance words, to which I have already had recourse in my discussion of rule breaking and its relation to 'mental illness'. There is perhaps no better way of describing this point than by quoting Wittgenstein himself:

> Consider for example the proceedings we call 'games'. I mean board-games, card-games, ball-games, Olympic games, and so on. What is common to them all? – Don't say: 'There must be something common, or they would not be called "games"' – but look and see if there is anything common to all. – For if you look at them you will not see something that is common to all, but similarities, relationships, and a whole series of them at that. To repeat: don't think but look! – Look for example at board-games, with their multifarious relationships. Now pass to card-games; here you find many correspondences with the first group, but many common features drop out, and others appear. When we pass next to ball-games, much that is common is retained, but much is lost. – Are they all 'amusing'? Compare chess with noughts and crosses. Or is there always winning and losing, or competition between players? Think of patience. In ball-games there is winning and losing; but when a child throws his ball at the wall and catches it again, this feature has disappeared. . . . And the result of this examination is: we see a complicated network of similarities overlapping and criss-crossing: sometimes overall similarities, sometimes similarities of detail.
>
> (Wittgenstein 1958: I, para. 66)

The fact that games have no common properties means that there can be no correct list of necessary and sufficient attributes that would define the word once and for all. Nevertheless we are able to use, understand and explain the word 'game' without major problems by giving examples together with an etcetera clause. What links the various activities called games together is the network of complicated and overlapping characteristics. Therefore the concept has no hard and fast boundaries. Boundaries can be drawn for specific purposes, for example games qualifying for Olympic events, but the boundary is only relevant to that purpose. We do not have to cease calling 'tiddlywinks' a game because it does not fit Olympic criteria!

'Mental illness' is in every respect similar. It is used in different but related ways with overlapping resemblances. Attempts to provide lists of defining characteristics fail because (i) there are always cases that do not fit, and (ii) there is a tendency to make one characteristic the dominant one, a mistake parallel to considering 'winning and losing' as the defining characteristic of a game. There are no sharp and rigid boundaries to the concept 'mental illness', although these can be, and often are, drawn for specific purposes.

SCIENTIFIC AND TECHNICAL DEFINITIONS

It might be argued that 'mental illness' as used by the general population is indeed vague and ambiguous, but its use within psychiatry is systematic and determinate, allowing it within that context to be defined by lists of necessary and sufficient criteria. Take salt for example. In lay parlance it is the white crystalline substance used to bring out the flavour of food, or the taste of sea-water. However, within the scientific domain of chemistry, sodium chloride is a specific substance made up of molecules each containing one atom of sodium and one of chlorine, with a precise molecular weight, defined attributes and reactivity. Cannot 'mental illness' be thought of in the same way?

Unfortunately not, for the term 'mental illness' is not reserved solely for scientific use within psychiatry but has widespread use in common parlance where it is related to other words like mad, crazy, cracked, touched, demented, deranged, lunatic and nervous breakdown. Moreover, the uses of 'mental illness' within and outside psychiatry are related within a complex and ambiguous web of meanings and associated social practices. They affect and contaminate one another, rather than being distinctive, different and used for divergent purposes. In any case, psychiatry does not have detailed definitions, except in a rather broad sense of ICD or DSM. When psychiatric professionals get beyond talking about 'mental illness' *in toto* to specific diagnoses, they soon lapse into the murky waters of asserting or rejecting illness status on a variety of grounds in a variety of circumstances – sometimes for the very same disorder. Finally, if there was a specific and agreed definition for 'mental illness' within psychiatry, this is how the term would be taught, rather than as it is, taken for granted as self-evident by most psychiatric texts.

LANGUAGE AS ACTION

Wittgenstein likened words to collections of tools in a tool-box, or to the different controls on a locomotive. By using this analogy he was asserting that words have a variety of different uses and functions, despite their overall similarity of appearance. Words enter into and are crucial parts of human activities or practices. Similarly the words 'mental illness' are part and parcel of a variety of formal and informal activities, and like a tool they can be used in various ways. If one wishes, therefore, to know what 'mental illness' is, it is necessary to look at the way the words are used in different ways and in different contexts towards different ends.

I must apologise for this short, superficial and partial rendering of the thought of one of the greatest philosophers of the age. I can only hope my explanation has been sufficiently complete for the reader to understand the discussion that follows. There are occasions on which some commentators come close to the appreciation that the meaning of 'mental illness' is embedded in the practices surrounding its use. Kendell (1975b), for example, shows that he recognises the systematic ambiguity of the words 'illness' and 'disease' when he likens our current vocabulary of illnesses to a collection of furniture in an old house, in which each successive resident has added a few more items without any being thrown away. Hence we are left with an idiosyncratic collection of objects from a succession of periods. Szasz (1987) at times clearly recognises that the meaning of 'mental illness' is directly related to the activities surrounding becoming and being a psychiatric patient, and that the term is used in practical circumstances in order to accomplish certain ends. However, neither of these two authors manages to get an overview of the nature and use of the term 'mental illness'. Some preliminary steps towards the provision of such an overview will be made before the close of this chapter. First a variety of understandings of the term 'mental illness' and their insufficiencies will be described, a process which will provide further clarification of the ways in which the phrase 'mental illness' enters into everyday discourse in practical circumstances.

METAPHORS AND MENTAL ILLNESS

The most notorious interpretation of 'mental illness' is that of Szasz (1972) who argues that it is a metaphorical expression only. Although this assertion is infamous, and is made repeatedly by Szasz in his writings, it remains hard to describe in detail. What Szasz appears to be saying is that the only real, literal form of illness is physiological disorder. Therefore when we say somebody is mentally ill, or sick in the mind, or whatever, we are using the term metaphorically and not literally. The person concerned is not really ill, only metaphorically so. In a similar way it can be said that economies suffer the disease of inflation. This position is further supported by the fact that there are obvious differences in the uses of the terms 'mental' and 'physical illness', just as there are always differences between metaphors and the literal meanings upon which they are parasitic. Most criticisms of Szasz from within the psychiatric professions have focused upon the phenomenological reality of 'mental illness', that people really do become agitated, manic, deluded, hallucinated, etc. Szasz (1987) rightly rejects these arguments as missing the point. He does not deny that people behave in these ways, but instead suggests that when we call them ill we are speaking metaphorically rather than literally.

Szasz's argument can be undermined in a number of different ways, if not by the above rather superficial attempt. For instance, he is seriously confused about the nature of metaphorical language. First, although he appreciates that whether a phrase is literal or metaphorical is determined by convention, he admits that he has to fight hard to persuade everybody that 'mental illness' is a metaphor. In fact, it is clear that their convention defines the phrase 'mental illness' as literal, which is why Szasz has a hard time persuading anybody otherwise. It is a universally recognised stupidity to take a metaphor literally, a situation fully exploited by comedians and comedy script writers. Taking a metaphor literally is clearly visible in what a person does or says, like for example, saying one will measure up the foot of a mountain for a pair of shoes. That 'mental illness' is used within and outside psychiatry without the appearance of obvious stupidity underlines the fact that our convention does not consider it to be metaphorical. Calling the doctor out to assess the state of a country suffering from the illness of inflation would be such a stupidity, indicating that use of the term 'illness' here is metaphorical.

Second, the logic of Szasz's assertion that a metaphor is at work here simply does not fit our use of language. Take the following pair: 'illness' and 'mental illness'. Here 'illness' is supposed to be the term used literally and metaphorically in different contexts. If this was so, though, why would we add the qualifying word 'mental'? By adding the word 'mental' we are already saying we mean something different from simply 'ill'. When using a word metaphorically we do not qualify it in this way, as it detracts from the illustrative picture a metaphor is intended to convey. For instance we do not say: 'the country is economically ill with inflation'.

Under the guise of deriving facts from the logic of our language use, Szasz is actually carrying out a moral and political crusade. He campaigns for the idea that what we currently call 'mental illness' should not be considered an illness, that the institution of psychiatry be dismantled and everybody be held fully responsible for their actions. He is fully entitled to make this argument and to suggest that we should use our language differently, or change the way we speak about and act towards that which we now call 'mental illness'. However, this position is not an analytic truth and cannot be derived as a logical conclusion from the way we currently speak and act. His argument is a moral one masquerading as logical.

MENTAL ILLNESS AS PHYSIOLOGICAL DISORDER

Of course, Szasz's position is also undermined if his case that the defining characteristic of all illness is physiological disorder can be shown to be false. He makes a number of initial false moves in this particular argument. Ignoring our everyday distinctions and different usages of words, he asserts that all illness is disease, and that both are structural or functional abnormalities, tissues, organs or bodies. On the grounds of a partial reading of the evidence, Szasz concludes that 'mental illness' is not a physiological abnormality and is therefore not an illness. Many organically-oriented psychiatrists might also agree with the former argument on the definition of illness, but disagree about the assessment of evidence and therefore derive the opposite conclusion to Szasz.

The most obvious counters to this position have been marshalled by Kendell (1975b). He points out that illnesses and diseases have been historically identified long before any physiological explanation for them was available, and thus their meaning cannot be that physiological explanation. Moreover, Szasz's criterion rules out any diseases/illnesses for which no cause has been found, a position which is absurd to maintain. Szasz (1987) in fact accepts the category of putative disease but argues that either any 'mental illness' that turns out to have a physiological cause should no longer be called a 'mental illness', or that no 'mental illness' qualifies as a putative disease. Kendell also indicates the impossibility of finding a clear physiological demarcation between disease and health in such illnesses as diabetes and hypertension. The conclusion can be drawn that if these boundary decisions have to be taken on social grounds, then the definition of illness itself is to some degree based on social criteria. It is clear that this must be accepted, and that on this point too Szasz's arguments should be rejected. At least part of Szasz's failure is based upon his inability to recognise that to find out what illness and disease mean we must look at how the words are used by people in practical situations, rather than attempt a single major a priori definition.

CROP AND BLIGHT

Sedgwick (1982) takes more or less a precisely opposite position to Szasz, arguing that the identification of diseases/illnesses is based upon social valuations. Sedgwick bases his position upon the three arguments of Kendell above, as well as his own 'Crop and Blight' argument in which he tries to demonstrate that there are 'no illnesses or diseases in nature'. This argument is worth quoting verbatim:

> All departments of nature, below the level of mankind are exempt both from disease and from treatment – until people intervene with their own human classifications of disease and treatment. The blight that strikes at corn or at potatoes is a human invention, for if we wished to cultivate parasites (rather than potatoes or corn) there would be no 'blight', but simply the

necessary foddering of the parasite crop. Animals do not have diseases either, prior to the presence of humans in a meaningful relation with them. A tiger may experience pain or feebleness from a variety of causes . . . . It may be infected by a germ, trodden by an elephant, scratched by another tiger, or subjected to the ageing process of its own cells. It does not present itself as being ill . . . except in the eyes of a human observer . . . . Outside the significance that we voluntarily attach to certain conditions, there are no illnesses or diseases in nature. . . . Are there not fractures of bones, the fatal ruptures of tissues, the malignant multiplications of tumorous growths? Are not these, surely, events of nature? Yet these, as natural events, do not constitute illnesses, sicknesses or diseases prior to the human social meanings we attach to them. The fracture of a septuagenarian's femur has, within the world of nature, no more significance than the snapping of an autumn leaf from its twig: and the invasion of a human organism by cholera germs carries with it no more the stamp of 'illness' than does the souring of milk by other forms of bacteria.

(Sedgwick 1982: 28–30)

Sedgwick is undoubtedly right that social valuations as well as biological criteria are part of the meaning of illness and disease. This has already been established by the arguments of Kendell. However, with the 'Crop and Blight' justification above, Sedgwick is asserting that all illness and disease is a matter of social definition. In making this argument Sedgwick believes he has legitimised the status of 'mental illness' by showing that all illness of every kind, not just 'mental illness', is socially defined.

Unfortunately Sedgwick too has failed to get to grips with the way we use words and language. His main problem is with the phrase 'in nature', for as he uses it, there is no room for any named object, item or activity. His argument can be used to say there is no sodium chloride, no mountains, no seas, no planets, no stars, no atoms, no light or dark, save for human beings calling them such according to their interests. Of course, all these are present in nature but nature itself does not call them by name. Were there trees in the Jurassic period before the existence of man? According to Sedgwick's argument there were not, for there were no men to make distinctions between trees and shrubs. Nevertheless, such items that we would now call trees did exist, and such plants that we would now call roses grew. All that Sedgwick has discovered here is that it is difficult to know how we should speak of these things. He has not undermined the fundamental objective physical reality of biological disease.

In any case, we are not trying to establish what we could say about the phenomenon we now call illness if no human beings existed. If no human beings existed, there would be no one to speak and no one to listen. The whole exercise is a metaphysical linguistic contortion. We can be brought back to earth by a consideration of the way we use the words 'illness' and 'disease'. When we do so we realise that at least one of the criteria we utilise on many occasions is that of physiological abnormality, disorder, malfunction or upset by infection. Thus although social judgements enter into definitions of illness and disease, so also do objective criteria of the breakdown of biological systems.

This means that Turner's (1992) resolution of the problem is not required. Turner argued, in an Orwellian manner, that although all things are socially constructed, some things are more socially constructed than others. The example he gives is that the equation $2 + 2 = 4$ is less socially constructed than a psychiatric diagnosis of anorexia. However, both are used by human beings as part of their actions, and it cannot be denied that in this sense both are social constructions through and through. Given the understanding of the nature of language reached above, the real import of Turner's argument is that anorexia may not be as useful within the domain of activity we call psychiatry, as numbers are in the domain of activity we call arithmetic. Thus Turner mistakes an empirical and practical question for a logical and ontological one, feeling that the only way he can escape complete relativism is to admit gradations of social construction.

ILLNESS AND INCAPACITATION

It is of interest to note that Sedgwick's idea of social valuation actually describes a process by which illness/disease is identified, without providing or describing the social criteria which he believes are used. Many have suggested deviancy from social norms as the answer to this question, and this solution has been examined in great length in Chapter 2. Sedgwick (1982), along with Kendell (1975b) and Lewis (1953), rejects the idea of simple statistical deviation from the norm because this over-inclusively incorporates anything from saintly virtue to rare eye colour under the title of illness. The rule-breaking perspective of deviancy sociology is not discussed by these authors. Previous consideration of this solution led to the conclusion that there were many types of social rules and norms, and that the specific sorts of norm breaking which we call illness could not be identified and separated from others. Thus deviancy from social norms could not be considered the defining characteristic of illness. Sedgwick offers a paltry attempt at clarification by suggesting that illness is deviancy from a desired state of affairs. Unfortunately by this definition my failure to win the national lottery is a disease! A more sympathetic reading of Sedgwick, putting together his examples with his statements on deviancy, is that under the title 'deviancy' he is really describing incapacity or disability, a factor which is itself determined by social norms of usual capability, relative to age and gender.

Incapacity is certainly another of the criteria we use in the determination of whether something should be considered an illness. It applies equally to mental and physical illness, both of which incapacitate. Once again, though, the temptation to utilise this as the one sole major defining criterion for illness should be shunned. Incapacity can have many causes, of which illness or disease is only one. Being in prison makes me incapable of going to work in my regular employment every day, but it is not an illness. Similarly, it is possible to be seriously ill, with say an early tumour, and yet not be incapacitated at all. Again this underlines the necessity to look at the complex ways in which we use the words 'illness' and 'disease' in our daily lives.

A neat and tidy way to acknowledge social and physical definitions of illness has been advanced by Morgan (1975) and Kleinman (1980). Both suggest that 'illness' or 'sickness' refers to the social aspects of disease, how the sick person and those around him respond to it; and disease is the biological disorder. This gross oversimplification might have a didactic utility, but does not reflect the complexity with which we use these terms. It assumes that to be useful, these words must have fixed representational meaning.

EVOLUTIONARY CRITERIA

Kendell (1975b) is unique in advancing the argument that illness is anything that produces biological disadvantage. By biological disadvantage he means reduction in fertility or shortening of life, or in other words survival disadvantage. Kendell is therefore making an argument from evolution. Although initially an attractive idea, this solution of the problem of the definition of illness has both theoretical and practical shortcomings. The theoretical flaw is that this simply is not the criterion that we use to decide what is or is not an illness. When asked 'Is Fred ill?', we do not try to imagine the impact of Fred's condition as it would be in a primitive, pre-literate, hunter-gatherer social group and then answer yea or nay depending upon our assessment of Fred's survival chances in that context. What is more, this attempted definition falls to meet Kendell's own critique of the Szasz position. If physiological criteria were not used to determine illness in historical epochs, neither were evolutionary ones. The practical problems with this evolutionary definition are the exclusion of many items that currently count as illness (neurotic disorders, some personality disorders) and incorporates many more that are not so counted (infertility, employment as a miner or fireman).

RESPONSIBILITY AND ABSOLUTION

Illness has another characteristic which is less often proffered as a defining one: reduction in responsibility. The most evident reduction in responsibility relates to the loss of capability to perform usual functions and roles. All illness offers this kind of 'time out' from the daily round of responsibilities to others. In some cases it goes further and absolves from socially undesirable action: the diabetic in a state of hypoglycaemia who crashes his car, the epileptic who in a post-ictal fugue insults his boss. In cases of physical illness this kind of absolution is rare and applies only to those disorders that interfere with the functioning of the central nervous system. The matter is complicated still further by the fact that for some physical illnesses the sufferers themselves are held in some way to be accountable for becoming ill. Examples here would be the heavy smoker with lung cancer, or the heavy drinker with liver failure.

The situation is obviously more complicated than illness providing a blank cheque of non-responsibility that can be cashed by the sufferers with respect to any activities or actions. Actual responsibility is negotiated according to situation within specific contexts. Allocation of freedom from responsibility is nearly always severely circumscribed to particular behaviours, situations and times, for to treat someone as completely non-responsible is to remove them from the human race and treat them as an animal incapable of volitional action, interaction, relationship and meaningful communication. Given that this is the case, a sick person can make a claim to not being responsible in a certain area, and others can make judgements about whether that claim will be allowed and to what degree. In some circumstances it is others who will attribute non-responsibility before it is claimed, or without it being claimed at all.

There are four relevant factors in a determination of responsibility. The first is in whose eyes or from whose perspective the determination is being made. A mother, lover or close friend is going to allow more leniency or latitude in their judgements than is any kind of institutional official. Second, for what purpose is the determination being made? If we take the example of smoking and lung cancer once again, the judgement of the sufferer's employer will be that they should be allowed paid sick leave, but the judgement of any health promotion officer may be that they only have themselves to blame. Third, for what action is the determination being made? The more serious or grave the action, the less likely exculpation is to be offered. Fourth, in relation to what claimed or perceived loss of control is the determination being made? Having a severe cold may absolve us from the necessity to work for a few days but would not be any excuse for parking a car in a no parking zone.

All of this applies equally well to 'mental illness', except that mental illness more frequently involves socially-disruptive and disorderly behaviour, and always serves as potential grounds for absolution because the sufferers' judgements are considered to be affected. All severe mental illnesses are reckoned to affect the ability to judge situations, discern right action from wrong and assess the consequences of actions. The more minor mental illnesses like anxiety and depression contain the same potential to absolve though to a lesser extent. In each and every case, whether the person is deemed responsible will depend upon who is making the judgement, for what purpose, about what action and what has been the perceived loss of control.

It is the circumscribed and context-specific nature of attributions of responsibility that makes 'moral treatment' possible within psychiatry. As discussed in Chapter 6, although people may be admitted to hospital through being assessed as not responsible for their actions and liable to harm themselves or others, once ensconced within a psychiatric ward the staff endeavour to hold them responsible for their actions in order to help them achieve increasing degrees of control. This may have the appearance of paradox or nonsense, but not the reality, for as described above, attributions of responsibility are context-dependent.

The two concepts, illness and responsibility, are mutually interdependent and interrelated. On the one hand behaviour that, because of circumstances, context and absence of clear motivation, suggests that the person is not responsible also suggests that the person may be mentally ill. Gaines (1992) makes this loss of inner direction or self-control the central feature of his definition of 'mental illness', and Williams (1985) describes how historically hypnotic trances were considered pathological because of the lack of voluntary control by the subject. On the other hand, a person who is evidently mentally ill (for example, expressing severe paranoid delusions and obviously hallucinating) may on those grounds be considered not responsible for certain actions in certain circumstances. It is therefore plain that the way that the term 'mentally ill' is used in daily activity is interrelated and overlaps with our determinations and attributions of 'responsibility'.

INSANITY AND RATIONALITY

The nature of 'mental illness' as a family resemblance word, in Wittgensteinian terms, is now becoming more clear. In some cases 'mental illness' means actual or putative physiological disorder of the brain, in others incapacitation, and in yet others a loss of control over actions with consequent reduction in attributed responsibility. There are also further additional overlapping characteristics, perhaps one of the most prominent of these being unreasonableness or irrationality. Despite the fact that historically insanity was seen as a loss of reasoning faculties, little attention has been paid to this notion by recent psychiatric theoreticians whose key ideas have been explored above. Yet in Chapter 3, on the relationship of rule breaking to 'mental illness', it was shown that it was not so much the breaking of social rules that invoked the identification of a person as mentally ill, as the fact that the rule breaking had no underlying reason or understandable motivation. Also, in Chapter 2 on labelling theory, I argued and concluded that Scheff's (1966) concept of 'residual rule breaking' as the identifying characteristic of 'mental illness' could be more coherently replaced with irrational or inexplicable rule violation.

Judgements of rationality, like judgements of responsibility, are made about specific behaviours in specific circumstances, by particular people and for particular purposes. Irrationality is not a blanket judgement about all of any person's behaviour all the time. Neither is the word 'irrational' precisely coterminous with 'mental illness'. It is possible in some circumstances to be quite rational and yet be mentally ill, and in other circumstances to behave irrationally and yet not be considered mentally ill. Irrational and unreasonable behaviour can be put down to all sorts of reasons other than 'mental illness': stupidity, lack of forethought, impulsiveness, stress, making a mistake, lack of sleep, etc. A social phenomenology of rationality has been provided by Schutz (1953) in which he describes the wide range of characteristics of actions to which the word 'rationality' is applied, from categorising to analysis of consequences. However, this does not provide us with any kind of typology of rationality by which we can indicate the particular type of irrationality that prompts attribution of the title 'mental illness'. Schutz's typology does underline the fact that to understand 'rationality', like 'mental illness', one must look at the way the word is used in everyday conduct. If the irrationality commonly displayed by those called mentally ill is examined, it is found that the irrationality must be of a certain kind and persevere for some time before people start to consider 'mental illness' as an appropriate category. In other words, the irrational behaviour should follow an already known pattern, including such things as disordered speech and communication, hallucinations, the expression of bizarre beliefs, inappropriate affect, and unpredictable conduct. What is special about the irrationality of madness is that it follows specific forms and generally corrupts wide areas of the person's life, calling their global judgement into question. In yet other cases, the irrationality may be narrow, only arising in certain aspects of the person's life, but so fundamentally and widely and importantly different, with such immense consequences, resistant to all forms of education or attempts to shed the light of rationality, and so linked to harmful behaviour to others, that 'mental illness' is declared.

Szasz (1987) concludes that because rationality is a socially-contexted judgement, 'mental illness' cannot be an objective physiological disorder. This is wrong on two counts, as I have shown in Chapter 2. First, irrational behaviour often indicates what is well known to be a physical disorder, as in toxic confusional state. Second, it is a mistake to believe that social categories are incommensurable with physical ones. How the two relate to each other is a matter for empirical investigation, not a priori rejection of any relationship.

There exists a strong temptation (which must be repudiated) to accept irrationality as the master characteristic of 'mental illness'. The desire to have words standing for one defined thing only is very strong. However, irrationality is not the only idea that is central to 'mental illness'. It is not the irrationality of the depressed which is at the forefront, but their suffering and inability to get on with rewarding lives. Rationality is not always the most salient issue for deciding the relevance of psychiatric treatment.

COMMON FEATURES

There are several other features of behaviour considered to exemplify mental illness that have usually been considered in isolation and therefore rejected for definitional use. This has been a typical failing in the search for one overarching definitive statement on what constitutes mental illness. However, as part of a family resemblance picture of mental illness these features can be restored to their rightful position – not present all the time in all that is considered mental illness, but nevertheless present repeatedly in differing combinations. Some have already been alluded to above. For instance, the pain and suffering of the depressed and anxious person is indicative that they have an illness, although obviously not all pain and suffering is due to mental illness or indeed illness of any kind. Also, not all sufferers of mental illness are obviously suffering all the time – sometimes the opposite is the case, as with mania sufferers at certain stages of their illness. Harmfulness to self or others is another link in the chain of concepts surrounding the usage of the term 'mental illness'. However irrational peoples' beliefs and actions are, if they are harmless they are liable to be left alone and called eccentric rather than mentally ill. Harm to others is linked to socially obnoxious and disruptive behaviour, or the breaking of social norms and rules. Lastly, although 'need for treatment' is a criterion scorned by everybody from Kendell (1975b) to Szasz (1987), nevertheless certain behaviours and problems come under the rubric of psychiatry not because they are first adjudged varieties of mental illness, but because psychiatric professionals have the technologies and resources to help. Both post-traumatic stress disorder and bereavement counselling can be thought of in this way.

It is possible therefore to compile a list of the characteristics that the mentally ill may display. These are:

Irrationality
Non-responsibility
Loss of control
Physiological disorder affecting brain function
Incapacitation
Suffering
Socially obnoxious and disruptive behaviour
Harm to others
Harm to self
Treatable with psychiatric techniques

This list is preliminary, not exhaustive. It does not mean that everything considered mental illness displays all these characteristics, but all mental illnesses will display some constellation of these features. Thus all members of the category will possess a family resemblance to each other. Which common human predicament is treated as this sort of phenomenon is a historical, political, organisational and cultural product. At any time, any condition is open to being reallocated to an alternative category, or indeed to being counted as normal variation, should some rationale for it become commonly accepted. The key question becomes, which is the most useful way of regarding each of these conditions, and what form of treatment has the best outcome? Moral questions of responsibility and blame also arise around whether the condition is taken to be voluntary or not, and such decisions may drive allocation to the category of mental illness or to some other such as crime. Discovery of a physiological cause sometimes confirms allocation to mental illness and psychiatry. The more intrinsically self-harming, as opposed to harmful to others, a behaviour is, the more likely it is to be perceived as irrational and therefore as mental illness.

Mental illness is therefore not one single sort of thing, but a hotchpotch collection of items with cross-cutting resemblances. Some mental illnesses may be physiological disorders of the nervous system, while others may be social or behavioural problems. For many we have no real idea of the precise nature or cause of the problems. Accordingly the boundaries of what is called and treated as mental illness are, to a degree, fluid and socially determined.

PROS AND CONS OF THE ILLNESS PARADIGM

Many of the critical psychiatric writers, Szasz foremost amongst them, argue that we should abandon the idea of illness completely, and that the phenomenon of insanity should either be dissolved under a number of different categories, or treated alternatively. Although, as has been demonstrated above, this argument cannot be derived from logic or language use, there is a moral or political case to be answered here. The term 'illness' is seen by many to imply actual or putative physiological cause, even if this does not match its daily and historical use. Baruch and Treacher (1978) have cogently argued that categorisation as illness creates what they call a 'treatment barrier'. Allocation to the illness category removes the responsibility for the situation from the person, who after all cannot be blamed for being ill. If their illness was caused by an intolerable interpersonal situation, then calling it illness removes from the individual any agency, responsibility or power to rectify or put right that situation. Thus effective treatment sometimes depends first upon convincing the person that they are not ill in the same sense as having influenza: the treatment barrier has to be crossed. The illness model may also facilitate a process of converting political and social problems into those of medical treatment, thus shunting them into a siding where they can be ignored. This is precisely what Scheper-Hughes (1988) described in her case study of 'nervios' in Brazilian plantation workers. Moreover, to the extent that psychiatry treats personal and moral problems as problems of faulty brain physiology, it can be said to depersonalise and dehumanise its subjects.

However, it should also be acknowledged that there are real advantages to working within the illness paradigm. It facilitates the treatment of 'mental illness' in a non-stigmatising humane manner. It promotes justice in that those who are clearly not fully responsible for their actions can be treated and cared for, rather than punished. Blame is removed from patients and their families, who may be freed from guilt and thereby be able to manage their situation better. New and effective treatments, resulting in the alleviation of the suffering of millions, can and have been found by physiological research.

Which position is correct hinges upon the actual nature and cause of individual mental disorders. For if some, all, or a few mental disorders really are physiological brain malfunctions, then in those cases none would dispute the applicability of the term 'illness' and its connected social roles. Vice versa, if some mental illnesses are disordered interpersonal relationships or situations, none would fail to see the difficulties posed by the use of the term 'illness'. It is obviously mistaken to apply one or other of these positions to all that goes under the title of 'mental illness'; instead each type of disorder needs to be taken on a case-by-case basis. Perhaps even more unfortunately, for many mental disorders we simply do not know or are not sure of their nature and cause. Rival aetiological theories can therefore very quickly transform themselves into moral battles about whether the disorder under consideration is properly to be called an 'illness' or not.

LINGUISTIC ANALYSIS

Throughout this book I have been using the term 'mental illness' as shorthand for 'that with which psychiatry deals'. This is a frequent usage, but only one of several, for the way in which we use a whole host of health-related terms is actually very complex. There are two ways to seek descriptions of the way words are used and how they link into human activities. The first is by simple reflection or philosophical analysis. This path has been taken by Champlin (1981), who has made a preliminary description of the logical grammar of our language use in this domain. He has shown that we make complicated distinctions between disease, having an illness, being ill, feeling ill, injury, poor health, etc. Consider the person who is overweight, or blind, or senile, or deaf, or has a broken arm, or who has toothache. None of these things is an illness but each of these people has something wrong with them. They may be ill as well, i.e. a blind man may also be ill, but his blindness is not an illness. Feeling ill generally equals aches, pains, nausea, weakness, faintness, discomfort. Champlin points out that this leads to some surprising facts. It is possible to have an illness without feeling ill – for example, I had measles but I did not feel ill. It is possible to be ill without suffering from an illness – a little boy can be ill from eating too many green apples but he does not have an illness. Injury is distinct from illness – the victim of a road traffic accident can be critically ill, but is suffering from an injury rather than an illness. Champlin argues that disease is a more technical term indicating malfunction, upset or disorder of a physiological process. Crops, plants and trees can have diseases, but not illnesses; many diseases are not illnesses at all, such as acne or dental caries. To be called a disease, physical evidence of structural deterioration is usually required.

Champlin's account shows how complex our language use is even for physical illness. More complexity is introduced when we start talking about 'mental illness'. Most mental illnesses are only putative diseases; we may guess that they are diseases, but we do not have much evidence as yet of structural deterioration. The question whether they really are diseases of the brain thus remains an open one. The illness of the mentally ill rarely makes them feel ill, at least not in the same way as physical illnesses do. Mental illness does not give you aches, pains, nausea and weakness. In some mental illnesses people actually feel much better than usual. When the mentally ill do complain of their condition, it is in very diverse ways, from complaints of uncomfortable moods/feelings to complaints of being out of control. Mental illness is never infectious, you cannot die of it, and it is always serious – you cannot have a trivial, short-lived mental illness. But both mental and physical illness incapacitate – they stop you from doing things you want to do, from getting on with everyday life.

The second way to achieve descriptions of language use is via ethnographic study. As far as I am aware, although much research is carried out in psychiatry, none has looked at the way we use the terminology of 'mental illness' and the like in everyday professional practice. Nevertheless, some tentative and preliminary remarks may be made.

In common lay parlance 'mental illness' is sometimes used as a term of abuse and derogation. The fact that it is so used is indicative and supportive of the stigma and fear of the mentally ill. Perhaps more frequently, when the statement 'He is mentally ill' is used in common parlance, it means that the person indicated is considered to need psychiatric help and treatment. As used by psychiatric professionals, most commonly 'mental illness' is used as a shorthand term for all those things with which the institution of psychiatry deals. Notwithstanding this use of the term, individual patients and types of patients can from time to time be considered 'not really ill', as female neurotic patients are sometimes so considered by psychiatric nurses (Macilwaine 1981). Being mentally ill is also a social status, entry to which is determined in the first place by general practitioners and secondarily by consultant psychiatrists. Like physical illness it absolves from the responsibility to work or do normal duties, and may provide the basis for a claim for official disability status. On other specific occasions the statement 'He is mentally ill', say after a violent incident on a psychiatric ward, would be a plea that the person could not help what they did, should not be held responsible, and therefore all anger and blame should be allowed to evaporate. On other occasions the contrary claim may mean precisely the opposite. The term also has a legal use in that to be detained in hospital under the Mental Health Act a person must be formally judged by several people to be suffering from a 'mental illness'.

SUMMARY

When we talk about 'mental illness' our language is not faulty or flawed. Nothing is wrong with this talk. It is not illogical or irrational, we understand what we are saying and we are able usefully to continue with our actions. We are not misunderstanding or mistaking each other, nor stupidly taking any metaphor literally. We use 'mental illness' in a coherent way that allows us to talk about the matters with which psychiatry deals. Actual everyday use of the words 'illness' and 'mental illness' has been shown to be significantly complex, a fact that underlines the uselessness of searching for a single definition of 'mental illness' by necessary and sufficient criteria. Instead 'mental illness' should be considered to have a number of overlapping meanings whose individual instances display a family resemblance to one another. The criteria which are typically present and which in a variety of combinations suggest candidates for consideration as 'mental illness' are irrationality, non-responsibility, loss of control, physiological disorder affecting brain function, incapacitation, suffering, socially obnoxious and disruptive behaviour, harm to self, harm to others, and the ability to be treated with psychiatric techniques. The criteria in this mixed bag are mainly socially defined, but objective physiological criteria are also sometimes present. It is open for anyone to suggest that we should change our language and the institution of psychiatry or its subject matter in any way. However, this would not be a matter of making our language more regular or logical, but a matter instead upon which the pros and cons of any significant change need to be carefully weighed. For example, the treatment of what we currently call 'mental illness' as illness creates specific benefits as well as handicaps, suggesting that cautious and careful thought should precede any attempt at creating new categories.

Chapter 9

Physiology

Although the word illness is used in a diverse number of ways, it takes only brief reflection to realise that in some usages the idea of physiological malfunction is at the forefront. Signs of this kind of malfunction are common on many of those occasions on which we call someone ill, and are sometimes the basis for so doing. These signs may be obvious, e.g. coughing, bruising, bleeding, temperature, vomiting, changes in skin colour, and others too numerous to mention. At other times these signs may be elicited by test or examination. These methods of determining illness are not new, but date back thousands of years. Our language use itself reflects the often intimate tie between concepts of physiological malfunction and of illness. We speak of the well person as having 'nothing wrong with them', just as we speak of something being wrong with our car when it will not start in the morning; the phrase thus indicates mechanical malfunction as common to both ideas.

In this chapter the idea of physiological brain malfunction will be explored from a number of different perspectives. In the course of this discussion the role of social, psychological and biological explanations of mental illness will be clarified in order to ascertain how, and to what degree, these different accounts are separable.

We should not, however, lose sight of the insights gained in the preceding chapter. Although illness in some usages indicates physiological disorder, this is not so in all cases. Moreover, 'mental illness' has different usages from the word 'illness' by itself, and is still less intimately connected with connotations of physiological disorder. It is Szasz's failure to take note of this that leads him into the fatal error from which most of his other errors flow; that is, that illness is either physiological disorder or it is not illness at all. Such a deduction perpetrates a grand injustice upon our language use, and leads

Szasz into making some absurd conclusions. For instance, he concludes (1987) that as mental illness is not real illness it must be fake illness. Coupling this with psychiatric accounts of hysteria that appear to validate this proposition, Szasz proceeds to infer that all mental illnesses of every variety are actually forms of malingering or imitation. He then pours scorn upon psychiatry for treating these fraudulent versions of illness as the real thing. This absurd conclusion is based upon an absurd premise. Physiological malfunction is one, but not the sole, criterion for the use of the word 'illness'.

PSYCHOLOGICAL MALFUNCTIONING

Along with many others, Lewis (1953) uses the idea of psychological malfunction as the defining criterion of mental illness. As with Szasz, this is also wrong for it does not tally with our actual everyday language use. Initially, however, the idea is appealing, and would appear to bring mental illness into congruence with physical illness. In the former, thought or affect may be disordered, while in the latter the stomach or liver (for instance) may be disordered. This way of talking does try to build a similarity between psychological and physiological malfunctioning. Unfortunately the parallel quickly breaks down upon further exploration. We do not talk about having something wrong with our feelings or thoughts. Instead, in order to make the parallel work, we have to import hydrodynamic, electrical or other mechanical analogies of cognitive functioning. Additionally, it is impossible to distinguish the concept of psychological malfunction from that of abnormality, and this drags in its wake all the problems of deviancy theory already described.

To take the analogy further, physical treatment should thus be paralleled by psychological treatment. At this point the parallel either again breaks down as one seeks equivalents for surgery or medication, this time into a clear picture of physiological brain malfunction, or becomes a powerful metaphoric picture. Psychological treatment is then seen as another word for psychotherapy, an activity that heals the hurts of the soul and relieves the pains of life. However profound this picture appears to be, its validity depends upon an aetiological account of mental illness in which emotional trauma is a significant causal contributor. The essential element of this metaphor is emotional injury coupled with emotional healing. Any other interpretation simply will not fit well enough – for example, to talk about psychological malfunctions as an infection of the psyche, and psychological treatment as parallel to the regular administration of antibiotics, just does not have the same illustrative power or weight of resemblance. Even if we are to accept some form of metaphor based upon the idea of psychological malfunction, the question of the efficacy of the psychological treatment remains an open one which requires empirical investigation and test.

RELATIONSHIP OF WORDS TO NEUROLOGICAL STATES

Reznek (1991) does not pursue the analogy this far, but instead suggests that every psychological malfunction is simply indicative of an equivalent and parallel brain malfunction. Somewhat crudely he argues that mental events are caused by physiological brain events, and that therefore abnormal mental states are caused by abnormal physical ones. He believes in looking for the 'twisted molecule behind every twisted thought'. There are great problems with this simplistic picture. Certainly a functioning person with a body, including a brain, is required to show psychological malfunction. Also, few would now wish to accept a dualist account of human beings which asserted that minds were separate from bodies and that therefore the former could malfunction without any malfunction of the latter. Nevertheless this does not mean that all psychological, cognitive or mental state words actually signify particular brain states. It would be a mistake to seek exactly corresponding brain activity for every psychological or behavioural item. It is possible to provide examples of several words that one can predict do not indicate anything like brain activity. 'Intention' is one, as Wittgenstein (1958) has shown, also 'understanding' and 'meaning'. For example, if I am waiting at the train station for Aunt Sarah, will you eventually be able to PET scan my head and see the 'waiting'? In everyday discourse, brains are not examined in order to determine whether a person is waiting for something. Instead the criteria for the use of this word are what a person says about what they are doing, or simply the context of their behaviour. Some activities like these have no equivalent brain states, or are not connected to a brain activity at all. They are truly social – but of course one needs a brain to do them.

Thus many words we use to describe actions and feelings will not correlate in a straightforward way with brain states because they are a matter of social and contextual relevance, not of neurophysiology. Consequently, finding the correlates will not be easy. Moreover, when descriptions of behaviour in neurophysiological terms are found, one may predict that they are going to seem very strange to us, if not startlingly weird. Most will probably not be useful except in the specific contexts of psychiatric and neurological treatments. However, some might creep in, creating new language games, patterns and contexts of activity.

The concept of psychological malfunction is not therefore very helpful in clarifying the nature of mental disorder. It either dissolves into accounts based upon physiological malfunctions, or becomes a poetic metaphor whose validity depends upon a particular causal theory of mental disorder. Reznek's attempted resolution based upon monism fails due to the simple picture he draws of psychological events being caused by physiological events. He fails to appreciate that psychosocial terminology refers often to matters of social context (for example, that I look in the train timetable, then at my watch, and walk down to the station and look in a certain direction, after having received a letter several days ago announcing the arrival of my Aunt Sarah) rather than some supposed brain state (for example, my 'waiting'). In the example given, the 'waiting' is no more a brain state than the letter from Aunt Sarah. Of course this does not mean that in no case is psychological malfunction caused by brain malfunction. It does however mean that careful analysis and empirical evidence are required before such a statement can be made.

EMPIRICAL ARGUMENTS DENYING PHYSIOLOGICAL CAUSATION

There are some writers, from sociology and psychology backgrounds, who argue that there is no significant evidence for physiological disorder in mental illness. In order to make this case they generally ignore well-known physiological syndromes such as Alzheimer's disease, toxic confusional states, Wernicke's encephalopathy, Korsakoff psychosis and the like. Instead they make the syndrome of schizophrenia the battleground, possibly because if arguments for physiological causation fail here, then most of adult psychiatry and psychiatric treatment is called into question, for evidence supporting the physiological causation of other adult mental illnesses like the neuroses is weaker than that for schizophrenia. In addition, some (e.g. Scull 1979; Pilgrim 1990) heap scorn upon psychiatry for its inability to deliver the promised physiological mechanism of insanity, a promise first made at least a hundred years ago.

There are two frequently travelled lines of argument here. Coulter (1973) and Bentall *et al.* (1988) attack the reliability and validity of the concept of schizophrenia. Coulter (1973) additionally attacks the methodology of twin and genetic studies. A detailed review of the evidence would be beside the point here. By engaging in these arguments the critics have admitted the logical possibility that schizophrenia may exist as a distinct syndrome and have a physiological explanation. Psychiatry has come a long way since the 'pink spot' débâcle, when due to poor research methodology it was thought that a chemical identifying schizophrenia had been detected in urine. Diagnosis is more rigorous, untreated samples are used, non-invasive brain scanning technology has advanced and shows differences in brain functioning. The case for the physiological aetiology of schizophrenia may still not be proven, but is suggestive, and is supported by other lines of evidence (for example, drug-induced psychoses, the efficacy of neuroleptics, and parallels with toxic confusional states).

General Paralysis of the Insane (GPI, tertiary syphilis) is an oft-quoted example used to demonstrate that mental disorders first identified on psychosocial grounds can be eventually discovered to have physiological causes. Prior (1993) describes how this has acted as a paradigm case for psychiatry. Perhaps predictably, Szasz (1987) disagrees that GPI can perform this function. He argues that there was never any doubt of the physiological aetiology of GPI as its presentation was always accompanied by physical signs, whereas in currently identified mental illnesses such signs are absent. Unfortunately for Szasz, this is not entirely true. Differences in frontal lobe functioning have been shown in schizophrenia (e.g. Buchsbaum *et al.* 1992), and several physiological correlates of severe depression have been discovered (see review in Cowen and Wood 1991). Even if this was not the case, Szasz's argument does not logically undercut the possibility of physiological cause in disorders that currently do not display them. First, the presence of signs is often a function of the sophistication of techniques to detect them, and such technology is improving all the time. Second, it is possible to point to other psychiatric disorders, like Alzheimer's disease, which also had no reliably detectable physiological signs until recent advances in brain scanning technology (Burns 1993).

It should also be borne in mind that studies which are equally as methodologically rigorous are demonstrating the significance of psychosocial factors in the genesis and outcome of schizophrenia. Leff and Vaughn (1985) have started a broad research tradition showing that relapse can be prevented by psychosocial methods. Lewis *et al.* (1992) have demonstrated the aetiological importance of urban environments in schizophrenia, using a very large sample of Swedish young men. These and many other studies have convinced most people that schizophrenia has a combined physiological and social aetiology, although the precise nature of the interaction and the relative contributory weights of the various factors are fiercely disputed. Evidence on the aetiology of the neuroses is much more ambiguous, leaving even greater territory open to debate. These are matters for empirical study rather than logical debate, although the combination of social and physiological aetiologies will be further considered below.

A PRIORI ARGUMENTS DENYING PHYSIOLOGICAL CAUSATION

The above-mentioned attempts to rule out a physiological cause for schizophrenia are based upon empirical evidence. There have also been endeavours to rule out physiological causes for all mental disorder on a priori grounds. One of these has been covered and rejected in previous chapters; namely, the argument that all social categories are incommensurable with physiological categories. The case made above about 'waiting' and similar words might be held to support this position. However, it is not being suggested that all social categories have no specific neurophysiological correlates, just that some do not and that we should be careful to distinguish those from others. Take a contrasting example to that of 'waiting': seeing a ship on the horizon. This does not mean that our everyday use of the word 'see' refers to particular brain processes and states. We do not examine people's brains in order to determine if they see something; this is not the criterion for the use of the word. Instead the criteria for 'seeing' are entirely social. If I want to know if my friend has seen the ship too, I ask him and go by what he says. If I have any doubts I ask questions about what he has seen, like 'How many funnels does it have?' and if he answers correctly I know he has seen it too. In this sense, as described by Ryle (1949), 'seeing' is an achievement word. However, just because the criteria for the use of this word are social, or normative as some would wish to say, this does not mean that 'seeing' cannot correlate with neurophysiological events. In the case of 'seeing', we know some of this quite well. An image must be cast upon the retina, converted into a pattern of nerve impulses that travel down the optic nerve, etc. We even have some preliminary ideas about how those impulses are dealt with by receptive fields in the brain (Hubert and Wiesel, reviewed in Kalat 1986). Thus our socially defined categories of mental disorder, or of particular symptoms, may also correlate with brain events. Finding out if they do or do not is a matter for further empirical study. Whether such correlations justify judgements of abnormality, disorder or illness will be further considered at a later stage.

There is a second way in which logical doubt has been cast upon the rationality of the possibility that mental disorder is a physiological disturbance. This has been accomplished by Szasz (1972) with his television (TV) set analogy, which I shall quote in full:

> I hold that mental illness is a metaphorical disease; that, in other words, bodily illness stands in the same relation to mental illness as a defective television receiver stands to an objectionable television programme. To be sure, the word 'sick' is often used metaphorically. We call jokes 'sick', economies 'sick', sometimes even the whole world 'sick' – but only when we call minds 'sick' do we systematically mistake metaphor for fact; and send for the doctor to 'cure' the 'illness'. It's as if a television viewer were to send for a TV repairman because he disapproves of the programme he is watching.
>
> (Szasz 1972: 11)

This is a strong picture that appears to undermine the possibility that mental disorder can be a physiological disorder and be treated as one. Szasz's arguments about metaphor have already been disposed of, but his analogy of the TV set still appears to have some force. This is only so, however, because the analogy trades upon a hidden dualist conception of minds being separate entities from bodies. Once detailed questions are asked about the analogy this becomes apparent, for if the TV set represents the body, what can the objectionable programme stand for but the disordered mind. To make the analogy work, we must consider the mind to broadcast through the physical body, a position which is essentially dualist.

Szasz has depicted his analogy very carefully so that morally bad behaviour is opposed to physiological functioning (the objectionable programme versus the broken TV set). A more illuminating picture would be a fault at the transmitter versus a fault on the TV (the 'Do not adjust your set' message). To be sure, we do not call in the TV repairman here, but neither are we making a moral judgement; and because moral judgements are out of the way we are now more able to see the dualist implications of the analogy being made between TV sets and human beings. Lastly, the real target of the viewer's complaint in Szasz's analogy is not the TV set, but neither is it the source of the transmission (the transmitter). It is the programme-maker who has made an objectionable programme. If we are to apply this accurately to human–human interaction, then certainly one person can object to another's behaviour. A number of remedies are open to that person, from verbal complaint to calling the police, but one does not instantly telephone for the psychiatrist – that only happens in certain scenarios and contexts, such as irrationality, lack of motivational explanation, the presence of delusions, hallucinations, obsessional rituals, deep depressions or other abnormal behaviour.

COMPUTER ANALOGIES

Reznek (1991), too, tries to demolish Szasz's TV set analogy, but in so doing he creates a host of new problems by substantively changing the analogy. Instead of talking about objectionable programmes and TV sets, Reznek changes the analogy to computer software and hardware. Any fault or disorder can then be in the software (mental illness) or in the hardware (physical illness). The mistake in calling out the TV repairman is paralleled by the mistake in calling out the computer service engineer to remedy a corrupt executable file. Reznek then demolishes his straw man by indicating that software errors have a physical presence too within the microchips of the computer, and by suggesting that we cannot distinguish the difference between hardware and software in the human brain. Unfortunately, Reznek's demolition does not work, and as analogies between human brains and computers are becoming more prevalent this requires some further elaboration, for maybe disordered computers could be analogous to disordered brains.

Reznek fails to undermine the analogy, first because his argument from monism fails as previously demonstrated, for not all psychological or behavioural descriptors necessarily have brain state equivalents. Second, contrary to his assertion that the essence of both hardware and software is physical, and that a fault in either remains categorically the same kind of thing, it is possible to pursue a differential hardware and software analogy in talking about brain function (although it must be kept clear that this is an analogy or model, not a factual description). There are in fact two ways to pursue the analogy.

1 Hardware is taken to mean the genetic or nature component of human beings, and software the learned social and cultural component, in other words nurture. These can be distinguished by careful physiological study, research on psychological development and by twin studies, albeit with great difficulty in most cases. However, the force of Szasz's argument has now disappeared, for it is not necessarily ludicrous to treat socially-caused problems by physical means. The alleviation of panic attacks in cases of sudden grief or loss with anxiolytic drugs would be an example. Additionally, use of a software/hardware analogy here carries no particular benefits – it is just another way of talking that might be of use in the teaching of psychology to computer experts but not elsewhere.

2 Hardware is taken to mean the physical structure of brain neurons and their synapses, and software the pattern of discharging activity of those neurons. It is therefore possible that if this latter pattern of activity became disordered there might be no change in the hardware or physical structure of the neurons themselves in terms of axons and synapses. There would still be a physical difference, a different pattern of neuronal discharging, and yet as far as could be detected there would be no physical change. There might be undetectable dysfunctions of brain activity, undetectable for it is unlikely that harmless and non-invasive techniques for the detailed monitoring of whole brain activity will ever be developed. On the other hand, it is possible that after a period of time this different patterning of activity may have detectable secondary effects on brain structure – for example changes in neurotransmitter concentrations, synaptic connections or neuromodulator accumulations. This may not necessarily occur, however, leaving open the possibility that some mental disorders may remain functional rather than organic,

even if they have a real physiological basis. Thus the software/hardware analogy may here really assist with hypothesis generation and research about mental disorder. Nevertheless, this interpretation of the Szasz picture also fails to support his argument that it is ludicrous to treat physically the equivalent of a software error in the brain. It would be in fact a thoroughly reasonable response should this be the case.

Szasz cannot therefore convince us that the physiological treatment of mental illness is ludicrous or nonsensical. His TV set analogy will only work for the convinced dualist, and neither interpretation of the hardware/software analogy undermines the possibility of physiological abnormality as a cause of mental disorder.

BRAIN CORRELATES AND CAUSALITY

For the sake of argument, let us suppose that we do find a clear physiological correlate for a mental illness (whether this be Munchausen by proxy, schizophrenia, depression or whatever). This will never be able to mean that it is an abnormal physiological process, because normality in this case is not determined by structure or process in the brain, but by function. And with the brain, function will always have entirely social and psychological criteria. We will not be able to look at a brain and say: there, that particular neuronal/biochemical system is abnormal, it's obvious, anyone can see it. It might just as well be considered normal. It is the symptoms that are the criteria for deciding normality/health, and these are always psychosocial with mental illness. Otherwise I could say that having less than average intelligence was abnormal and an illness, and perhaps be able to point to a discernible difference in brain function. Difference or variation in brain activity does not by itself equal malfunction.

The function of other organs is defined by their structure. Kidneys produce urine. This is what they do, why they are structured the way they are. It is built into them, physically. Any defect or abnormality is always obvious and visible against that background. Similarly, blood and the circulatory system are constructed in such a way as to carry oxygen around the body, while the function of the digestive system can be read off from its structure. However, when we turn to the brain, matters are less clear because in many respects we can only determine the function of the brain from the actions of people, and not so readily from its structure. Because our brains are formed out of the interaction between our biochemical inheritance and our experience of life, who is ever going to be able to determine what physiological functioning is normal solely from anatomy and physiology? Abnormality is therefore only visible against a background of behaviour, not a background of physically- and structurally-determined function. The implication of these arguments is that neurophysiological investigation and the discovery of differences in brain biochemistry cannot logically place psychiatry on a natural science footing.

There is of course a gaping hole in this line of argument. How then do we account for gross brain abnormality, like the organic dementias? These are undoubtedly differences in brain function. They do indeed have behavioural criteria too, but nobody would wish to argue that they are not physiological diseases. In the light of this we can see that there might be a variety of kinds of detectable brain biochemical differences. Many of these we would accept without arguing as physiological diseases, but why? I would suggest that in the following cases any differences in brain function detected would be readily counted as diseases:

1 Where that difference is demonstrated to involve tissue destruction or damage.
2 Where that difference is similar to or parallels abnormalities which arise in other body systems and which are determined to be diseases in terms of their interruption of that body system's functions. One thinks here of parallels like peripheral nervous system degenerative diseases, tumours of other organs, etc.
3 Where there is disruption of known physiological events, or metabolic pathways which have been well investigated and described in other tissues.

So the question now becomes, do any mental illnesses other than the organic dementias meet any of the above criteria? Are we liable to be able to find specific tissue damage in the other mental illnesses? Interestingly, to demonstrate this we would have, at least theoretically, to provide for the event which damages the tissue (there are several different kinds of things we call illnesses, from tumours to infections – if we could show mental illness as one of these the case would be proved, and we would have to count it a disease). On the other hand, we are back on psychosocial territory if all we can point to is a small neurometabolic difference, or structural variation, without an obvious cause. For then we have no grounds other than psychosocial ones to say that this is abnormal in the sense of being a disease.

All this thinking can be directly applied to depression and neurotransmitter work. Even if shown that depression and 5HT transmission differences go together, this does not establish that it is a brain abnormality. We might just as well think of it as normal brain function variation, or a brain correlate/expression of a particular pattern of behaviour.

It strikes me that what I have done here is to give a more sophisticated statement of the argument that 'even if you find a brain correlate of depression, it doesn't mean that you have established that it is a physical disease'. Thinking, believing, normal mood, and reliability, all might have brain correlates, but that does not make them diseases. The biochemists' reply might be that diseases are obvious differences, but as I hope I have shown, when it comes to the brain they are not.

Additionally, how well correlated does the brain 'symptom' (neurotransmitter differences) have to be with the condition (depression) in order for the two to be considered identical? Or does the physiological criterion become a competing one, and if it is given precedence on what grounds can it be given that precedence? Precedence here would mean an alteration of psychiatric diagnostic categories to match the physiological criteria.

I am not here attempting to construct an argument about the cause of mental illness *per se*. Instead I am asking what evidence we would need to demonstrate that any one mental illness was a physiological disease like diabetes or cholera. My conclusion is that the simple demonstration of a physiological (and I would now add structural) difference in the brains of those people suffering from a defined mental disorder does not by itself prove that this is a disease. This is because difference in body system or organ functioning is not necessarily equivalent to disease. Such things may be abnormal without being pathological. In order for that brain difference to be accepted as a disease, it must be proven to be dysfunctional in physiological terms. To show this in the case of brain functioning would require proof of tissue damage or destruction, and/or parallels with other known diseases in other body systems, and/or disruption of known physiological events or metabolic pathways.

For example, 5HT function is known to be abnormal in depression.

Nevertheless, the question I would wish to raise is, does the phenomenon meet any or all of the three criteria I have described above? Can it be shown to be a dysfunction in physiological terms?

Aetiology is of course a related issue here, but it is not quite the same thing. Even if evidence can be offered that 5HT abnormalities meet some or all of the criteria above, the question of cause still remains open. Those abnormalities might be caused by a metabolic disorder or by psychosocial factors. Even structural changes may have psychosocial causes. Although I find it unlikely, it is quite logically possible that the brain atrophy of the frontal lobes that occurs in severe Obsessional Compulsive Disorder might be a consequence of a psychological disorder with a psychosocial aetiology.

Much similar doubt exists around all the other biological markers of depression. Those that have been identified (platelet and lymphocyte 5HT binding site density, cation transport, and cortisol secretion) are not present reliably enough for firm conclusions to be drawn. Even if they were, the same question arises: if they are direct evidence of biological abnormality or are themselves that abnormality, is such abnormality pathological or mere physiological variance?

DISEASE STATUS AND PHYSIOLOGICAL CAUSATION

Let me now turn to a consideration of aetiology and how it may have a bearing on the issue of deciding whether a mental illness should be considered to be a disease. The definitive establishment of physiological cause for a mental illness would, I believe, logically and conclusively establish the status of a mental illness as a pathophysiological disease. However, by definitive establishment, I would mean either (i) evidence for a dominant or recessive gene which fully explains the presence of the disease in the phenotype, or (ii) evidence of infection, injury, neoplasm or the like fully correlated to the start of the illness. Evidence of this strength is largely lacking. The hardest evidence we have, I believe, is for schizophrenia. Even there, genetic inheritance seems to account for only half of the incidence. However, together with other indicative evidence I would find this enough to conclude that schizophrenia should be regarded as a physiological disease. In the case of other mental disorders, we are still struggling with a multifactorial aetiological picture that is even less clear. Thus, as the question of aetiology remains open, so must the question of the nature of the phenomenon.

At this stage it may be suggested that the efficacy of physical treatments in psychiatry surely means that we are dealing with a pathophysiological phenomenon. Kramer (1993) uses this rationale to assert that shyness, distress, timidity and dysphoria are biologically determined and dysfunctional because they respond to treatment with Prozac. However, the efficacy of physical treatment does not logically establish either physical aetiology or the nature of the phenomenon as pathophysiological. Suppose I were in a numbing state of shock following a narrow escape from death in a car crash. The fact that a dose of diazepam would calm me down in no way indicates that I have been suffering from a physiological disease. In a similar way, the efficacy of neuroleptics in schizophrenia (by itself) carries absolutely no logical implications about the nature or cause of schizophrenia.

On the other hand, even if evidence causes us to conclude that a mental disorder is a psychosocial phenomenon, that does not mean nothing physiological is happening in the brain. After all, one does need a brain to be depressed. It is an interesting question to ask exactly what is going on in the brain that correlates with depression. Such work may lead to new physiological methods of helping the person who is very depressed, as well as to our understanding other functions and systems of the brain. All this I agree with and I am also excited by the possibilities, but the question of whether these phenomena are pathophysiological or not is of great moment. Either way, it affects the social and moral status of those who suffer them. We need to be sure before issuing conclusive declarations, because these are consequential decisions, particularly in the case of depression, for it carries so many implications about the nature and value of human suffering, loss, grief, failure and achievement.

PHYSIOLOGICAL HYPOTHESIS GENERATION

Not only are there problems in determining whether variants of brain functioning are malfunctions or not. Often the models of brain dysfunction used by researchers are crude and simplistic. Theories of schizophrenia or affective psychosis based upon speculated variations in neurotransmitter concentrations are a case in point. It has already been described above how it is possible that the brain might produce undetectable malfunctions of activity that pass without physical trace. The picture of dopamine synapse system fault in schizophrenia may simply be very wrong. It may be there is one very small single point of brain failure that sets in motion a whole series of imbalances, of which the dopamine synapse system is just one. Or neuroleptic drugs may just act like putting a wet blanket on top of the fire, with the heart of the fire still burning away underneath, the real cause being elsewhere. Perhaps schizophrenia is a whole brain dysfunctional pattern, rather like an epileptic fit. What if once you lapse into this state, it is hard to get out, and makes it more easy to lapse into again? This would mean that all single system research is a waste of time, because the dysfunction is in the way the whole brain works as a unit. What is more, this would mean that we will not understand the physiology of schizophrenia until we understand normal whole brain functioning. We need to open up the range of possible pictures for ourselves in order to facilitate research.

BIOPSYCHOSOCIAL AETIOLOGICAL ACCOUNTS

Reference has been made earlier to the possibility of combined physiological and social causes for some mental disorders. This initially appears to be quite a simple idea, but it becomes rather more complex when considered in detail for social causative accounts enter into everything about human beings – even into being struck by lightening (if I hadn't gone for that walk . . .), or in genetic diseases (the choice to have a child, the timing of conception, the choice of partner . . .). Cholera epidemics are another example. One can consider that they are caused by a particularly virulent variety of bacteria, or by war and a consequent lack of clean water. These are not new facts, but have long been recognised by epidemiologists.

The shape and content of a causal account depends upon the purposes of the person seeking it. Suppose I catch influenza. Is this because I have breathed in a droplet containing the virus which has now entered some of my body cells and started to replicate? Or is it because I failed to get my flu jab? Or because Fred came into work when he was ill and I caught it? Or was it because we are all threatened with redundancy and so Fred came in and therefore I caught it? Or was the cause that someone travelled back from a foreign country with the new mutation of the virus? Or was it that I had not been eating properly and taking enough rest so that my immunity was suppressed?

Any or all of these causal explanations may be equally as valid.

None of these explanations has priority over others. The microbiological, genetic or physics explanations are still explanations for particular purposes. They have no priority as explanation – they are not logically or rationally more perfect, fuller, more true, nor do they necessarily make all other explanations false. The advantage they have is that sometimes they provide leverage/control over events by physical means and manipulations.

The pebble you throw when playing ducks and drakes can be talked about solely in terms of forces acting according to the set laws of Newtonian physics. That is what caused the pebble to move in the way it did. On the other hand the reason why the pebble skipped across the water is because you threw it, and maybe you threw it to entertain your child whom you were taking for a walk. The two causal accounts overlap, but only in places. They are not entirely commensurable or parallel. You cannot lay them side by side and say this equals this, but both accounts have their place. They are used for different purposes.

However, starting from the position of a health professional who wants to treat, cure or prevent disease, understanding of the physiological cause might be the most essential step towards achieving that goal. Control, treatment, alleviation of suffering, cure and prevention are the matters that determine for health professionals the relevance of causal accounts. Even here though, the socio-environmental factors are important, but only those which exhibit a regular pattern rather than those which are incidental. For example, a decision to take more exercise might be purely incidental to being struck by lightening, but that that exercise is taken by walking in the park during thunderstorms would not.

It is tempting to make a distinction between reasons and causes, as do Johnston (1989) and others. If this distinction can be clearly made, then we can talk about people acting because of the reasons they have, whereas causal accounts can only be given for inanimate objects. The division so produced is used to justify non-positivist views of knowledge and research in the social sciences – people are not caused to act in certain ways, therefore law-like statements cannot be made about social behaviour and the social sciences will never be equivalent to the natural sciences where causal accounts are valid. Avoidance of the language of 'cause' applied to human beings also side-steps difficulties in matching a deterministic picture of people with our language of options, choices and free will. This does not mean, however, that regularities in social behaviour cannot

be described, and the admission of such accounts does not constitute a surrender to positivism. These regularities of conduct and
practice are the nuts and bolts of social interaction and language,
but they do not have to be thought of as law-like causal forces.

Thus the social cannot be subtracted from aetiological accounts
of illness. It remains an important part of causal accounts of everything, even those diseases which are genetic, infectious, or otherwise
capable of being characterised. This is recognised as a reality everywhere from public health and health promotion to epidemiology.
Biological accounts are neither dominant, nor always the most
important. Neither does the existence of such explanatory accounts
determine whether something is accounted a disease/illness or not,
although it may be a factor, perhaps even occasionally the dominant
one. Natural science explanations of illnesses are therefore never
complete by themselves.

That this is so poses particular problems for thinking about the
cause of mental disorder. In psychiatry this becomes more confused
because physiological accounts are often not available, or are
unknown, or possibly even absent. All explanations apart from the
incidental (or perhaps even that too) are counted in as possibly of
significance. Therefore all psychosocial accounts have a blanket
equivalency, except for those few based on empirical study. The only
competitor to these is natural science guesswork based upon small
quantities of tentative indicative evidence. In this position it is hard
to distinguish the relevant explanations (ones which expose the
regularities contributing to the condition) from the merely incidental. Therefore my depression might well be due to departmental
overwork, not just from the point of view of my colleagues but also
from the point of view of the psychiatrist.

A further complicating facet of the problem is that the social and the
physiological intricately interact with each other. It is possible to
regard stressful events and childhood trauma as actual tissue-
damaging events, almost exactly parallel to the damage left in the wake
of an infection or the structural damage caused by an infarct or head
injury. Plentiful evidence indicates that the placebo effect operates in
schizophrenia, major depression and in physical illnesses, underlining
the fact that social and psychological factors operate to change physiology. Kleinman (1988) speculates that powerful symbolic healing
ceremonies in other cultures induce brain changes that counteract
depression. These moves may have the potential to remove some
mental illness back into the neurophysiological disorder category.

Further reflection leads to the conclusion that the functioning of nervous tissue both affects and makes possible all social interaction all the time. We should therefore be wary of using the word 'multi-factorial' to gloss over these complex issues. If we are ever to produce full causal accounts of what we consider to be mental illnesses, it will be necessary to describe this complex interaction of the interpersonal and the physiological, in detail and over time. Whether we will then be able, or still wish, to make efforts to change the causal patterns that emerge remains to be seen.

SOCIOBIOLOGICAL INFLUENCES

There is a further vector through which physiology might affect mental disorder. Although the argument for strong deviancy theory, that societal response and rejection is causative of mental disorder, has been countered, it is undoubtedly true that social processes are important in the moulding of the presentation and outcome of psychiatric illness. This is supported by the form and content distinction which can be validly made during cross-cultural comparison of mental disorder. It is also supported by historical data showing that differing responses to mental disorder in differing ages influenced the behaviour of the mentally ill. Therefore if the social response to mental disorder, in particular the stigmatisation and rejection of the mentally ill, was itself biologically determined, then it could be said that physiology was having a significant and indirect influence on the presentation, course and outcome of mental disorder. I have argued previously that the potential for stigmatisation of the mentally ill is derived from three factors: orderly social behaviour, the tendency of human beings to form groups, and natural fearful responses to unpredictable and strange behaviour on the part of others. However, it is of course also possible that these factors and the consequent stigmatisation process are instinctual and therefore biologically determined.

Szasz (1971) indicates he believes this might be the case with his story of the painted bird. Roughly paraphrased the story goes like this: one day a bird is captured from a flock, its captors paint it a different colour, release it, and it is rejected and pecked to death by the flock because of its difference. Szasz therefore challenges us to ask on what grounds we could confidently assert that the rejection of the mentally ill is a similar, natural, biologically determined process.

Review of the sociobiological literature (e.g. Gribbin and Gribbin 1988; Dawkins 1989; Ruse 1979; Wilson 1978; Kitcher 1985) shows that three components are used to construct arguments that certain behaviours are instinctual as opposed to learned or cultural. These are universality, provision of an animal example, and a theory linking the behaviour to a survival advantage. We will consider each in turn.

1 *Universality*. Rejection and exclusion of the mentally ill, sometimes mistreatment, do appear to be fairly, although not completely, universal phenomena. But simple evidence of a continuously present tendency does not establish this as a biological drive, force or motivator. Human beings do lots of things in common, for example, talk, eat, write books, tell stories, tell lies and work. These cannot all be considered the outcome of instincts. Hilgard *et al.* (1979) describe how the theory of instincts was dropped by psychology for this reason, for eventually it applied to everything and explained nothing. So although stigmatisation is fairly universal, this does not establish definitively that it is instinctual or biologically determined.

2 *Animal example*. The sociobiologists provide a profusion of examples of animal social behaviour which they use to illuminate similar human behaviour. However, none of those examples I have been able to locate refer to any group of animals rejecting members because of differences in appearance or behaviour. There does not appear to be an animal paradigm of stigmatisation of the mentally ill. Even if there was, by itself a similarity or parallel would not prove identical cause. Animals and men might behave in a particular way that seems the same but actually has different rationales or causes. In addition, Kitcher (1985) shows that many of the examples used by the sociobiologists trade upon a covert anthropomorphism; descriptions of animal behaviour are made first with human social terminology which imports with it certain suppositions and assumptions which may not be valid. Kitcher is particularly scathing and effective in demolishing the sociobiologists' manipulation of such terms as monogamy and polygyny. Therefore if an animal example was provided, we would have to be very careful that that example really paralleled the human social process of stigmatisation, rather than just appearing to do so. Even in Szasz's fable the

parallel is not accurate, for human beings do not all immediately attack a member whose appearance changes, killing them.

3   *Survival theory*. The above two factors are usually coupled with a theory that attempts to explain how the behaviour helps survival. Dawkins' (1989) enhancement that the unit of selection is the gene allows tentative theoretical explanations of altruism based on kin selection. The concept of evolutionary stable strategies in animal social behaviour, developed by Maynard Smith (1988), also enables more complex theories to be constructed. However, nothing seems to explain the survival advantage of the stigmatisation of the mentally ill. If any difference led to rejection by the society, be it animal or human, then all evolution would grind to a halt. Evolution is based upon the continuous production of differences, some of which prove to be of survival advantage. A sociobiological position on stigmatisation could be defended by arguing that only certain changes are rejected, not those which are advantageous, but this assumes the unlikely idea that both animals and people carry out a survival calculus before reacting.

By themselves each of the arguments above is fairly weak. Together they do make a stronger picture, if the evidence for universality is good, if the tendency to anthropomorphism is avoided and if the survival theory makes sense. None of these criteria is met for that behaviour which we call stigmatisation of the mentally ill. For other behaviours of human beings, only those clearly biological, for example eating and drinking, cannot be denied to be of biological origin. However, these too are strongly psychosocially mediated, for people can wait a long time to eat, and eating behaviour is intricately enmeshed with social routines. For those behaviours in which biological necessity is not directly apparent, alternative explanations are often possible or available. Even for paradigm cases like incest taboos, alternative social explanations are possible. Therefore for these behavioural items the question remains open and is likely to remain so.

This is not to say that human beings and their societies are unconstrained by their physiological nature. Hunger, tiredness, the need for warmth/shelter, how fast one can run, having only two hands, the necessity to breathe, death, birth and childhood all constrain, set boundaries or give direction to human activities. However, for human beings the physiological cannot be abstracted or separated from the psychosocial. There is no action, no movement, uncontaminated by language, the way we talk about it, act towards it, after it, respond to it, prepare for it, see it and intend it. What it is is nothing until socially contexted – just a series of movements, a chemistry, actions and reactions, mass gravity and electrons, without meaning. The physiological by itself explains little about human behaviour.

PHYSIOLOGICAL EXPLANATIONS AND PROFESSIONAL LEGITIMACY

There are those who assert that physiological aetiological models of mental disorder are supported by psychiatrists in order to legitimate their profession and expand its influence. This charge is parallel to the accusation that psychiatrists are expanding the diagnostic lexicon in order to increase their earnings, and Scull's (1989) account of the rise of psychiatry in the nineteenth century which gives priority to causal accounts utilising the assumption that psychiatrists were at all times seeking more power and legitimacy. These arguments have been examined in previous chapters and found to be one-sided.

The question whether physiological aetiology does legitimate medical psychiatry has not, however, received inspection here, but is treated at length elsewhere (Bowers 1991). In that work I proposed that the causal chain of 'physiological cause, leading to physical treatment, leading to treatment by doctors' was not robust when subjected to detailed consideration. Physiological cause, as I have shown above, is only separable from psychosocial causes for particular purposes and does not constitute a full explanation of mental disorder. Even in cases when physiological cause is at its most strong, like Alzheimer's disease, much treatment and rehabilitation is psychosocial rather than physical. Also, in stress responses which are clearly social in origin, physical treatment is sometimes appropriate. The connection of physiological cause to physical treatment is not as strong as cursory inspection suggests. Lastly, in cases when physiological cause is established and physical treatment appropriate, there is no necessity that the treatment should be carried out by the medical profession. Only insofar as the medical profession has complete control over the delivery of physical treatment does physiological aetiology lend some legitimacy to their activities.

Other professions within psychiatry, not just the medical, have sought to advance their professional position by arguing for particular conceptions of mental disorder. For example, Bentall (1991) seeks to advance the power of psychologists based upon a cognitive conception of mental disorder. Again, this argument gives legitimacy to psychologists only insofar as they have full control over the delivery of cognitive therapies. Thus discussion about the nature of mental illness can readily be submerged into professional power battles, a fact that does not help us to arrive at an objective point of view. Moreover, many are tempted to believe that the connection between a particular point of view on mental disorder and the legitimacy of a profession is a necessary one. In fact the connection is socially contingent. A new occupational group could be launched tomorrow and given the training and responsibility for physical treatment of the mentally ill. It might have nothing to do with the medical profession. Physiological cause and physiological treatment do not logically force treatment by doctors.

SUMMARY

In this chapter I have explored the logic of physiological explanations in psychiatry. It has been shown that psychological abnormalities cannot be straightforwardly translated into physiological abnormalities. Even when physiological differences exist in the brains of those we call mentally ill, several additional criteria will need to be met before these can be considered malfunctions. It remains a possibility that for many mental illnesses this evidence will never be attainable. As very few determinations of mental illness are made on physiological grounds, currently decisions as to whether a behaviour is mental illness or not is made on political and moral grounds. It is a social issue, one for decision by people on the basis of pros and cons, utilitarian assessments of consequences, deontological rules and the like. In the absence of physiological criteria, psychiatrists and other professionals have little specific expertise to offer in the making of this decision. I have shown in addition that physiological accounts of cause in mental illness are always partial, and relevant only for a restricted number of purposes. Nevertheless, physiological aetiology for mental disorder cannot be ruled out on logical grounds.

Chapter 10

Social construct

Many papers and books written from the varied backgrounds of deviancy, transcultural or historical psychiatry reach a common conclusion which is summed up in the phrase 'therefore mental illness is a social construction'. This deduction is usually made upon the basis of social process effects upon the generation and development of mental illness, or evidence for the variability of mental illness across cultures or epochs. Alternatively, the same conclusion is reached by those who argue from first principles that all illness is socially defined, mental illness included. Having considered how these ideas are applied in the varying realms of the sociology of deviance, transcultural psychiatry, the history of psychiatry, psychiatric practice and reflection, we are now in a position to say in exactly what ways this statement is correct or incorrect.

A clear appreciation of the meaning this conclusion might hold does contain certain implications for the institution of psychiatry. While these are by no means as radical as some of the anti-psychiatric writings may suggest, they are nevertheless important pointers to areas which require further reflection and possible change. Conversely, much of the argument in this book supports the legitimacy, rationality and morality of psychiatric practice. Indeed it is a major weakness of the literature considered in this book that, in the main, it fails to describe how psychiatry should change on the basis of its conclusions, or to consider the effects any such changes might have upon psychiatric service users.

I make no apology for calling some of the literature considered in this book anti-psychiatric, although perhaps it would be better to describe it as critical of psychiatry. Many may have been hoping that what had been previously characterised as 'anti-psychiatry' had slipped into the past and could now be left behind. Unfortunately, many of the ideas that reared their heads under this title in the 1960s and 1970s not only had a rather lengthy academic history, but continue to crop up in renewed forms in sociological, anthropological and historical writings about psychiatry. These concepts and arguments have not gone away at all, as they continue to fuel critiques of psychiatry from a whole variety of sources. Effective rebuttal of these critiques depends not on arguments about the interpretation of empirical data, but upon achieving clarity about what we already know and are able to say. When correctly understood, the phrase 'therefore mental illness is a social construction' is neither wholly incorrect nor a criticism of the best in psychiatric practice. In some ways it might be a challenging source of research hypotheses and moral reflection. With this in mind, we will first consider how this phrase can be wrongly interpreted.

PHYSIOLOGICAL CAUSE A POSSIBILITY

Arguments covered repeatedly in previous chapters show that no amount of evidence regarding social forces, factors or definitions in mental illness rules out the possibility of physiological cause. Even if mental illness is determined by wholly social criteria, this does not mean that those social criteria are incommensurable with physiological ones. This is straightforwardly demonstrated by known cases of brain disease like GPI, Alzheimer's disease and the like. It is in any case a deduction based upon a false picture of the relationship of talk about social actions and talk about human physiology. The diagnostic enterprise in psychiatry, or any other attempted classification of psychiatric disorder, is as we have seen, also logically legitimate. It should not however be seen as implying a physiological cause to all the items it so classifies.

Neither can 'socially constructed' mean determined by social rules, moral judgements or conventions. This is to give mental illness the same ontological status as bad manners, making it a matter entirely socially, historically and culturally relative. In fact, as I have shown previously, not only are there many categories and varieties of socially made rules and conventions, but also mental illness does not fit a rule-breaking picture properly. In addition, there exists considerable evidence for both cross-cultural and transhistorical continuity for mental disorder. In the course of struggling to demonstrate or exaggerate that social relativity does exist, a number of false interpretations of language or manipulated mistranslations are made. Within the historical field, evidence for comparable relativity is drawn from speculation based upon historical generalised depictions of madness, similarities between the institution of psychiatry and witchcraft trials which simply do not exist on close inspection, and changes in numbers of patients with an accompanying unsubstantiated claim that conceptions of insanity also changed.

Linked to the above misconceptions about the social construction of mental illness are a number of false conclusions. Most prominent among these is the idea that mental illness could be defined, treated and dealt with other than it is. Although there is a grain of truth here, there is also much chaff to be separated before it can be discovered. All human activities have to fit around the obdurate characteristics of the natural world. Insofar as mental illnesses have or may have physiological causes to some degree, then human responses must fit around these realities. In addition, some things, even though social, cannot be otherwise dealt with, for there are universal social characteristics dictated by the nature of life and the necessities of social interaction. Moreover, there are only limited numbers of ways to cope with and solve certain problems like the management of those we call mentally ill. Thus even if the mentally ill could in some cases be conceived of otherwise, or dealt with otherwise (and this is the grain of truth of the argument), there are good reasons why they are cared for as they are. This is why those scholars who mount this challenge seldom or never provide the detail of what type of institutions they believe should replace psychiatry.

To the degree that physiological causation in mental illness is not established, scholars like Szasz are perfectly entitled to argue that we should dispense with the term 'mental illness', and treat those currently so considered in a radically different way. However, Szasz cannot derive this from his propositions about the metaphorical use of the term 'mental illness'. These assertions are not borne out by the way we talk, and Szasz has been shown to be seriously confused about the identifying criteria of metaphorical speech. He is not actually exposing the logic of our talk, but is instead making a covert moral or political argument, and should be challenged to say in precisely what way he wants psychiatry to change, and be invited to consider the possible consequences. The arguments of Szasz in this area illustrate that there is considerable confusion between theoretical/philosophical issues and moral/political ones. The former cannot be used to force conclusions in the latter domain, although the clarity provided by good theoretical discussion can sometimes make the choices so clear that it appears to do so. In any case, much critical writing in this area so far has amplified rather than minimised our puzzlement.

The confusion between the theoretical and the moral is nowhere more apparent than in those discussions about professional power, generally the power of psychiatrists. Conclusions about the nature of mental illness reached on the basis of flimsy theoretical arguments are used either to undercut the legitimacy of psychiatry *in toto*, to justify exercises in academic infiltration (for example of anthropologists into psychiatry), or to legitimise the power of a specific professional group. The charge that 'mental illness is a social construct' has been just as much misused in this sense as the rather older claim that mental illness is a brain disease. Not only do these professional conflicts provide strong motivations to bias in assessment of the arguments, but they also hold less force than is commonly credited to them. Even worse happens when statements about the nature of mental illness are linked to one-sided accounts of professional groupings that talk solely about self-interest and never about service to humanity, as does Scull (1979) in his historical account of the rise of psychiatry. The danger here is that we reject the theoretical premise not because it is faulty, but because it is made to appear to have justified professional power-building at the expense of the mentally ill.

POSITIVISM AND THE SOCIAL SCIENCES

A further common mistaken line of argument starts with the conclusion that positivistic study of humanity is both misconceived and impossible. It goes on from there to argue that if mental illness is socially constructed then psychiatry can never be a scientific study. Once again there is some truth here that needs to be carefully disentangled. First, to the degree that physiological cause for mental illness can be established, then law-like natural science investigations are entirely appropriate. Indeed they are appropriate in order purely to discover whether physiological causes can be determined. Even if they cannot, physiological study of the correlates of mental illness may provide many ways of ameliorating suffering or exercising a control over the phenomena that we do not now have. Second, it must be asked what constitutes a science. If being a science means attaining objective accounts from which all human agency is removed and laws derived, then yes, the argument may hold. But if science means rational, systematic action based upon the maximum achievable objectivity, then it is possible in the field of psychiatry as it is in other human endeavours. In the absence of evidence about physiological causation we are not absolved from the requirement of trying to determine the consequences of treatments, different forms of service organisation, outcomes, effectiveness and efficiency. It would be a failure of trust if we abandoned the attempt to plan and test services purely because such investigation did not meet the canons of natural science.

Similar arguments are made in some cross-cultural psychiatric work, in particular that emanating from radical social anthropologists. These scholars argue that the nature of the self is differentially socially constructed across cultures, and draw the conclusion that therefore mental illness is also substantively different. They then proceed to rule out the possibility of empirical comparisons of mental disorder across cultural boundaries in order to tease out the social from the universal or physiological components. Instead they recommend a study policy of detailed ethnography and exposition, so that wholly different conceptions of mental illness can be displayed, and our own categories questioned. Coupled with misconceptions about the difficulties of translation originating with Whorf, who argued that language determines thought, experience and metaphysics, the radical social anthropologists appear to have produced a strong case for psychiatric cultural relativity. However, these arguments are based upon a misunderstanding of language that gives too much weight to differences of names and grammar, and too little to the ways in which they are used in everyday life. Once a vocabulary and grammar are located in the everyday life of a community it is possible to see that straightforward translation and understanding are possible. If the validity of the form (culture-free) and content (culture-determined) distinction is allowed for symptoms of mental illness, then it is clear that cross-cultural comparisons can be systematically made. 'Socially constructed' does not therefore mean that mental illness is wholly different in dissimilar cultures.

Neither can 'socially constructed' be interpreted as meaning that mental illness is in some way socially functional. The high importance given to secrecy and confidentiality in psychiatric practice means that psychiatry does not provide public occasions for the ventilation of emotion or anger. Although psychiatry may have the effect in some places and on some occasions of explaining away what may be a moral or political problem, this is not the overt aim of professionals or patients. As activities can only logically have functions in relation to the purposes of the participants, then this is not the function of psychiatry either. Nor does psychiatry ensure that the mentally ill take the blame for social problems, as it takes only a moment's reflection to realise that today's social problems are not laid at the door of the mentally ill at all. Psychiatry could, of course, be politically exploited in this way – but this still does not make such exploitation the social function of psychiatry. The only way to determine the function of psychiatry is to look at the everyday reasoning and purposes of those engaged in making it work. Then it can be seen that psychiatry is first and foremost a struggle to provide relief from suffering and distress, and to manage in a humane way those who suffer from mental illness.

LANGUAGE AND SOCIAL CONSTRUCTION

There are however ways in which the phrase 'mental illness is a social construction' makes perfect sense. The most superficial, although frequently misunderstood, is that it is named by human beings, embedded in language and therefore through and through a social construction. It is the last part of this argument that leads to much confusion. The failure here is to appreciate properly the implications of being named or otherwise identified by people. For in this sense all the material world is socially constructed, from stars to the soil upon which we stand. One of the implications of the fact that all language socially constructs the world is again that we could choose to distinguish and talk about things differently. If we so wished, or had not thought of it, we could not make distinctions between planets and stars, or between sand and clay. This would not change the world one jot, but it would alter the utility of our language and our ability to carry out astronomy or agronomy. The language of psychiatry is precisely parallel here, and the crucial issue is not whether mental illness is socially constructed in this sense, but how well our language matches the realities of the world, and what we can do effectively with the tools it provides.

Another way that 'socially constructed' in relation to mental illness can be construed is that it is significantly socially influenced. That is, mental illness is modified by the beliefs and actions of the sufferers and those around them. This is not a proposition with which one would want to argue, as it is so obviously correct. How the sufferers interpret their experience, what they call it, how they respond to it, to whom the problem is taken, within what organisational context, how the general public respond to problems of this nature formally and informally – all these have a tremendous impact upon the shape, course and outcome of what we call a mental illness. It is this variation which is illustrated by transcultural, some historical and most sociological psychiatric studies. This does not imply, however, that there are no obdurate phenomena here, and that all is created by the social process. Transhistorical and transcultural continuity exist to such a degree as to make this most unlikely. In any case, such attempts to turn the sufferers of mental illness into the equivalent of 'innocent victims' of social processes fail to account for human choice and agency on the part of the sufferer, turning them into actors putting on a play at the behest of social responses.

Perhaps the most important way that mental illness can be said to be socially constructed is that it is identified and determined by social criteria. Mental illness is exhibited by actions and behaviour. Only in very few cases are physiological criteria actually used. Even in cases where physiological difference is or may be present, judgements of abnormality are made on the basis of behaviour. As I have argued previously, the function of most organs of the body can be read off from their structure and activity, with dysfunction clearly visible against that background. For much of the brain, however, structure and function can only be determined from social activity. Therefore in the absence of evidence for structural deterioration in one form or another, simple differences in brain chemistry are only physiological correlates of behaviour. Determinations of mental illness are still made on social grounds, and are thus moral matters which are decided, not physiological malfunctions which have been discovered. It is this that carries important implications for society's relationship to psychiatry.

This does not mean that mental illness is or can be anything at all. It is a quite specific phenomenon identified by certain family resemblances: irrational inexplicable behaviour, evident loss of control, reduced responsibility for actions, incapacitation, suffering, disruptive behaviour, etc. A body of people with these cross-cutting resemblances are identifiable in all cultures and ages. They are universally treated as ill and sent to healers, and they are universally stigmatised. Mental illness may be shaped in various ways by social processes, it may be determined on social criteria, and there may be borderline cases coupled with doubts as to what is to be included or not; nevertheless, there exists an unyielding core which seems to be an inextricable part of the human experience for many, and which has always accompanied the society of man wherever he has made his home.

CONSEQUENCES FOR PSYCHIATRY

There are several implications to be found here for academic psychiatric study, research and professional education. Some similar attempts to clarify or define mental illness have closed with the plea that there should be more research attention given to psychosocial factors (Eisenberg 1988; Engel 1977; Kleinman 1988). Psychosocial research does get carried out, so it is unclear whether these pleas are efforts to persuade those who have extreme organicist views about the causation of mental illness, or whether they are efforts to influence the politics of research funding and academic appointments. However, although the conclusions reached in this book underline the legitimacy of psychosocial research, they by no means imply that psychosocial research is going to be the most productive in finding ways of helping those suffering from mental illnesses. This remains to be seen. Recommendations on the distribution of research funding cannot therefore be made on these grounds. It should also be remembered that extreme points of view are fruitful generators of research hypotheses, and provide strong motivation to test them. As to matters relating to academic appointments, the distribution of these among those with particular research interests is rightly related to the production of meaningful research, peer evaluation and consensus. As such they are matters for academic departments and professional groupings to determine.

In professional education, particularly of psychiatric nurses and social workers, it can be confidently recommended that labelling and deviancy theory should be dropped from curricula. It has been shown that this approach is seriously confused and in many respects simply wrong. Mental illness is not helpfully seen as social rule breaking. Aetiological theorising based upon this line of argument, far from emphasising the humanity of the mentally ill, actually portrays them as passive responders in the face of social pressures. In addition, labelling theory is commonly mixed up with challenges to diagnostic systems in psychiatry, and to interprofessional conflicts. These arguments at times have a real negative effect upon the care of those with serious mental disorders. Also, there is a very real moral argument to be made about the depersonalisation of psychiatric patients by certain uses of diagnostic tags. This argument could be clarified if it could be separated from the labelling/deviancy debate and shown to be a completely different issue.

It is a shame that the sociological study of mental illness appears to have entered a cul-de-sac with the labelling and deviancy topic. Useful and important research on psychosocial processes and factors in mental illness has been taken over by mainstream psychiatric researchers, often from professional backgrounds. Large research traditions on psychosocial factors in the course of schizophrenia, or life events and neurosis, have been generated and maintained mostly by psychiatrists and psychologists, but not by sociologists. If the sociology of mental illness is to be reborn, this is the type of research within which their expertise is needed. The other area in which sociological study can be so useful is in the political and moral critique of psychiatry. Challenging interpretations of psychiatric practice which identify interest groups, or possible exploitative practice, are good remedies to complacency and act as spurs to political discussion and action. Aetiological theorising in psychiatry and determinations of the boundaries of practice both commonly carry political implications, and are therefore matters for widespread debate.

Academic psychiatry could usefully exercise a little more humility. Vast vistas of ambiguity and ignorance about aetiology and treatment exist. It would seem that psychiatry deals with a wide variety of differing phenomena, some of which are physiological diseases and others which may be of a completely different order. Nearly all the matters with which psychiatry deals are determined by social criteria which are themselves matters of social consensus. Psychiatry exists therefore to serve society, not to dictate to it from a position of expertise which is in most cases in reality very restricted. Two examples will serve to illustrate this point.

In cases of psychopathy, diagnosis is made solely upon the basis of conduct. There are no known physiological tests or criteria – they are wholly socially determined. Amoral conduct which is impulsive and takes no account of consequences and is unaccompanied by any signs of guilt are commonly taken to be indicators of psychopathy. Such behaviour appears to the ordinary person irrational, without sensible motivational reason, a characteristic that leads to the troubles of psychopathy being accounted matters for psychiatry to deal with. Should a person like this commit a serious criminal act, be caught and plead insanity, he is likely to be assessed by a psychiatrist as suffering from a psychopathic disorder. However, the psychiatrist who makes this judgement has no expert basis on which he can make his decision. He has no sophisticated test by which he can determine someone who is psychopathic from another person who is not. Society has already decided to account for the actions of the psychopath in this way, and all the psychiatrist does is provide a smoke-screen to the place where the real decision is made. The question being asked by the court – does this person suffer from a mental disorder? – hides the real question: should we treat people who do these things in this way as suffering from a mental disorder? Psychiatry should make it clear in this situation that when they give an answer to the former question, it depends upon the latter question as already being agreed and answered. The limited expertise of psychiatry can then become visible: by inter- viewing the defendant they are able to make a judgement as to how similar the person is to other people who have previously been accounted by psychiatry as suffering psychopathic disorder. If these distinctions are not made clear, psychiatrists appear to be the possessors of specific expertise that allows them to identify an entity, mental disorder, in others when no one else can. In addition, society at large loses its consciousness of the choices it has in whether to account a phenomenon as mental illness or not.

The second example is that of the boundary that needs to be drawn between normal distress, and anxiety/depression as a mental illness. Currently, in everyday life, whether a distressed person is referred to a psychiatric professional depends upon whether they choose to go and see their GP, whether they show their distress, whether the GP favours psychiatric referrals, and other similar factors (Goldberg and Huxley 1980). In parallel with this, system- atic diagnostic scaling techniques have been developed whose criteria are derived from previous psychiatric practice and general social judgements, with finer distinctions about the precise bound- aries of 'caseness' being made largely on the basis of the requirements of the research undertaken at the time. The distinction between who is or is not suffering a mental disorder or normal distress is therefore made on the basis of criteria drawn up by psychiatric researchers, as well as on the basis of criteria generated by describing existing psychiatric patients. These scales are then taken out into everyday practice and used by some GPs and others to determine who should be referred to psychiatry. Once again a decision that belongs to society at large has been obscured rather than subjected to widespread debate. To state that criteria for who is or is not a psychiatric case have been determined by describing existing cases does not give the criteria objectivity. Instead this hides the fact that decisions on the criteria for these distinctions are not being taken at all, and that psychiatric practice continues to be based on a combination of tradition and contingency. These criteria have also been drawn up, in part, by a small band of people whose motivation was research rather than the prescription of social policy. These distinctions are morally crucial, for if people who are possibly normally distressed due to life factors and events are treated as sufferers of mental disorder, then their essential humanity and the meaningful nature of their life is to a degree eroded. This is the threat posed by Kramer's (1993) eulogy of Prozac consumption: the tie between cause and effect, life choice and consequent feelings, is weakened, and we are made less human as a result. Vice versa, a psychotically depressed person who believes his bowels are blocked and thinks he is responsible for the ills of the world, may be made worse if forced to own his depression, rather than helped.

In this field, cross-cultural psychiatric studies show that, although the experience of depression and anxiety is universal, in different cultures these reactions may not be identified as abnormal, or as an illness, and that the course of these disorders/problems may run through culturally-provided channels that ameliorate their impact. Scholarly work in these areas shows that the way different cultures organise their social and political structures determines, in a variety of ways, which people in society will suffer frustration and loss. In addition, cultures may offer structured opportunities for protest, grief, anger and sadness, and the provision of such opportunities may reduce the incidence of what we in the West call clinical depression and the harm it causes. These structures are frequently entwined with religious and social beliefs about the meaning of life and suffering.

Drawing the line between normal distress and anxiety/depression therefore requires wider social debate, and has consequences for how meaningful we allow our lives to be. The conclusion might be reached that there are different boundaries to be drawn for psychotherapeutic work and for organic treatment, or different ways to regard organic treatment itself. These decisions may carry implications about the organisation of psychiatry and its responsibilities. It is also worth noting that many of the explosions of new diagnostic entities over the last few decades may actually be subsumed under this heading. Several solutions are possible. One would be that after general social debate and agreement, professionals make and monitor the boundary based on a calculus of numbers, severity and duration of symptoms. Another would be that individuals themselves decide after discussion with professionals whether they wish to consider themselves ill or not.

Furthermore I look forward to a wider public debate on whether disputable syndromes are to be accounted illness or not. Psychiatry needs to make more effort to find, achieve and keep a social consensus and agreement. Psychiatry is the servant of public debate, opinion and consensus. Boundary issues should be decided this way, not by fiat, nor by a professional group with vested interests, nor by scaling techniques which lend a spurious aura of objectivity. The views of the sufferers themselves should also be solicited and heard. It was, after all, the political activities of homosexuals that obtained their removal from the lexicon of psychiatric disorders. Greater discussion about these decisions would also help prevent us from transforming political or social problems into psychiatric ones.

Of course, this still leaves many syndromes, especially the psychoses, where there is little disagreement over the fact that they are called mental illness and treated for by psychiatric professionals. In these cases there would appear to be no grounds for change. Nevertheless, the judgement that these things are mental disorders and should be so treated rests upon a social consensus as well as upon the attributes of the phenomena themselves.

Finally, social processes are of acknowledged importance in the course and outcome of psychiatric disorder. Stigmatisation of the mentally ill is both harmful and widespread. Its roots have been shown to be found in the group-forming tendency of human beings coupled with natural negative reactions to mental disorder. Given that this is the case, in order to promote the well-being and quick rehabilitation of the mentally ill, active efforts need to be made all the time to minimise the natural process of stigmatisation. This is a battle that will never be won and needs to be continuously fought.

Bibliography

Anonymous (1982) 'Labelling someone mentally ill: a case study', in W. R. Gove (ed.) *Deviance and Mental Illness*, London: Sage.

Arendt, H. (1966) *The Origins of Totalitarianism*, London: George Allen and Unwin.

Austin, J. L. (1965) *How To Do Things With Words*, New York: Oxford University Press.

Baker, G. P. and Hacker, P. M. S. (1980) *Wittgenstein: Meaning and Understanding*, Oxford: Basil Blackwell.

Baker, G. P. and Hacker, P. M. S. (1985) *Wittgenstein: Rules, Grammar and Necessity*, Oxford: Basil Blackwell.

Banks, C. G. (1992) '"Culture" in culture bound syndromes: the case of anorexia nervosa', *Social Science and Medicine* 34(8): 867–84.

Banton, R., Clifford, P., Frosh, S., Lousada, J. and Rosenthall, J. (1985) *The Politics of Mental Health*, London: Macmillan.

Barham, P. (1992) *Closing the Asylum: The Mental Patient in Modern Society*, Harmondsworth: Penguin.

Baruch, G. and Treacher, A. (1978) *Psychiatry Observed*, London: Routledge and Kegan Paul.

Basaglia, F. (1980) 'Breaking the circuit of control', in D. Ingleby (ed.) *Critical Psychiatry: The Politics of Mental Health*, New York: Pantheon.

Bateson, G. (1972) *Steps to an Ecology of Mind*, San Francisco: Chandler.

Bateson, G. (ed.) (1974) *Perceval's Narrative*, New York: William Morrow.

Becker, H. (1963) *Outsiders: Studies in the Sociology of Deviance*, New York: Free Press (2nd edn).

Beeman, W. O. (1985) 'Dimensions of dysphoria: the view from linguistic anthropology', in A. Kleinman and B. Good (eds) *Culture and Depression*, Berkeley: University of California Press.

Beiser, M. (1985) 'A study of depression among traditional Africans, urban North Americans, and Southeast Asian refugees', in A. Kleinman and B. Good (eds) *Culture and Depression*, Berkeley: University of California Press.

Bentall, R. P. (1991) 'Explaining and explaining away insanity', in R. Tallis and H. Robinson (eds) *The Pursuit of Mind*, Manchester: Carcanet.

Bentall, R. P., Jackson, H. F. and Pilgrim, D. (1988) 'Abandoning the concept of "Schizophrenia": some implications of validity arguments for psychological research into psychotic phenomena', *British Journal of Clinical Psychology* 27: 303–24.

Berrios, G. E. (1984) 'The psychopathology of affectivity: conceptual and historical aspects', *Psychological Medicine* 14: 303–13.

—— (1985a) 'Descriptive psychopathology: conceptual and historical aspects', *Psychological Medicine* 15: 745–58.

—— (1985b) 'Obsessional disorders during the nineteenth century: terminological and classificatory issues', in W. F. Bynum, R. Porter and M. Shepherd (eds) *The Anatomy of Madness*, vol. 1, *People and Ideas*, London: Tavistock.

—— (1996) *The History of Mental Symptoms: Descriptive Psychopathology Since the Nineteenth Century*, Cambridge: Cambridge University Press.

Birchwood, M., Mason, R., Macmillan, F. and Healy, J. (1993) 'Depression, demoralisation and control over psychotic illness: a comparison of depressed and non-depressed patients with a chronic psychosis', *Psychological Medicine* 23(2): 387–96.

Blum, A. F. (1970) 'The sociology of mental illness', in J. D. Douglas (ed.) *Deviance and Respectability*, New York: Basic.

Blumer, H. (1969) *Symbolic Interactionism: Perspective and Method*, Englewood Cliffs, NJ: Prentice Hall.

Bowers, L. A. C. (1991) 'Community psychiatric nursing in description and action', unpublished M.A. (Econ.) thesis, University of Manchester.

Boyle, M. (1990) *Schizophrenia – A Scientific Delusion?*, London: Routledge.

Brown, G. (1973) 'The mental hospital as an institution', *Social Science and Medicine* 7(6): 407–24.

Brown, G. W. (1981) 'Aetiological studies and the definition of a case', in J. K. Wing (ed.) *What is a Case?*, London: Grant MacIntyre.

Brown, G. W. and Harris, T. (1978) *Social Origins of Depression: A Study of Psychiatric Disorder in Women*, London: Tavistock.

Buchsbaum, M. S., Haier, R. J. and Potkin, S. G. (1992) 'Frontostriatal disorder of cerebral metabolism in never medicated schizophrenics', *Archives of General Psychiatry* 49: 935–42.

Burns, A. (1993) 'Accuracy of clinical diagnosis of Alzheimer's disease', *Alzheimer's Review* 2(1): 25–8.

Busfield, J. (1986) *Managing Madness: Changing Ideas and Practice*, Wolfboro, NH: Longwood.

Bynum, W. F. (1981) 'Rationales for therapy in British psychiatry, 1780–1835', in A. Scull (ed.) *Madhouses, Mad-Doctors and Madmen: The Social History of Psychiatry in the Victorian Era*, London: Athlone.

—— (1985) 'The nervous patient in eighteenth and nineteenth century Britain: the psychiatric origins of British neurology', in W. F. Bynum, R. Porter and M. Shepherd (eds) *The Anatomy of Madness*, vol. 1, *People and Ideas*, London: Tavistock.

Bynum, W. F., Porter, R. and Shepherd, M. (eds) (1985) *The Anatomy of Madness*, vol. 1, *People and Ideas*, London: Tavistock.

—— (1985) *The Anatomy of Madness*, Volume 2, London: Tavistock.

Caplan, G. (1964) *Principles of Preventive Psychiatry*, London: Tavistock.

Castel, R. (1988) *The Regulation of Madness: Origins of Incarceration in France*, Oxford: Polity.

Castel, R. Castel, F. and Lovell, A. (1982) *The Psychiatric Society*, New York: Columbia University Press.

Chamberlin, J. (1977) *On Our Own: Patient-Controlled Alternatives to the Mental Health System*, London: MIND Publications.

Champlin, T. S. (1981) 'The reality of mental illness', *Philosophy* 56: 467–87.

Chauncey, R. L. (1975) 'Comment on "The Labelling Theory of Mental Illness"', *American Sociological Review* 40: 248–52.

Conklin, H. (1955) 'Hanunoo color categories', *Southwest Journal of Anthropology* 11: 339–44.

Cook, J. (1978a) 'Whorf's linguistic relativism, part I', *Philosophical Investigations* 1(1): 1–30.

—— (1978b) 'Whorf's linguistic relativism, part II', *Philosophical Investigations* 1(2): 1–37.

Coulter, J. (1973) *Approaches to Insanity*, London: Martin Robertson.

—— (1975) *The Operations of Mental Health Personnel in an Urban Area*, PhD thesis, University of Manchester.

Cowen, P. J. and Wood, A. J. (1991) 'Editorial: biological markers of depression', *Psychological Medicine* 21: 831–6.

Dawkins, R. (1989) *The Selfish Gene*, Oxford: Oxford University Press (2nd edn).

Dean, C., Surtees, P. G. and Shashidharan, S. P. (1983) 'Comparison of research diagnostic systems in an Edinburgh community sample', *British Journal of Psychiatry* 142: 247–56.

Department of Health (1994) *Working in Partnership. A Collaborative Approach to Care. Report of the Mental Health Nursing Review Team*, London: HMSO.

Der, G., Gupta, S. and Murray, R. M. (1990) 'Is schizophrenia disappearing?', *Lancet* 335: 513–16.

Dowbiggin, I. (1985) 'Degeneration and hereditarianism in French mental medicine', in W. F. Bynum, R. Porter and M. Shepherd (eds) *The Anatomy of Madness*, vol. 1, *People and Ideas*, London: Tavistock.

Durkheim, E. (1938) *The Rules of Sociological Method*, New York: Free Press.

—— (1964) 'The determination of moral facts', in K. H. Wolff (ed.) *Essays on Sociology and Philosophy*, London: Harper and Row.

Eagles, J. M. (1991) 'Is schizophrenia disappearing?', *British Journal of Psychiatry* 158: 834–5.

Eisenberg, L. (1988) 'The social construction of mental illness', *Psychological Medicine* 18: 1–9.

Endicott, J. and Spitzer, R. L. (1972) 'What! Another rating scale? The psychiatric evaluation form', *Journal of Nervous and Mental Disease* 154(2): 88–104.

Engel, G. L. (1977) 'The need for a new medical model: a challenge for biomedicine', *Science* 196(4286): 129–36.

English National Board for Nursing Midwifery and Health Visiting (1996) *Learning from Each Other*, London: English National Board for Nursing Midwifery and Health Visiting.

Evans-Pritchard, E. E. (1976) *Witchcraft Oracles and Magic Among the Azande*, Oxford: Clarendon (originally published in 1937 by the same publisher).

Eysenck, H. (1985) *Decline and Fall of the Freudian Empire*, London: Viking.

Fabrega, H. (1989) 'Cultural relativism and psychiatric illness', *Journal of Nervous and Mental Disease* 162: 299–312.

—— (1991) 'A cultural analysis of human behavioural breakdowns: an approach to the ontology and epistemology of psychiatric phenomena', in W. S. Flack, D. R. Miller and M. Wiener (eds) *What is Schizophrenia?*, New York: Springer.

—— (1992) 'The role of culture in a theory of mental illness', *Social Science and Medicine* 35(1): 91–103.

Falloon, I. R. H. and McGill, C. W. (1984) *Family Care of Schizophrenia*, New York: Guilford.

Foucault, M. (1967) *Madness and Civilisation*, London: Tavistock.

Freud, S. (1910) 'Leonardo da Vinci and a memory of his childhood', in *The Pelican Freud Library*, vol. 14, *Art and Literature* (1985), Harmondsworth: Penguin.

—— (1939) 'Moses and monotheism', in *The Pelican Freud Library*, vol. 13, *The Origins of Religion* (1985), Harmondsworth: Penguin.

—— (1985) *Civilisation and Its Discontents*, Harmondsworth: Penguin.

Gaines, A. D. (1992) 'From DSM-I to III-R; voices of self, mastery and the other: a cultural constructivist reading of US psychiatric classification', *Social Science and Medicine* 35(1): 3–24.

Garfinkel, H. (1967) *Studies in Ethnomethodology*, Oxford: Polity.

Goffman, E. (1961) *Asylums: Essays on the Social Situation of Mental Patients and Other inmates*, Harmondsworth: Penguin.

—— (1963) *Stigma, Notes on the Management of Spoiled Identity*, Englewood Cliffs, NJ: Prentice Hall.

—— (1972) 'The insanity of place', in E. Goffman (ed.) *Relations in Public*, Harmondsworth: Penguin.

Goldberg, D. (1992) 'A classification of psychological distress', *Social Science and Medicine* 35(2): 189–93.

Goldberg, D. and Huxley, P. (1980) *Mental Illness in the Community: The Pathway to Psychiatric Care*, London: Tavistock.

—— (1992) *Common Mental Disorders: A Biosocial Model*, London: Tavistock.

Good, B. J. (1977) 'The heart of what's the matter: the semantics of illness in Iran', *Culture, Medicine and Psychiatry* 1: 25–58.

Good, B. J., Good, M. D. and Moradi, R. (1985) 'The interpretation of Iranian depressive illness and dysphoric affect', in A. Kleinman and B. Good (eds) *Culture and Depression*, Berkeley: University of California Press.

Gouldner, A. W. (1970) *The Coming Crisis of Western Sociology*, London: Heinemann.

Gove, W. R. (1975) 'The labelling theory of mental illness: a reply to Scheff', *American Sociological Review* 40: 242–8.

—— (1976) 'Reply to Imershein and Simons (1976) and Scheff (1975)', *American Sociological Review* 41: 564–7.

—— (1982) 'The current status of the labelling theory of mental illness', in W. R. Gove (ed.) *Deviance and Mental Illness*, London: Sage.

Gribbin, J. and Gribbin, M. (1988) *The One Per Cent Advantage: The Sociobiology of Being Human*, Oxford: Basil Blackwell.

Haafkens, J., Nijhof, G. and van der Poel, E. (1986) 'Mental health care and the opposition movement in the Netherlands', *Social Science and Medicine* 22: 185–92.

Hardman, C. (1981) 'The psychology of conformity and self-expression among the Lohorung Rai of east Nepal', in P. Heelas and A. Lock (eds) *Indigenous Psychologies: The Anthropology of the Self*, London: Academic.

Hawkins, P. and Shohet, R. (1989) *Supervision in the Helping Professions*, Milton Keynes: Open University Press.

Hilgard, E. R., Atkinson, R. L. and Atkinson, R. C. (1979) *Introduction to Psychology*, New York: Harcourt Brace Jovanovich (7th edn).

Horwitz, A. (1979) 'Models, muddles and mental illness labelling', *Journal of Health and Social Behaviour* 20(September): 296–300.

Hughes, E. C. (1971) *The Sociological Eye*, Chicago: Aldine Atherton.

Hunter, J. F. M. (1973) *Essays After Wittgenstein*, Toronto: University of Toronto Press.

Hunter, R. and Macalpine, I. (1963) *Three Hundred Years of Psychiatry, 1535–1860: A History Presented in Selected English Texts*, London: Oxford University Press.

Huxley, P. (1993) 'Location and stigma: a survey of community attitudes to mental illness, part 1: enlightenment and stigma', *Journal of Mental Health* 2: 73–80.

Hyler, S. E., Gabbard, G. O. and Schneider, I. (1991) 'Homicidal maniacs and narcissistic parasites: stigmatisation of mentally ill persons in the movies', *Hospital and Community Psychiatry* 42: 10.

Imershein, A. W. and Simons, R. L. (1976) 'Rules and examples in lay and professional psychiatry: an ethnomethodological comment on the Scheff–Gove controversy', *American Sociological Review* 41: 559–63.

Ingleby, D. (1980) 'Understanding "mental illness"', in D. Ingleby (ed.) *Critical Psychiatry: The Politics of Mental Health*, New York: Pantheon.

Johnson, J. (1993) 'Catatonia: the tension insanity', *British Journal of Psychiatry* 162: 733–8.

Johnston, P. (1989) *Wittgenstein and Moral Philosophy*, London: Routledge.

Jones, K. (1955) *Lunacy, Law and Conscience, 1744–1845*, London: Routledge and Kegan Paul.

—— (1960) *Mental Health and Social Policy, 1845–1959*, London: Routledge and Kegan Paul.

Jones, K. and Fowles, A. J. (1984) *Ideas on Institutions*, London: Routledge and Kegan Paul.

Kalat, J. W. (1986) *Biological Psychology*, Belmont, CA: Wadsworth.

Kelly, M. and May, D. (1982) 'Good and bad patients: a review of the literature', *Journal of Advanced Nursing* 7: 147–56.

Kendell, R. E. (1975a) *The Role of Diagnosis in Psychiatry*, Oxford: Blackwell Scientific Publications.

—— (1975b) 'The concept of disease and its implications for psychiatry', *British Journal of Psychiatry* 127: 305–15.

Kitcher, P. (1985) *Vaulting Ambition: Sociobiology and the Quest for Human Nature*, London: MIT.

Kleinman, A. (1980) *Patients and Healers in the Context of Culture*, Berkeley: University of California Press.

—— (1988) *Rethinking Psychiatry*, New York: Macmillan.

Klerman, G. L. (1989) 'Psychiatric diagnostic categories: issues of validity and measurement', *Journal of Health and Social Behaviour* 30: 26–32.

Kramer, P. (1993) *Listening to Prozac*, New York: Viking.

Kuhn, T. S. (1962) *The Structure of Scientific Revolutions*, Chicago: University of Chicago Press.

Laing, R. (1965) *The Divided Self*, Harmondsworth: Penguin.

Leff, J. (1988) *Psychiatry Around the Globe: A Transcultural View*, London: Gaskell.

Leff, J. and Vaughn, C. (1985) *Expressed Emotion in Families: Its Significance for Mental Illness*, New York: Guilford.

Lemert, E. M. (1951) *Social Pathology*, New York: McGraw Hill.

—— (1962) 'Paranoia and the dynamics of exclusion', *Sociometry* 25: 2–20.

—— (1967) *Human Deviance, Social Problems and Social Control*, Englewood Cliffs, NJ: Prentice Hall.

Levy, R. I. (1973) *Tahitians: Mind and Experience in the Society Islands*, Chicago: University of Chicago Press.

Lewis, A. (1953) 'Health as a social concept', *British Journal of Sociology* 4: 109–24.

Lewis, G., David, A., Andreasson, S. and Allebeck, P. (1992) 'Schizophrenia and city life', *Lancet* 340: 37–40.

Lienhardt, G. (1961) *Divinity and Experience*, Oxford: Clarendon.

Lindow, V. (1994) *Self-help Alternatives to Mental Health Services*, London: MIND Publications.

Link, B. G., Cullen, T., Frank, J. and Wozniak, J. F. (1987) 'The social rejection of former mental patients: understanding why labels matter', *American Journal of Sociology* 92: 1461–1500.

Link, B. G., Mirotznik, J. and Cullen, T. (1991) 'The effectiveness of stigma coping orientations: can negative consequences of mental illness labelling be avoided?', *Journal of Health and Social Behaviour* 32: 302–20.

Lovell, A. and Scheper-Hughes, N. (eds) (1986) *Psychiatry Inside Out: Selected Writings of Franco Basaglia*, New York: Columbia University Press.

Lutz, C. (1985) 'Depression and the translation of emotional words', in A.

Kleinman and B. Good (eds) *Culture and Depression*, Berkeley: University of California Press.

Lyon, M. L. (1996) 'C. Wright Mills meets Prozac: the relevance of "social emotion" to the sociology of health and illness', in V. James and J. Gabe (eds) *Health and the Sociology of Emotions*, Oxford: Basil Blackwell.

Macalpine, J. and Hunter, R. A. (1969) *George III and the Mad Business*, London: Allen Lane.

Macilwaine, H. (1981) 'How nurses and neurotic patients view each other in general hospital psychiatric units', *Nursing Times* 77(27): 1158–60.

McKeown, M. and Clancy, B. (1995) 'Media influence on societal perceptions of mental illness', *Mental Health Nursing* 15(2):10–12.

Mahendra, B. (1981) 'Where have all the catatonics gone?', *Psychological Medicine* 11: 669–71.

Marcuse, H. (1966) *Eros and Civilisation*, Boston: Beacon.

Marsella, A. J. (1982) 'Introduction: cultural conceptions in mental health research and practice', in A. Marsella and G. White (eds) *Cultural Conceptions of Mental Health and Illness*, Dordrecht, Holland: Reidel.

Martin, J. P. (1984) *Hospitals in Trouble*, Oxford: Basil Blackwell.

May, D. and Kelly, M. (1982) 'Chancers, pests and poor wee souls: problems of legitimation in psychiatric nursing', *Sociology of Health and Illness*, 4: 279–301.

Maynard Smith, J. (1988) *Games, Sex and Evolution*, New York: Harvester Wheatsheaf.

Mead, G. H. (1936) *Mind, Self and Society*, Chicago: Chicago University Press.

Menninger, K. (1948) 'Changing concepts of disease', *Annals of Internal Medicine* 29: 318–25.

—— (1963) *The Vital Balance: The Life Process in Mental Health and Illness*, New York: Viking.

Mental Health Act, 1983, London: HMSO.

Merton, R. (1957) *Social Theory and Social Structure*, New York: Free Press.

Meyer, A. (1955) *Psychobiology: A Science of Illness*, Springfield, IL.: Charles Thomas.

Miller, W. R. and Rollnick, S. (1991) *Motivational Interviewing: Preparing People to Change Addiction Behaviour*, New York: Guilford.

Mirowsky, J. and Ross, C. E. (1989) 'Psychiatric diagnosis as reified measurement', *Journal of Health and Social Behaviour* 30: 11–25.

Mor, V., Sherwood, S. and Gutkin, C. (1984) 'Psychiatric history as a barrier to residential care', *Hospital and Community Psychiatry* 356: 368–72.

Morel, B. A. (1857) As quoted in Dowbiggin (1985).

Morgan, D. (1975) 'Explaining mental illness', *European Journal of Sociology* 15: 262–80.

Murphy, J. M. (1982) 'Cultural shaping and mental disorders', in W. R. Gove (ed.) *Deviance and Mental Illness*, London: Sage.

Nuckolls, C. W. (1992) 'Toward a cultural history of the personality disorders', *Social Science and Medicine* 35(1): 37–47.

Obeyesekere, G. (1985) 'Depression, Buddhism, and the work of culture in Sri Lanka', in A. Kleinman and B. Good (eds) *Culture and Depression*, Berkeley: University of California Press.

Parry-Jones, W. L. (1972) *The Trade in Lunacy*, London: Routledge and Kegan Paul.

Parsons, T. (1951) *The Social System*, New York: Free Press.

Peterson, D. (ed.) (1982) *A Mad People's History of Madness*, Pittsburgh: University of Pittsburgh Press.

Philo, G., Secker, J., Platt, S., Henderson, L., Mclaughlin, G. and Burnside, J. (1994) 'The impact of mass media on public images of mental illness, media content and audience belief', *Health Education Journal* 53: 271–81.

Pichot, P. (1994) 'Nosological models in psychiatry', *British Journal of Psychiatry* 164: 232–40.

Pilgrim, D. (1990) 'Competing histories of madness: some implications for modern psychiatry', in R. P. Bentall (ed.) *Reconstructing Schizophrenia*, London: Routledge.

Pilgrim, D. and Rogers, A. (1993) *A Sociology of Mental Health and Illness*, Milton Keynes: Open University Press.

Pollner, M. (1974) 'Sociological and common sense models of the labelling process', in R. Turner (ed.) *Ethnomethodology*, Harmondsworth: Penguin.

Popper, K. (1963) *Conjectures and Refutations*, London: Routledge and Kegan Paul.

Porter, R. (1985) '"The hunger of imagination": approaching Samuel Johnson's melancholy', in W. F. Bynum, R. Porter and M. Shepherd (eds) *The Anatomy of Madness*, vol. 1, *People and Ideas*, London: Tavistock.

—— (1987) *Mind Forg'd Manacles: A History of Madness in England from the Restoration to the Regency*, London: Athlone.

Prior, L. (1993) *The Social Organisation of Mental Illness*, London: Sage.

Ramon, S. (1983) '*Psychiatria democratica*: a case study of an Italian mental health service', *International Journal of Health Services* 13: 307–24.

Rapoport, R. N. (1960) *Community as Doctor*, London: Tavistock.

Reich, W. (1949) *Character Analysis*, New York: Farrar, Straus and Giroux.

Reznek, L. (1991) *Philosophical Defence of Psychiatry*, London: Routledge.

Rogers, A. and Pilgrim, D. (1991)'"Pulling down churches": accounting for the British mental health users' movement', *Sociology of Health and Illness* 13(2):129–48.

Rogers, A., Pilgrim, D. and Lacey, R. (1993) *Experiencing Psychiatry: Users' Views of Services*, London: Macmillan.

Romme, M. and Escher, S. (1993) *Accepting Voices*, London: MIND Publications.

Rose, N. (1986) 'Psychiatry, the discipline of mental health', in P. Miller and N. Rose (eds) *The Power of Psychiatry*, Oxford: Polity.

Rosenhan, D. D. (1973) 'On being sane in insane places', *Science* 179: 250–8.

—— (1975) 'The contextual nature of psychiatric diagnosis', *Journal of Abnormal Psychology* 84: 462–4.

Ruse, M. (1979) *Sociobiology: Sense or Nonsense?*, Dordrecht, Holland: Reidel.

Ryle, G. (1949) *The Concept of Mind*, Harmondsworth: Penguin.

Samson, C. (1995) 'Madness and psychiatry', in B. S. Turner (ed.) *Medical Power and Social Knowledge*, London: Sage.

Scheff, T. (1966) *Being Mentally Ill: A Sociological Theory*, London: Weidenfeld and Nicolson.

—— (1974) 'The labelling theory of mental illness', *American Sociological Review* 39: 444–52.

—— (1975) 'Reply to Chauncey and Gove', *American Sociological Review* 40: 252–7.

—— (1976) 'Reply to Imershein and Simons', *American Sociological Review* 41: 563–4.

Scheper-Hughes, N. (1988) 'The madness of hunger: sickness, delirium and human needs', *Culture, Medicine and Psychiatry* 12: 429–58.

Schieffelin, E. L. (1985) 'The cultural analysis of depressive affect: an example from New Guinea', in A. Kleinman and B. Good (eds) *Culture and Depression*, Berkeley: University of California Press.

Schutz, A. (1953) 'The problem of rationality in the social world', *Economica* 10 (May).

Scull, A. (1977) *Decarceration: Community Treatment and the Deviant – A Radical View*, Englewood Cliffs, NJ: Prentice Hall.

—— (1979) *Museums of Madness: The Social Organisation of Psychiatry in Nineteenth-Century England*, London: Allen Lane.

—— (1981) 'The discovery of the asylum revisited: lunacy reform in the new American republic', in A. Scull (ed.) *Madhouses, Mad-Doctors and Madmen: The Social History of Psychiatry in the Victorian Era*, London: Athlone.

—— (1989) *Social Order/Mental Disorder. Anglo-American Psychiatry in Historical Perspective*, London: Routledge.

—— (1993) *The Most Solitary of Afflictions: Madness and Society in Britain, 1700–1900*, New Haven: Yale University Press.

Sedgwick, P. (1972) 'Mental illness is illness', *Salmagundi* 20: 196–222.

—— (1982) *Psychopolitics*, London: Pluto.

Sheridan, A. (1980) *Michel Foucault, The Will to Truth*, London: Tavistock.

Shotter, J. (1981) 'Vico, moral worlds, accountability and personhood', in P. Heelas and A. Lock (eds) *Indigenous Psychologies: The Anthropology of the Self*, London: Academic.

Shweder, R. A. (1985) 'Menstrual pollution, soul loss, and the comparative study of emotions', in A. Kleinman and B. Good (eds) *Culture and Depression*, Berkeley: University of California Press.

Sournia, J. (1990) *A History of Alcoholism*, Oxford: Basil Blackwell.

Spitzer, R. L. (1975) 'On pseudoscience, logic in remission, and psychiatric diagnosis: a critique of Rosenhan's "On being sane in insane places"', *Journal of Abnormal Psychology* 84: 442–52.

Spitzer, R. L. and Williams, J. B. W. (1982) 'The definition and diagnosis of mental disorder', in W. R. Gove (ed.) *Deviance and Mental Illness*, London: Sage.

Spitzer, R. L., Endicott, J., Fleiss, J. L. and Cohen, J. (1970) 'The psychiatric status schedule: a technique for evaluating psychopathology and impairment of role functioning', *Archives of General Psychiatry* 23: 41–55.

Spitzer, R. L., Fleiss, J. L., Endicott, J. and Cohen, J. (1967) 'Mental status schedule: properties of factor-analytically derived scales', *Archives of General Psychiatry* 16: 479–93.

Steering Committee of the Confidential Inquiry into Homicides and Suicides by Mentally Ill People (1994) *A Preliminary Report on Homicide*, London: Steering Committee of the Confidential Inquiry into Homicides and Suicides by Mentally Ill People.

Strauss, A., Schatzman, L., Bucher, R., Ehrlich, D. and Sabshin, M. (1964) *Psychiatric Ideologies and Institutions*, London: Free Press.

Strauss, J., Rakfeldt, J., Harding, C. and Lieberman, P. (1989) 'Psychological and social aspects of negative symptoms', *British Journal of Psychiatry* 155 (suppl. 7): 128–32.

Susman, J. (1994) 'Disability, stigma and deviance', *Social Science and Medicine* 38(1): 15–22.

Szasz, T. (1971) *The Manufacture of Madness: A Comparative Study of the Inquisition and the Mental Health Movement*, London: Routledge and Kegan Paul.

—— (1972) *The Myth of Mental Illness*, London: Paladin.

—— (1987) *Insanity*, New York: John Wiley.

Turner, B. S. (1992) *Regulating Bodies: Essays in Medical Sociology*, London: Routledge.

Vico, G. (1725) 'Scienza Nuova', cited in Shotter (1981).

Walk, A. (1954) 'Some aspects of the moral treatment of the insane up to 1845', *Journal of Mental Science* 100: 807–37.

Wallcraft, J. (1996) 'Some models of asylum and help in times of crisis', in D. Tomlinson and J. Carrier (eds) *Asylum in the Community*, London: Routledge.

Warner, R., Taylor, D., Powers, M. and Hyman, J. (1989) 'Acceptance of the mental illness label', *American Journal of Orthopsychiatry* 59(3): 398–409.

White, E. (1989) 'Trieste: a personal view of an Italian community mental health service', *Community Psychiatric Nursing Journal* 9(1): 14–17.

Whorf, B. (1964) 'Language, thought and reality', in J. B. Carroll (ed.) *Language and Thought*, Englewood Cliffs, NJ: Prentice Hall.

Wieder, D. L. (1974) 'Telling the code', in R. Turner (ed.) *Ethnomethodology*, Harmondsworth: Penguin.

Williams, J. P. (1985) 'Psychical research and psychiatry in late Victorian Britain: trance as ecstasy or trance as insanity', in W. F. Bynum, R. Porter and M. Shepherd (eds) *The Anatomy of Madness*, vol. 1, *People and Ideas*, London: Tavistock.

Wilson, E. O. (1978) *On Human Nature*, Cambridge, MA: Harvard University Press.

Wing, J. K. (1978) *Reasoning About Madness*, Oxford: Oxford University Press.

Winick, C. (1982) 'The image of mental illness in the mass media', in W. R. Gove (ed.) *Deviance and Mental Illness*, London: Sage.

Wittgenstein, L. (1958) *Philosophical Investigations*, Oxford: Basil Blackwell.

Wolfensberger, W. (1972) *The Principle of Normalisation in Human Services*, Toronto: National Institute on Mental Retardation.

—— (1987) *The New Genocide of Handicapped and Afflicted People*, Syracuse, NY: Author.

World Health Organisation (1979) *Schizophrenia: An International Follow-Up Study*, Chichester: Wiley.

Yap, P. M. (1965) 'Koro, a culture-bound depersonalisation syndrome', *British Journal of Psychiatry* 111: 43–50.

Zubin, J. (1985) 'Negative symptoms, are they indigenous to schizophrenia?', *Schizophrenia Bulletin* 11(3): 461–9.

Name index

Arendt, H. 129
Austin, J. L. 43

Baker, G. P. 34, 43, 147
Banks, C. G. 99
Banton, R. 136
Barham, P. 129
Baruch, G. 81, 162
Basaglia, F. 132–4
Bateson, G. 51, 100
Becker, H. 8, 10, 12, 15–16, 37, 107–8
Beeman, W. O. 53
Beiser, M. 70
Bentall, R. P. 170, 187
Berrios, G. E. 98, 100, 117
Birchwood, M. 86
Blum, A. F. 17–20
Blumer, H. 11
Bowers, L. 186
Boyle, M. 75, 91–2
Brown, G. 51, 82, 88
Buchsbaum, M. S. 170
Burns, A. 171
Busfield, J. 106
Bynum, W. 94, 140

Caplan, G. 10
Castel, R. 94, 102, 108, 140–1
Chamberlin, J. 136–8
Champlin, T. S. 163–5
Chauncey, R. L. 9
Cook, J. 51–5
Coulter, J. 15, 17, 170
Cowen, P. J. 170

Dawkins, R. 184–5
Dean, C. 88
Der, G. 106
Dowbiggin, I. 101–2
Durkheim, E. 11, 15, 26–7

Eagles, J. M. 106
Eisenberg, L. 195
Endicott, J. 75
Engel, G. L. 195
Evans-Pritchard, E. E. 115
Eysenck, H. 136

Fabrega, H. 39, 50, 63–4
Falloon, I. R. H. 81
Foucault, M. 10, 94, 96–7, 102–4, 109–10, 112
Freud, S. 97, 135

Gaines, A. D. 71, 158
Garfinkel, H. 31–3, 35, 37, 80
Goffman, E. 17–19, 24, 82
Goldberg, D. 81, 93, 124, 197
Good, B. J. 55, 68
Gouldner, A. W. 119
Gove, W. R. 9, 22–3
Gribbin, J. 184

Haafkens, J. 136
Hacker, P. M. S. 34, 43, 147
Hardman, C. 49
Hawkins, P. 79
Hilgard, E. R. 184

Subject index